Pear Tree H

A Gloucestershire Ch

First memories are of a white cottage and black orchard; then later farm-cart rides, harnessed horses jigging in the sky, gates and wagon tracks and elm clumps melting with mystery and distance.

Things like this remain suspended in the dark, set in one's consciousness like jewels flashing in their first light. Like that too were the apple boughs where the dog and I caught bees; and beneath them, scarcely recollected now, the abandoned sleep in the tufts where the green heat raced over us like water and the high trees soared in the summer day.

All this though was back there, along the road, far away; and my new life began in the back of the furniture lorry when I was four years old . . .

First published in 1993
by Ashford, Buchan & Enright Publishers,
31 Bridge Street, Leatherhead, Surrey KT22 8BN

A CIP catalogue record for this book is available
from the British Library

ISBN 1-85253-242-4

Typeset by Priory Publications,
Haywards Heath

Printed in Great Britain by
FotoDirect Ltd, Brighton

Pear Tree Hollow

A Gloucestershire Childhood

Gerald Roberts

Ashford, Buchan & Enright
Leatherhead

CONTENTS

Bending the Twig 1

Them Next Door 17

School 34

War Games 66

Father 83

Lads and Landgirls 100

The Hill 113

Mother 136

Yanks 158

Outings 170

Down in the Village 188

End Days 203

**For
Neila**

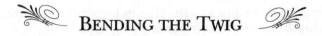

BENDING THE TWIG

March was everywhere: in the heatless sun gliding in the empty trees, in the raging woods along the roadside, in the bright fields flowing smoothly past. Perception moved round needles of light striking over the tailboard. The sun tapped morse on the brass coal scuttle, and in its glare I slowly observed the contents of my rocking chrysalis, cluttered high and wide with chairs and tables, mats and beds, trunks and bundles.

Dazed by the swift solid air through which we cleaved, and the thunderous uproar and motion, I turned my bewildered gaze upon the two figures hidden behind the aspidistra, and recognised again my Mother and sister, those two pillars of all my early years. We came out from the trees and the sunlight rushed round, and I saw who they were. They stared past me at the reeling bushes and spinning grit, and their faces said we would never see anything else.

I welled with the sensations of my new life: head and body hitherto independent suddenly fused into a giant whole, and no more would I ever separate one from the other, or ignore the hungers they spawned.

I was missing my dinner. I had a hole under my ribs and my legs were like straw but I sensed it was useless to mention it. Myra was unhappy too. White legs drawn up under her chin, socks round her ankles, shoulders bowed as if she were carrying the world: these were speechless codes of distress, flags flying mast high. Her eyes found mine and I discovered what they were for; more eloquent than words, louder than trumpets – passing the fear that this lorry was home and we would ride the roads forever.

It was about dinner time. There were no tables and chairs, no blue soup bowls or large brass spoons, no meal of heat and content, no potatoes, Oxo or swedes. Till that time came again (if ever it did) Mother fed us with surprises, hot lumps plucked from the passing cauldron speeding by the lorry.

'Oh look! Just you look at that!' 'See that pond? All those ducks?' 'There goes a fire engine, see!'

She chased the ends of her hair, tucking them into her bun, then, gently squeezing it into shape, rearranged the pins, sighing loudly at the bumps and bends.

'Lord, how much further?'

That light, loving voice was the first to lodge in my memory: crystals like wild-blown seeds gathering and taking root.

I was startled soon afterwards by another voice which seemed to come from the roof of the lorry. It was Father, and what he said instantly inspired and thrilled Mother and Myra. I remember their necks growing long out of their coats, and looking round I grabbed their arms, surprised. The moment broke, stillborn in frowns and partly opened mouths; my touch changed them and they turned, looking at me. Then I found that I too had a voice. 'What?' I whimpered. 'What? What?'

They never answered.

On the common we changed direction down a narrow drive, where the air slapping the fence posts sounded like someone gently stroking a cymbal. When it stopped we jumped through the ruts of a gateway into a field and everything fell around us. Saucepans, buckets, bowls and boxes lifted into the air, smashing forward. I thought we were turning over and leapt for the exit, but Mother grabbed me, held me by the belt, and tugged me back inside just in time.

Wallowing like a boat in a running sea, we plunged down a long bank and came to rest outside the cottages under a wood. It went very quiet. A ringing silence enveloped us completely, and only the natural gusting wind bid us welcome.

Standing in the field, the first thing I noticed was the sky: a great cloudless dome resting on a distant land across the valley. It latched under the wood and stretched right round behind us to the common. Blue and clear, the verdant height acted like a magic potion.

I was as stiff as a board and half frozen from the ride but the impact of that view set something working inside; it dazzled like a bubble and every day would grow bigger, wider, higher.

Bob, nearly a man now, came round from the front of the lorry. He stuck out his spotty chin, acting as if he'd known of this place for years.

'I knew I should 'a brought me kite. Wouldn't 'e go up 'ere a day like this!'

We joined him, Myra and I, the three of us with our faces turned upwards. We stared at heaven, sucked at the green, tasted the wind and raced back up the bank in a straggle.

'Wait for I!'

But they got away from me, two frantic figures weaving over the rolling slope, flapping like broken crows. I found them at the top by the wall where the wind punched us dizzy; and breathless, intoxicated by green and air, we flung ourselves down in the surging grass.

In the bottom Father and Mother and the lorry man trailed in and out of the cottage like laden coolies. When Father stepped away and waved us down, the great escape was over. Mother held aloft the food basket, swinging it from side to side over her head, and the rush down, into the wind, was like swimming to the bottom of a lagoon.

With wedges of sugared bread we perched like birds at roost round the warm radiator of the lorry, pecking at our fingers. We heard Father coughing with the effort of lifting and Mother telling him to sit down on the wall and rest: he'd ruptured himself twice in like manner.

For Bob and Myra this rest was temporary respite, the sandwich a part bribe, for in a moment they were fetched from me and put to work. They joined the slave line with the others, up and down the cinder path straining with boxes, iron beds, trunks; and chairs and mattresses that looked as if they had been shelled.

The aspidistra, protected all the way in Mother's lap, finally had two leaves amputated by a chair leg and she nearly broke down over it, though the thing still looked like a bush.

'Oh, daamn! Just you look at that! I've had it from a shoot too!' She kissed it, wiped its leaves with a flannel, and afterwards Myra flung a bucket of water over it for good measure.

I lay on my stomach under the lorry, watching them loom past me in the sky, a parade of legs, in pairs or sets, waltzing in the tufts.

Bob meanwhile sauntered about like a foreman, always with the lightest load, casting advice to the wind.

'They'll never get that in through *there!*' 'Ah, just you wait till they come t' lift *that!*' 'Snow good tryin' t' get all this damned stuff up them stairs!'-'What a blasted place!'

He stuck out his chin, put his hands in his pockets, and started his big whistling. He'd had enough of it.

The pieces and bits came apart, familiar remembered comforts unwedged and scattered in the grass, our home of that other place and life, not then noticed any more than a bird notices its nest. And here was that nest spoiled and ragged, strewn about in a puzzle: dusty pictures, cracked mirrors, pokers and black shovels, a marble top that looked like solid water, rolls of lino, a fire guard, boot brushes and ten boxes of stuff wrapped in newspaper. I was dry with questions and thought we were giving away our home.

'I wanna go 'ome our Mam. I be cold!'

I shivered and wailed at the wind, kicked the grass and bashed the wall and wondered what we were doing. Where was this place? Where were we? Why had we come here?

'I wanna go 'ome!'

They put me to hold open the garden gate. Green it was, old and broken with squeaky red hinges, and after each load I had a swing. Faces passed me, under boxes or looking over them, hissing, grunting, swearing.

Then suddenly it all stopped, and there was only me on the quickly gate racing in the wasted wind; and after my millionth swing I was fetched indoors.

Our home was heaped in a mountain on the red tiled floor of the kitchen, with deep canyons running between the piles. In one of these Father was pumping the primus into a hell blast; and hidden somewhere in another Mother searched for the tea pot. 'Well, it's not here, that's all there is to it. Damned things all wedged in like this! I don't know how you ever expect me to find anything.'

Her back aching, hair round her face, she talked to the hated boxes and the commentary never flagged.

'Look at all this! Who packed that? It's all over the auction here!'

Myra must have heard the commotion for I remember she came running in looking wide-eyed and sorrowful, ready to climb onto the roof if only it would help. Afterwards she hopped back outside and hid behind the plum tree just in case of trouble.

I crawled into the window, twisting round with one leg under me, watching the lorry man. Who was he, where had he come from? Was he here to stay, what was he called? He had wet eyes and a blue nose and looked like a dog. He rubbed his hands, sucked at his pipe and watched the kettle like a dying friend.

As usual, Bob had escaped, had vanished completely for over an hour. It was a trick he had, and for much of my early years I thought him a wizard gifted with the power to come and go in a puff of smoke. He appeared now in our midst as if he had just walked through the wall.

'I be goin' down the wood,' he said.

He had found his air gun, called the dog, and went off among the screeching trees. I knew he was whistling and breaking sticks, just for

4

the devil of it, but the sounds of that first exploration were lost in the mighty gusts.

Soon afterwards, Myra came in, skidding to a stop with sensational news: 'The lav's at the bottom of the garden under a bush!'

This sounded like something wonderful.

'I wanna 'ave a look!'

So she lifted me off the ledge and lead me out and round the house and down the back. The door creaked open two feet and absolutely refused to go wider then or ever. Dry leaves filled the corners, and cobwebs as thick and grey as blankets draped the walls, with spiders as big as raisins watching from their black holes. The privet hedge whose sweetness all through summer was like a cloying drug, threw a shoulder over the front of it and you had to walk round to get to the door. Soft shady green moved on the whitewashed walls and I quickly discovered that sitting therein, with or without intent, gave a temporary immunity to punishment, as well as providing the distraction of big black beetles which I made race each other along the seat to the very edge of destruction.

Under the bush, under the wild apple tree, in this lonely outpost, I'd listen half the day for sounds along the footpath, the first fearsome noises of strangers straying in from beyond the wood . . .

A shout brought us back indoors and Mother was holding up the tea pot, rubbing it like Aladdin's lamp. Till Father got the range working, this big brown pot would stand regally on a box with a packet of sugar, domestic totems of tribal continuity amid the desolation.

'Our Gerald's nose is runnin', Mam.'

Myra announced this with the biscuits, bending over me with a concern that filled me with a powerful dread, for the seriousness of her expression must mean, at the very least, another rash of warts, and I already had enough of those.

'Oh, wipe it for him, there's a good girl – and keep him away from the primus!'

We sipped our steaming tea and stared along the windswept field; the farm and all else lay over there hidden from view. Fresh paint and plaster mingled with wood smoke as the range picked up, exploding like fireworks and throwing gouts of choking smoke into the room, where it congealed under the ceiling like an indoor sky.

We squeezed round, feeding its flames through the bars with bits of a broken orange box, strangling every time it blew back in our faces.

'The wind's wrong for 'n today,' said Father, and he was more right than he knew. The wind was always wrong for this chimney, except on very warm calm days, the smoke pouring into the room and out through the windows and doors, which were kept permanently open.

Eventually we got used to it, or put up with it, but on this first day we coughed and wheezed and our eyes streamed like an epidemic. Before he caught it the lorry man finished his tea, buttoned up his overcoat and said he had to be off. I followed him to the door and watched from the front step as the lorry rumbled back up the field out of sight, wondering sadly whether he would ever come back to us . . .

A longed-for warmth spread out with the smoke, and for the first time that day we took off our coats. After bread and butter I lay down with the dog, a thing I'd done from birth, but was held back from sleep by the roar of whispers, the tea chest inches from my face, the chimney bumping, the dog's wet nose. I remember Mother coming from a cave and bending over me.

'Just look at the poor little mite!'

She touched my forehead and I seemed to float away over the bank.

Our bed was set up in the little back room and here I was carried that first night, shrunk to an atom, a speck who knew nothing of day or night, only the conscious weight of itself among other atoms. Myra was there curled to the wall, and in I squeezed beside her, quickly anchoring myself to her friendly lump. The sheets were slick and cold, the room bare and unfriendly. I heard the door latch click, Mother's pattering feet on the stairs, the hushed voices again in the kitchen below.

Night snuggled round the cottage, the little window rattled in the wind, and I stirred to the owls and the whispering wood, till at long last there was no sound at all.

I well remember that first day, but succeeding days flowed on unmarked, constantly changing yet always the same, like an unheeded endless river.

Daylight came from somewhere behind the wood, slanting across the bank in jets of gold, suddenly as if God had pressed a switch. Or it came out of the ground, grey and muddy and still dripping from the bullying night. Or the day formed itself in parts through the racing rain; long graceful curtains of it coming down the valley from Nailsworth, lashing us in torrents.

Some days stayed half-made and eclipsed, with the tops of the trees floating on the mist like weeds in a silent pond; or the sinuous mist itself, in the wood, shined like silk in the early sun and hung like drapes over the branches.

There was no apple orchard here, no ripe treasures to grovel for in mattresses of grass. Instead we had a large garden with a low stone wall right round the cottages – there were two – and nothing beyond but fields and woods that went on over the hill out of sight.

The joined cottages were T-shaped, with the back kitchens making the leg nearest the wood. They were brick roughcast with high tiled roofs, not old or young but somehow very worn and tired with use and isolation.

The kitchen chimney, which smoked for evermore, had a long yellow pot fitted over it to improve the draught, though it never did. But because it was crown shaped and yet clean, it made me feel that the house had been built especially for us, and I inwardly reckoned this chimney pot a symbol, put there to mark our coming, like heraldry over a throne.

I sat in the weeds and studied this chimney a lot in these first days. I watched the smoke pour from it in long coils, flutter along the garden and cartwheel up the bank. More often it hammered down into the kitchen and stayed there, wavering like translucent veils. None of the windows fitted properly (except the one in the back bedroom which had tiny leaded lights and secret ways with the wind). Lucky this was, for otherwise we would have died of fumes. The smoke poured out through these gaps and little rags of it took one's throat as you passed along the garden path.

In that first summer the dog and I joined the birds and squirrels in the dungeon trials of nettles, bean sticks, nightshade, cold slugs, hot hedgehogs and sharp bottles, all of which left a mark on me one way or another. In the afternoons the dog and I slept under the plum tree. It bent over us like a net and plopped fruit every minute. One merely reached out in hot half-dreams for the mouth-filling sweetness, often swallowing stone and all. The juice, slowly congealing over my fat face, hardened like shellac and I'd nudge the dog to lick it off, which he did with little tender probes of his tongue, as gentle as a nurse dabbing a wound. He was a black and white spaniel cross with red eyes and a fake bark, a sort of half-choked growl loaded with menace which kept everyone at the gate.

We called him Godsell after the people who gave him to us, and he and I in these first times of remembered summer tired first of the garden, then the field, and eventually spent most of our day in the copse, my first walk among massed trees, which scratched the sky and turned day into night.

The tower of the thicket was a massive beech tree holding the earth in its claw, and round its plush roots, behind the brambles, we found evidence of earlier settlers: rusting bicycle frames, colanders, wheels, batteries, tyres, rotting chairs. I lay the stuff around on the leaves: unexpected, unnatural wealth dragged from the bushes, green-tinged derelicts thrown there before I was born.

I lay with the dog in the sun dapple; we came here every day, a cool sighing land of birds and hot puddles of light thrown sideways into the trees. The cottages were only a hundred yards away, and the acrid smell of that chimney found me even here; but that was an irrelevance, for I lived here more or less permanently till I went to school.

The sky lay over me, the bank under me, and I knew of the village and valley; the farm was round the hill out of sight, there was nothing more to know and my life would remain this way for ever . . .

Wash-day Monday was the capital of the week, the beginning of counted time. Not that I understood name-days then, only recurring cycles of habits. But Mondays I knew belonged to the back kitchen and Mother in a soapy fog. I watched out for her in the steam, from the top of the pantry steps where we chopped wood to save bending down. I stood on the topmost step, grooved by the chopper, alert like a coast-guard and shouting warnings whenever she got too close to the high steps, which would skin her knees. An arm or shoulder was all I'd see in the fetid cloud: buckets crashed, water splashed, cross words spat like gun shots. The open door let out the steam, but it never got further than the old water butt just outside, where it met the cold air of the wood; not like the smoke, which you tasted and stirred.

This wet, fevery place changed our Mother completely. She was never bad tempered, but on Mondays in the back kitchen it was different. Even her voice changed, acquired a timbre and range never heard except at this weekly task.

She had plenty to howl over: the mangle which never worked, the damp wood and small coal, the green soap hopping out of her fingers along the stone slabs gathering dirt and dog's hairs.

The white walls streamed, the windows went blind, the cobwebs collapsed. I drew faces on the misty glass amid the debris of a dozen discarded chores: paint brushes soaking in jam pots, a clogged dog's brush, rusty razor blades, a tin of turpentine, broken pencils, half a puncture outfit, buttons and dead butterflies.

Mother wrung everything by hand. The sheets I remember were like pythons coiling along her arms, over her shoulder and down her back to the floor. Her face, young and smooth then, without a line in it, would be nearly expressionless. Panting hard, she'd fight its coils, wrestle it round the back kitchen and finally choke it to death over the sink.

'Don't get under my boots,' she would say, and her hand on my back directed me firmly into the weeds of the soap-gassed garden. I'd run under the billowing line, punching the fat pillow cases, while the dog yapped his Monday distemper, which always had a manic edge to it.

Mother imprisoned in the mist, the dog temporarily gone crazy, I'd leave them both and wander away to the furthest edges of the garden. A cluster of red poppies, startling eruptions like jets of blood, was where I always went. I walked into them, shoving my face to theirs, sniffing hard to overcome the soap. Also I had been told not to do it, and this was the first renouncement of authority, the first of many to be crossed off that charter of rules.

'Don't smell the poppies or they'll send you to sleep,' Mother had said. So I took a good long sniff and held my breath; but the excitement of this rebellion was swiftly followed by a disappointment even greater. I sat on the wall waiting for the sleep, but nothing happened; so I peevishly ran my nail along the calyx of the buds to ease their birth, and when they did not immediately spring into full round flowers I realized what I was up against.

On other days I gathered dock seed and hid it in the dark behind the coal pile, where it turned naturally to farthings and half-pennies, an unquestioned phenomenon, a gift of nature like puddles and seats in trees. Or I sat on the wall and sang of dogs and removal men; chewed the air, talked to the birds, shouted at the wood, chased continents of shadows over the rolling bank, lay suspended in the surprises of each separate day. Hot, cold or wet, one day never gave less than another; it was *today* always; ever the same day. Roaring, splashing or baking, it never really changed.

When I was bored with it all – the day, the bank, the chimney pot – I'd shut myself up in a cupboard and wait for Ted the baker.

He came the day after wash-day, so it was easy to remember. Coins on the table were another sign, and on my swinging gate I'd wait for him to turn in at the top of the field. I heard him long before he came into sight, and shouted his arrival across the garden.

'Ted's comin' with the buns, Mam!'

He came in a three-wheeled contraption, part motorcycle, part van, slewing sideways down the bank and making neat circles in the clover as he swung round in front of our gate. He charged into our morning like Mercury with all the news of that other world beyond. With his sandy hair cut like a brush and his long freckled face, Mother thought he looked a bit like Stan Laurel, and that is what we always called him among ourselves.

'Go and wait for Stan; he'll be here directly,' she used to say. I knew it was a secret though and that his real name was Ted, and when he came in I ran after him up the path.

'Let I see, Mister Ted. Let I see!'

He would lower the basket so that I could see the hot loaves and bag of cream buns with the grease coming through the packet, and the thought of that tea time was like the continual rehearsal of a birthday. Sometimes we had dough cakes, which Father liked, and tall black crusted loaves – cottage loaves Mother called them. Cut through, they looked like a figure eight, and one thick slice smothered with butter and jam, shared with the dog out in the weeds, would underwrite my good behaviour till bedtime.

All the sweetness and dust of the bakehouse was in Ted's old brown smock and I coveted it more than anything in the world. Its taste of flour and currants lingered in our kitchen for hours.

Sitting at the table, he'd take the red pencil from behind his ear and add up what we owed from a book so soiled that it looked itself like a piece of hardened dough. He sipped his tea, blew his nose and quickly reeled off the world's news without any extra charge. For these were the days when few had wireless sets and up there we were far from newspapers or gossip.

It was from Ted that we learned of the Spanish Civil War which had just begun. A lot of foreigners, clashing and bashing, black of hair and eye; bull-fighting people sniping the mountain roads and blowing up their own cities – Lord knows what for.

He told us of an Italian called Mussolini and of the invasion of Abyssinia: more bombing and sniping there. 'You never know where it'll all end,' he warned. Mother poured out the tea, lost with the geography

10

but full of sadness with his stories. 'Fancy. Mmm. Yes, well, you'd know I'm sure,' she'd say.

I could not then read or write but somehow the names stuck; names so gravely picked over by Ted and Mother that I thought it must all be happening somewhere over the hill.

One day he came with really shocking news: he said the king had run off with a woman. Their faces told me we were done for and I thought we would have to pack up and leave the hill that night. The shock of Ted's news made their eyes drift about the floor, their mouths drop, their voices plop like water. 'It's baad,' said Ted, and Mother's look confirmed it. They turned their gaze upon me and their silent stare made me wonder whether there would ever be a tomorrow, or another warm sun, or another lavender sleep.

Mother sighed the way she did when her head was bad. 'He loved that Mrs Simpson I suppose, that was the trouble.' Ted blew his nose, slung his basket over his arm and shook his head. 'I don't know! God knows what the world's a-comin' to.'

Ted never missed, never let us down. When the ground held lakes or the drifts sealed us off he still got through somehow, walking from the common in snow up to his waist. On days like this his face would be redder and shinier than ever, and longer too, as if the cold had stretched it, and he would open his coat and bend over the range for the heat to get at his chest. Then he'd go back out into the head-high drifts whistling like a bird.

I remember once he brought breathless news that the Crystal Palace had burned down; said it was all the talk. I thought it was in the village and wanted to have a look at it, but he laughed at that. ''Tis in London, bwhoy,' he said. 'Miles an' miles away. I went there once on a charabanc outin'.' 'All these things going on,' said Mother sadly, and I knew the bad news would later make her wander away up the bank and stare longingly down the valley: motionless, there on the hill, with the wind blowing her frock.

Of course there was good news too, and one day Ted told us that we had a new king and queen. He brought the newspapers and showed us, and I wondered where in the village they lived, and whether they knew about us up here in the fields. It turned out to be the last bit of good news he ever brought us.

After that things just seemed to go from bad to worse. He talked a lot of the Dictators and much about war. 'We're headin' for summat, that's for certain,' he said. And for certain we were, and so especially was Ted.

When the war he feared broke out he was called up almost at once; no one took his place, and now we fetched our bread from the village. With a few thousand others, Ted was shipped off to the Far East among brown, slant-eyed people who ate rice and not bread. The hot bakehouse he'd known was nothing compared to that full-blown sun, and sweating in the green steam of the Burma jungle he trained his thoughts on the wild white gales of our hill, the glassy frosts and sideways rain.

That day beyond the bamboo redoubt, the Japanese came like moving bushes, stealthily, with fixed bayonets in pursuit of our baker. Cut off and surrounded they all surrendered, and were led off and made to hack a road through the tangle, wide enough and long enough for a railway. Ted was lucky I suppose in that he survived the beatings, the snakes, the dysentery and beri-beri, and kept himself going by remembering his old rounds, his customers, where they lived, the names of their children, and what their orders were.

But when he came home again after the war, he was nearly white though still only in his thirties, and often seemed not to recollect that he had ever been our baker at all.

I tracked over the field in front of our cottage, measuring its face yard by yard. First to the water trough along the hedge, then to the lonely clump of ash trees, then the hay rick at its furthest point; prospects so new and different, so high and hidden, the source of lingering scents about my pillow, that now I beheld them face to face their mystery merely deepened.

Once, exhausted with miles of discovery, I found myself at the end of the drive, going back to that other place which was my real home. Out on the common, which opened before me like a featureless ocean, I trembled at its immensity, watched it quiver and slide and roll in the heat of day. I think it was here that I first realized how far and wide the world might become, if I let it, and sounds drifting up from the valley below were like prophecies struck out with hammers.

I remember it especially well, that day, because on the way home I was attacked by a dog. I was hemmed in with a wire fence all round and he had me down with one blow of his paw. He was a chesty, eye-sagging monster called Nero and he stood over me with his black muzzle brushing my wind-pipe. He ripped off my shirt then started eating my sandals, buckles and all. In terror and outrage, I screwed up a fist and slammed him under the jaw. He gulped and started choking on the sandal, and somehow I got from under him, clambered under the wire, and raced home bare foot through the thistles; my first reprieve, the first of a long, daunting catalogue of near misses.

The dog, a bloodhound, belonged to the Old Man – Father's employer. He slipped an extra three shillings in Father's pay packet on Friday night and hoped we'd keep quiet about it: two million men on the dole ensured that we did.

However, there was a curious sequel to this. A day or so later the dog began wetting and howling. He jumped clear through the lounge window and raced round the paddock half mad, and in minutes collapsed stone dead of a brain-storm. A coincidence, surely, but my indignation had aroused a benevolent spirit in my defence, of that I had no doubt. After that I began feeling even more separate and extraordinary. I saw strange figures waving in the wood, and the sprite's beside me in the empty fields now knew my name and I knew theirs.

With my sandals gone and never replaced, I went barefoot along the tracks and paths about the house. One path, the best, the one I ran on all day long, passed by the back of our cottage, connecting the village to the common. It was seldom used except on Sundays, and that was so much of an event that we ran shouting to the garden wall, watching the couples go by like an occasion. It was a briar-snagging, fern-fringed crease between the wood and the copse, ending in a stone stile, which was nearly as far as I ever went. Just over the wall, on the bank amid thick ferns, was a flat of bluebells and primroses, which sweetened our cold bedrooms.

To this lost place I came all that first spring and summer, hidden within its walls where the fronds towered over me like palm trees. Later, out of this desert-dry bracken, I lumbered to the wet, melting mowing grass and let it rush over me like tumbling water. The sun burned recklessly above, shreds of its light torn and thrown around my shaking cell like cusps of vibrant glass, flashing, always in motion. My fingers found the heat of the sod as I lay on my back under fans of verdant light, waiting for the dog to find me, the way he did, in these moats and turrets of my land. He came over the undergrowth like a porpoise leaping through waves, and got me to my feet. Then, barking, led off through the mat till he'd brought me safely to the gate.

I had a strange fever for solitude, something that was to stay with me for evermore. When the corn was grown tall I'd plunge into its molten veil and let it close around me. In its crawling bottom I'd lay on beds of speedwell waiting to be rescued. Too long and I fell asleep, till my Mother, calling through the heavy afternoon, brought me awake. She had a special voice for me, neither words nor music but an alloy of both, which rose brightly above the charm of the thicket. MeeeWeeee! MeeeWeeee! Like this her call carried through all the long summers of my early years, and finds me still at each day's ending. She would cup her hands and sing out from the doorstep, the bedroom window, or from the big five-bar gate under the oak tree; soaring, trembling chords echoing through the glittering wood.

Some days down in the wheat I'd take off all my clothes and with racing heart let the warm wind wrap me round and the stalks crash against me like many living fingers. A throb, warm and powerful, rolled round my stomach, and soon even the anticipation of being out there naked drugged my mind, made me feel animal and cunning and half mad for the pleasure. Once I tried it on a wet day, lost half my clothes, got chilled right through and came home with bronchitis. After that it lost much of its frail sensuality, and that part of me was only reawakened by the village girls years later.

This out of doors life, alone without eyes or ears, except those I made up, was a spill of that other life which was real, a rack of habits, beginning with light on the window and blackbirds calling in the hollow spinney.

I was always the last down, long after the others had gone and the house was quiet round my Mother. I came down the steep brown stairs one step at a time, with my trousers in my hand, wandering into the day-long kitchen of potato peelings, the sting of onions, the table hills of flour and breadcrumbs, bitter apple cores, wet pastry and lordly spoons of jam and Nestlés milk, these last two handed over as my due, the last worthy survivor of indulgence, the final presumptive connoisseur of empty tins and jars, the scraper of saucepans and bowls.

All through the quiet day I savoured my exclusiveness: we beat rugs, washed floors, chopped wood, made beds; chores that were in some ways games while Mother chanted songs by the dozen:

> *Goodbyee, don't cryee,*
> *Wipe a tear lady dear from your eyeee.*

Or for me:

14

I've been a soldier, I've been a sailor,
I've also been a policeman on the beat;
When I was a copper I was a failure,
Because I didn't have the regulation feet.

She might sing a dozen an hour or only one, or she'd suddenly grab me and dance round the table, pointing her toes and lifting her chin as we waltzed in circles to the tunes in her head.

It ended when Myra came home from school. Those carefree hours of preference vanished when she glided in, silently and unobtrusively, a withdrawn, bushy-headed object wandering round the kitchen, visiting it anew.

First the dinner bag hooked over the chair. 'I ate it all up, Mam.' Then the corner of the window with a piece of bread and jam through which she mumbled and splashed the latest news from Standard Two.

'Tim Green's bin at it again. Stole a tanner out the cloakroom.' Munch, munch. 'Pinched it out a somebody's coat on the peg 'e did.' Munch, munch. 'The boss 'it 'im sideways an' 'e fell on the piano; went tinkle tinkle.'

But sometimes she came in with quite interesting news, though was always slow to impart it. Once, after ten minutes and three large slices of bread and golden syrup she casually said: 'Oh, the chimney's on fire, Mam. I saw the flames a comin' out.'

One could imagine her coming home and with equal serenity announcing: 'I 'ad to kill the teacher' or 'There's bubonic plague in the village.'

It always took a good ten minutes to crack open her defences.

'What you done at school our Myra?'

'Summat.'

'What? What then?'

'Things.'

'What things? What? What things then? – make 'er tell I, Mam!'

'Sums 'n' writin'.' You'll find out one of these days!'

'Is school 'ard?'

She said it was just about the hardest thing there was, and it was about time someone put a stop to it. It began taking hold, that curiously strident fear that I too would one day have to go there, and even my dark thinking place behind the lavatory door failed to obliterate that sickening realisation: the thought of that far away village in the bottom where the king lived, and where children were herded to school and punished.

I'd come back into the light with my head still spinning and wait on the swinging gate for Father to come home from work. I watched for his head to come bobbing into view over the field, and followed him into the back kitchen where he washed away his special outdoor smell. What he did out there, in the fields, I did not yet know. I knew only that I wanted to smell that way too, and hung over his chair watching him eat, marking each careful mouthful, each slow swallow and taste; tasting it with him.

I especially liked the way he removed his hard boots, glittering with studs and as heavy as iron. The laces were like wire and the undoing of them a smart relief of grunts and whistles, a compulsion that meant something to men. Drawing them into a pair he'd drop them inside the fender and then set about his corns with a sharp penknife, paring the rough skin till it was soft and comfortable.

This was the prelude to his nap when we all had to keep quiet; even Bob who came in last of all, smelling of metal from the foundry. He was black and stayed that way till Saturday night when he went into Stroud to the pictures; a rather remote, self-possessed brother whom I observed from afar, oiling his air gun, mending rabbit nets, playing the mouth organ, smoking. He was finicky about his meals too and allowed to cultivate all manner of eccentricities. On his way home from work he would buy a sixpenny tin of salmon at Gortons which he ate like a starved animal, quite ignoring the sizzling sausages Mother put in front of him. Afterwards, he'd wedge the tin in the wall and use it for target practise, before vanishing into the wood where he would go without a word, as if he intended staying there and never coming home.

He was a good shot, and after he left the foundry and started at the piano works, saved enough to buy a bolt-action rifle for eighteen shillings. After that we lived on rabbit stew and our back kitchen became foul with skins, flypapers and wet coats and boots.

A thin, dungareed shadow, a prowler of dusk and dawn, he came home from the woods well after dark, and long after we were all in bed. We heard him softly whistle the dog, like a sentinel calling all was well; and his return, and the moon on the bank, at last brought a quiet over our cottage.

⤳ THEM NEXT DOOR ⤳

Summer Sunday evenings before the war were the rose of all these early remembered days, our walk to Amberley something we looked for but could never be quite sure of, a wish growing with the fine weather or promptly abandoned with rain rushing into the water butt.

So, then, warm days started the hope, lifted our eyes over the valley, and after our mutton dinner we'd wait. Father would look at the sky, reading cloud and wind. This meant he had already made up his mind. 'Might take 'em out later,' he'd say. Then he'd close the stairs door on us and moments later would be fast asleep in bed.

At that we hopped into the back kitchen and Mother scrubbed us over the sink. Hands and knees lost their weekend contamination, our Sunday best was unpacked like regal robes, and out in the field we were placed, stiff as dolls, afraid to move and nearly too smart and clean to breathe.

The fear was that Father might oversleep, for his slumber was a sort of coma, with thunderous struggles between life and death. To take our minds off it we looked for four-leaf clovers in the field. It was too easy; so we searched and found five-leaf clovers, then six and seven. In time we got up to eight, which we hoped doubled our luck, and I have no doubt that it did.

Every five minutes Myra sent me like a page to the kitchen window, and on tip-toe I'd peer over the sill. 'Our Myra said, "When's our Dad comin'?"' Mother, rolling pastry at the table, waved me away with a floury hand. 'Soon. Soon. Don't keep on, there's a good boy.' I'd run back with the message and wait for further instructions while Myra stared at the wall, frowning.

But eventually and greatly relieved we'd see Father at the bedroom window where he sat pulling on his socks; and for some reason we grew wide-eyed with surprise at this, as if receiving an unexpected compliment.

Mother never came with us, though we begged her to. She liked her own company, liked the easy house when we were gone. So on these Sunday evenings she baked cakes and tarts and sang to herself and went to bed early.

Off at last, straggling down the track, we heard her love song dwindle. As clear as glass it was, a sweet despairing sorrow drifting through the green wood. Before we reached the lane the church bells would begin and follow us down through the village, along the main road and up the far hill.

Our first stop was at The Bear, at the edge of the common. We sat outside at tables marked by previous callers and waited for Father to bring us lemonade and crisps. Here the valley changed her face; we looked at it in reverse, and from its dark bottom rose a blue mist which collected round the trees.

Here we drank to the sun and moon and all the Sundays there ever were or would be, holding up the lemonade to see the fire reflected in it. We drained our glasses upside down and ran our fingers round the crisp packets for the salt, before inflating and bursting them. Acid rose, our noses burned with it, and we watched the sun sink lower.

''Ope our Dad's not goin' 'angin' about,' said Myra, impatient with men and their drinking. In fact we seldom did linger here for this was a genuine thirst-quencher after the climb, and we had miles in front of us before it grew dark. He came out wiping his moustache, and we followed him up over the common. Warm it always was, with a rising dew, sunlight on the grass, and our shadows sliding along in front of us.

Bob was too big, too independent for this sort of thing; he was in long trousers now. Instead he would walk to Stroud with Ernie Powell, searching the empty weekend streets for girls to wink at, and it seldom went further than that. It was a sort of game, this waiting and looking, that would seem odd today, and so were the Brylcreem and creases. It was courtship laden with theory and tactics, and if they were lucky they would walk the girls home, no matter how far they lived. It was high-level romance one day a week, and the unions from such innocent beginnings never ended in divorce.

Just the three of us then it was, on these walks, though our Mother was there in our puzzlement. Over the left shoulder we watched the low sun roaring down behind our Elysium hill, where our cottage, under the wood, was half hidden and as lonely as a beacon. Sometimes we saw Mother in the garden, and shouted and waved. But a mile of air washed between us and we were just specks from there.

This common of Sundays only had been worked by Neolithic man, and the deep ditches he'd left were for Cowboys and Indians, or cover for impromptu lust. In them one came suddenly upon couples writhing like roots. They would jump apart, hands fluttering, smoothing dresses and combing hair – and one withdrew backwards so as not to miss anything.

These formal walks and times of best-clothes treats had a touch of immortality. We thought we might walk on to the end of the world, that there would be no sunrise, no tomorrow or school, just always the same warm endless dusk, and cake and sleep at the end, if it had to end. In that drowsy suspense we searched for flowers to fill Myra's scrapbook. It was a haphazard search and seldom fruitful: this common was too bare and grazed over. Ad hoc it had become the aim of our enterprise, though once, at the very beginning, it had had meaning. But now the scrapbook was bulging, the search no more than symbolic, though we still found treasures now and then.

Back there our hill darkened further in the last low light till all its features were gone, and only the glinting windmill at Top Barnes was visible in the fields. By Rodborough Fort we turned for the valley, for Rooksmoor and The Fleece. The cold lemonade made us shiver now as we watched the separate cars go by to Stroud. Men with sideways caps came out and put ginger beer in front of us. 'Yer dad wunt be long,' they said, winking. We knew them not but they knew us, and we guzzled the stuff effortlessly.

Glasses clinked, arguments turned to brawls on the forecourt; it sounded like an asylum. Beer gas and uproar rose in volume when the door opened and closed.

'G'night all! Don't be late in the mornin' Billy!' Guffaws from what seemed a thousand throats followed that smirking remark, but they laughed at anything on Sunday nights.

The light was gone now, the village lost in dark; just the ashes of the day lay cooling behind the climbing woods. At last our beer-polished Father tottered out to us with eyes glittering like sunlit water, though he had had no more than three pints all evening. For him though it was too much, and we took his arm and led him off up the hill.

One each side, Father in the middle, we began the steep climb back to Selsley Common, back to our own fields and woods which smelled different from any other. The long road half buried by banks and trees cleared Father's head, and took the very last of my strength, hoarded all week and willingly spent on these marathons. From now on I merely dreamed I was walking; the grass was black and bottomless, the ground moved under my every step. Myra wandered away scouring the deep black dips for orchids, though she was as tired as me. Somewhere along here I'd give up the struggle, cuddle into a pillow of grass, kick my boots off, and refuse to go on.

Father would turn and come slowly back and swing me onto his shoulder. 'You're gettin' too 'eavy fer this, little un',' he'd say, and so I was, at four.

The warm air stirred with all the sweet of the day in it, and holding round his neck I watched Myra hobbling behind, her little fuzzy head nodding at the grass, the precious flowers falling one by one from her dying fingers. Down under the wood, near home, the midges dived on us, and we carved through them with sickles of fern and elderberry, glad of the little pockets of cold air where they never followed: then we smelled the privet, and coming out of the trees our cottage rose up blackly, as sharp as a cliff, and I slid down at last onto our doorstep.

Mother was snoring upstairs in bed, and the warm kitchen longed for us. Father took off his jacket and cut three large lumps of cake. Exhausted by the air I found my mouth by instinct, my jaw and stomach were on their own. I held up my head with the flat of my hand, looking at Myra sideways. She was nothing to look at, just a wild bush of hair into which she poked crumbs, and her mouth moved slowly like a fish. By her plate the few wilted flowers were history of our walk, the picking of them already forgotten, belonging to memory.

Father lighted the candle and waited, one hand on the latch. The walls moved like silk around us, and when he lifted the light, higher holes appeared on the floor. Under the wavering glow we climbed ahead up the hard bare stairs to the dusty warmth of our bedrooms, and were asleep even before he closed the door.

Our neighbours, the Bolwells, were the first outsiders I ever really knew, and I studied them from the safety of our cabbage patch with that detachment and bold curiosity excused only in the very young or very old.

Old Bolwell, with his bulging voice and biceps, shouted his tribe into submission, or clouted them heavily round the ears. He was no man of compromise. His temper spelled danger and sent his family scampering for cover. As they fled from his wrath into the woods, the squirrels leaped chattering about the branches and pigeons whirred away over the copse. His little fat wife ('Er next door), though always planning his murder, never quite got round to it. Some women enjoy martyrdom, and she was one. His anger and flashing fists she herself willingly put up with, if it meant he left the children alone – that strange collection of halfwits and brilliant brains that made up their wide-aged brood. She accepted all their wrongdoings, and, although he had the strength, she had the tongue and invariably won on points.

Battle-hardened and blowing hard from their latest encounter, she'd come to our back door to tell us all about him and borrow all she could. She knocked and called out at the same time, very breathless.

'You in, missus? Only a minute.' She would ask if Mother was going to the village. 'I ain't got nothin' for Bolwell's tea; no, not a mouthful. I daren't think what 'e'll do!'

Mother handed over a quarter of a loaf and a pinch of tea.

'Bless you, missus! You'll get it back like always when I can get down to Gortons. I didn't want to go in this heat.'

In whispers she explained her 'inconvenience', ending as always with the story of her legs. 'They ain't bin right missus, not since our Harry was born they ain't.'

Occasionally she offered Mother advice as part payment for these favours. 'I see you got washin' out; sheets too, an' there's a blow comin', I can tell.' Her raspberry ripe face would turn to the sky over the bank. 'Oh it do look right enough now I grant, but its comin' on all the same an' you best get some of it in or lose it down in the wood.'

She told again how, once, the wind had sprung up out of nowhere, and she came home from Stroud to find all her washing blown away into the wood. 'Never did find me clothes line, an' our Jim 'ad to shin up the trees to fetch everythin'.'

The wind really did frighten her (whereas on Mother it acted like balm) and was her constant terror. She repeated the warning over and over, as if she feared for our lives.

'Wind, when it do blow up 'ere, missus, it *do* blow!' But we knew that already.

The Bolwells had five children, only two of whom, Polly and Harry, were still at school. Jim, Sam and Daisy were all out at work in the valley. For a long time I thought Polly was a boy. She wore her brothers' old clothes, cut her hair short, wore boots, and climbed trees faster and higher than any boy I ever remember.

But I knew she was a girl afterwards, by the way she cried when I kicked her, and her soppy punches were but feeble resistance, sorry imitation of her brothers who clouted me into the currant bushes twice a day.

When that happened I'd pick myself up and go sobbing to Daisy's arms, to her relish of bones and scent.

I'd let her cuddle me and stroke my head and tell me not to cry, that she would always look out for me. She was as delicate and frail as mist, somehow not quite real, not quite flesh and blood; and she was as tender and vulnerable as her flower name. Like that flower too she opened only when the sun shone. She would put on her bright petals and go out into the deep fields with all the other flowers, floating in the grass trying to capture a thought, a feeling, a hope that was her own. I remember her always in white, and when she went for her lost and lonely walks, on summer evenings, she'd mix with the haze of the back path and vanish out of this world. They said she was unfortunate, like her brother Jim, and there was some talk of a man, a stranger, who laid hands on her, dragged her into a barn when she was young, though she was even now only seventeen. It seemed likely, for she had a play of sadness about her as if her life had already ended; a wistful, searching elf bothered by wishes that she was too shy to grasp.

And her misfortune continued. Coming home from a walk one mellow evening, a gang of fellows surrounded her on the common, started teasing her and getting fresh. She made a dash for it, squealed for help, but they caught her and dumped her into the cattle pond. Ripped and soiled, poor Daisy came home and cried for a week.

'That poor girl! I've never heard the like of it,' said Mother.

'It's 'er dress,' Mrs Bolwell explained. 'It's the only decent thing she 'ad – an' all shrunk up; ruined like a bit of old rag.'

We gathered in the garden, wondering what to do.

''Tis that lot from Leonard Stanley,' said Mrs Bolwell, and she spoke of them like the hordes of Attila. 'They tried to get 'er before; laid in wait for 'er they did, an' 'er not knowin' what's right nor 'ow to stop 'em; but our Sam come along an' punched their 'eads for 'em an' 'er was spared the ground.'

News of this latest assault sent Harry and Sam racing away up the bank, fists and cudgels ready, their blood up. While they vainly searched the common, Jim was upstairs making a device to catch Daisy's attackers. He had several ideas in fact, one of which was to stake Daisy out like a goat and surround her with electric wires hidden in the grass. When the mob approached, licking their lips, he would throw the switch from his hiding place and fry the lot. He was perfectly serious about it and we had more sense than to laugh.

He made his lethal plan on odd scraps of paper; carefully made up words and meaningless diagrams which were supposed to represent electrical circuits; then he started assembling the bits. But the three hundred feet of copper wire, generator, engine and switchboard all came to rather more than the ten shillings that was his weekly wage, so he reluctantly dropped the idea and went on with other schemes in that half-awake world he inhabited.

He worked at the sawmill by the brook, and the men made his life a misery. Sweeping up, filling sacks with sawdust, he waited for the miracle which would one day put him upstairs in the office, where he would have the power to sack his tormentors. Those laughing devils who filled his dinner bag with mice and spiders would be the first to go; there would be no more of that when he was in charge. With a nice polished desk and a big brass ashtray, he would buzz the girl to bring him tea, and all day would do nothing but sign papers and give orders instead of taking them.

In the meantime there were other enemies to conquer. Like Satan-black winter nights, when the woods murmured about him, menacing him all the way home. He was all right till he got to the top of the lane; the houses with their chinks of light gave assurance till then. But as he climbed the gate into the Park, with the pitchy cold pressing round the hill like a wall, fear rose in his boots, shook his knees, hit him in the middle, chilled him with every improbable terror. Not childlike things of goblins or shapeless ghouls, but real blood-drenched assassins lying in wait with keen knives and heavy clubs.

He knew they were there, waiting to take him off guard, and it did not take him long to outwit them. He carried two torches, one in each hand, and talked to himself in two voices. It must have worked for he was never attacked and urged us to follow the example. Even so he half expected a murderous assault every winter's night, quite convinced that such would be his end sooner or later.

Coming home through the wet foggy fields, waiting for the dagger thrust, was about the only time his mind was on anything other than his inventions. It was just a question of hitting on the right thing, he said. Marconi and the Wright Brothers, they had done it, and so would he. He'd show them all.

He once had an alarming little scheme for recharging accumulators and batteries direct from the discharge of lightning. The difficulty was getting feckless nature to cooperate.

All that summer the assembled apparatus lay ready and sheeted against the wash-house wall. He sat on the bank looking down the valley where all the bad weather came from. At long last, one Saturday afternoon, it arrived: a boiling black mass riding on a skirt of rain, and in ten minutes it would crash on Jim's invention. The distant thunder sounded like barrels rolling slowly over cobbles, and with a whoop he began hauling his equipment into the field – to our relief well away from the cottages. His strength and temper were such that it would have been folly to try and stop him. His father might shout at him and even box his ears, but knew how far he dared go; for, once, when they sent him to get firewood, he came home with a tree, roots and all.

We saw the rods go up, watched him connect the wires to the twelve batteries set around in the grass, and he had barely time to get everything organized when the first spots of rain, as big as shillings, hit the windows and we all took cover. In seconds the field disappeared in the downpour; till the probing sun burst upon it and the copper masts blinked in the rising steam.

Then it darkened like a deadly dream, the sky zipped, the cottages shivered in the barrage, and the air squeezed like hot iron. Jim wandered about in this as happy as he could be, shirt plastered to his robust body, his cap wedged flat on his ears by the weight of water. But Ajax was merciful and sent all his darts well wide into the wood. The sky cleared, and a cold, very pale blue spread behind the storm.

Solemnly we put on our coats and went out to pick up his body, his mother already wailing the loss of her eldest. But he was far from dead and took no notice of us, wandering about with his hands on his head, like a disgruntled child, watching the thunder rumble away.

'Damn 'n' blast!' he said. 'It missed I!'

Although he tried twice more to kill himself in like manner, he was never afterwards quite as keen, and henceforth took his batteries down to the garage like everyone else.

The Bolwell boys (and Daisy too perhaps) acted like a magnet on the young men of the village. They came up two and three at a time, strutting about like Indian braves, showing off their knives and guns. Their shooting matches, through the trees, would have killed anyone using the footpath. Volley after volley snapped into the wood at the tin swinging on a branch. It was not quite rifle practice; rather it expressed the rules of the clan, extended recognition of their fraternity. The disputes over the scores were part of it too, the payment of wagers with Woodbines a binding ceremony. Daisy kept watch from her bedroom, trying to catch the drift of their primitive secrets. She had her eye on Bej, a frequent visitor and a hardy legend. But Bej had no eye for the girls. His love was the wild rabbit warrens of the hill, and he knew no other. He had the hue and brightness of an apple, was as tough as leather and nature's robust foil to disease. Varnished by rain and shine for sixteen years, he was both supple and enduring, and in all my life I never saw anyone so nobly tough.

''E'll be ate up with the rheumatic when 'e's older, you mark my words,' said 'Er Next Door. It was a reasonable prognosis all things considered, for he wore nothing but a shirt summer and winter, with just an old raincoat to confound the bitter winds. He preferred Wellington boots in summertime. 'They'd protect me legs from thorns 'n' stuff.' In winter he wore canvas pumps. 'They'd dry out quicker.'

He needed to be fit, living half his life in the woods, and carried a ferret everywhere he went, curled up inside his shirt next to his skin – a black-maned, pink-eyed killer which devoured bread and milk by the plateful. Bej fed it before setting it to work, to prevent it killing in, which would mean hours of digging by torchlight. On the other hand he never gave it too much either, for it would simply go to sleep in the burrow with the same result. Its snack had to be nicely judged, and at the end of the day, as reward, it received choice bits of heart and liver still warm from the kill.

Bob, Bej and Sam were the hunters of our hill and they met under the oak tree every Saturday afternoon. They loosed their guns into the wood as an overture, then dawdled round the hill to First Holes, a wild copse of oak and birch banked by fern, on a steep slope.

I went with them once, the only time I was ever allowed to. I could not have been more than seven at the time and was fed up after the first ten minutes. They shoved me under a bush and told me to keep quiet, while they looked around for the best holes, where the mud was smooth and covered in droppings. They pegged out a dozen nets and Bej put in the ferret. We squatted in the wet tangle, rather self-consciously. The flicking of ash from cigarettes was too exaggerated, too precise. They were old hands, had done it all before, yet were nervous in a way that they would not have been had they been alone.

Waiting was part of the game, so was silence, and I was no good at it. For a long time nothing happened. The high branches creaked; there was no other sound. Bej semaphored; he thought he heard something. Sam spat at a log and ignored him; Bob just looked puzzled. I held my breath and counted the ants running up my legs.

I was relieved when the ferret appeared, wriggling under the net. Bej grabbed him by the neck and thrust him down another hole, but disappointment was growing and we had only just begun.

They tried the ferret in three holes, but no more than three, and empty handed we gave up and came on round to Second Holes, a quarter of a mile in the next fold of the hill. This was a heavily worked area with a hundred holes pock-marking the clay on a very steep bank below a screen of bushes. The whole slope was a bone yard, the site of an ancient massacre when foot and mouth had ravaged the valley and eighty sheep had been slaughtered here. To the disturbed earth, rabbits came in droves, throwing out the skeletons as they went. Badgers and foxes added their havoc and flung the green bones far out among the coarse tufts.

The boys put down the nets again, banging the pegs in with their heels, though that was bad practice when ferreting. But we were cold and tired and careless, and silence had been dispensed with. It was Bej of course who kept hope alive, fanned dead enthusiasm back to life, made us disregard wet and hunger.

'We always get sommat 'ere. We *always* do, you know that. Who's got the fags?' Bob passed the fags around but it did nothing to quell the growing mutiny.

'It's that messin' ferret of yourn,' said Sam, always the first to crack. 'I wouldn't 'ave a messin' thing like 'im, would you, Bob? 'E's cross-eyed for a start.' Bob said nothing and chewed on a stalk.

'Somebody's bin round already most like: Old Smokey, or Dibbs or Barrett – one of 'em,' said Bej. He rubbed his purple hands, bit the nails and tried to raise morale. 'We shall be all right 'ere. Remember last time, Bob? We got 'undreds we did.'

Bob shivered, a thin purple line spreading slowly round his lips. 'Well I ain't diggin' 'im out this time any road. Not again I ain't,' he said. Sam puffed and nodded in agreement, as if he could already feel the shovel in his blistered hands. 'No nor I ain't. 'Tis too damn 'ard, you!'

But nothing shook Bej's permanent cheerfulness. 'I bet we get 'alf a dozen, there y'are. I bet we do. I bet we get three any road.'

Bob was miles away, shrinking down into his jacket, curling up like a snail. 'James Cagney's on at the Gaumont. It ain't 'alf good they reckon,' he said quietly. No one took any notice, though Sam opened his mouth as if to second the insubordination.

Bob kept asking me if I was all right. 'You ought not to 'ave come. Tis too cold.' I shivered as if the devil had hold of me, but denied that I was freezing.

'I be all right,' I said, chattering like a spring.

Then a rumble underground like the start of an earthquake shot us alert. The fags were pinched out and tucked behind ears, and we crouched round like wicket keepers. A net reared, a flash of white belly fur, a yell among the trees; now our luck was running. They laid the rabbits out in the grass and the boys seemed a foot taller. Bej drew his sheath knife, made a parting in the fur, and paunched each victim deftly. The long hours, the pain of cold and empty stomachs were immediately forgotten. 'See, I said didn't I! I *said!*' Never more would Bej's judgement, or the prowess of his ferret, ever be questioned.

The night stalked round, the moon came up and still they were at it above the blue woods. But they sent me home long before this. 'Tell our mam to get the fryin' pan ready!' Bob had shouted as I stumbled away over the bank. And at an hour that seemed like the middle of the night, he burst in, yellow with cold.

'Look what I got! We got two apiece!' Holding up a rabbit in each hand, he looked round for our praise. Raw air, fur and blood surrounded him in a warp. 'Bej lost 'is ferret. 'E's comin' up tomorrow to dig'n out.' And dig him out he did, though it took all of a weary day to do it.

They were not always so successful or so lucky. Bej lost three ferrets in the tangled chambers of Second Holes and grieved over each one like a lovely lost child. He hung round the banks for days, forgot work and meals, watched the ground like a hawk but never found them. Years later it was undoubtedly one of these which, one night, gnawed its way into a hutch and killed all my tame rabbits.

Prowling the fields and woods at night, Bob had nervy encounters with stray animals; unseen creatures that growled, flattened briars, left trails of startling proportions. Lights hovered on the grass; voices called near and far; images and shapes sliding under the moon. Much of it of course hallucinatory, engendered by hunger and fatigue – for he often stayed out twelve or fourteen hours at a stretch.

But there was one occasion when something extraordinary happened which neither he nor we ever understood or could explain. He was coming home alone, at dusk, along the bottom, when he heard the sound of breaking glass below, in a shed among trees at the end of a grassy track, and thought it must be boys smashing the windows. Putting his rifle in the hedge, he whistled the dog and started down the bank.

'Let's sort 'em out boy!'

In minutes they were at the bottom, where a short avenue of poplars made a cowl over Collet's shed. The noise had stopped now; all was quiet. He thought about rushing the stile, leaping down onto the track and clouting a few ears. It would be Murv Hollis and Des Turner again; they'd already done in two barns and been dragged off the church roof. He softly called the dog to heel, but all Godsell did was pant and sink down whining. Bob patted his knee to urge him up, but Godsell kept his head down between his paws; he wanted nothing to do with it.

The black trees broke among the stars and there was not a breath of air. Uneasily, Bob climbed the stile and dropped down onto the track. Looking round, thinking the dog must have followed, he saw him in the wash of light above the ridge, streaking for home, where he came howling at the door and dived behind the coal pile . . .

The blackness of the path now seemed total, the bank a wavy line across the empty sky. Thirty feet away stood the shed, doors agape. Moving forwards on his toes, he suddenly stopped dead, paralysed: something was taking shape between the doors! It grew out of nothing this thing, had its origins perhaps in the freakish mist rising from the moss, a calamity of condensation and fractured light. Yet, whatever it was took human shape, and stood there menacing and waiting.

Self-preservation broke the terror and he was half way up the bank before he came to his senses; but fear of that thing following, in the dark, was a spur in his flank, and he was dropping when he got home.

He burst in, sagging against the wall. When at last he recovered his breath, he looked around wildly, as if his brain had gone.

'You know what they say about ghosts?' he gasped. 'Well, I've just seen one!' Then he sensibly collapsed onto the sofa.

Father laughed at the very idea; we had never seen him laugh as much before. Practical as ever, he went straight down with the torch to retrieve the gun which was still in the hedge, while Myra and I hid in the pantry lest we catch the madness. Her frown thrusting over her eyes told me just how serious this was. She whispered we were done for if the thing had followed him.

But Mother, to whom stories of ghosts and ghouls were like tales of cherished friends, radiated assurance and complete belief. Of course it was true! Such a wonderful experience would be unnerving to say the least. And look at him! See how he trembled, how pale he was – that would be the shock, and him not yet sixteen!

She held his hand, poured sweet tea into him till he choked, and welcomed him to the brotherhood of believers.

After that Bob wandered among us like a chief, someone the other world had touched, and for days afterwards we watched him for signs of the spirit, or in case his blood dried up, but nothing very much happened. He had passed through fire and come through unsinged and unharmed so far as we could tell, and from what Mother said he was privileged and special.

Father continued to pour cold water on the whole thing of course, and perhaps it was a good thing he did, for we went to school that way. Next morning he and Bob went down to look at the shed, but there was nothing very much to see and not a single window broken anywhere.

So Father laughed again and said the boy had heard nothing but the wind in the telephone wires and imagination had done the rest, but we never believed it. For several months Bob moaned in his sleep, cried out loud as a grey misty thing wrapped round and drew him down, and Godsell would never go near the place again.

The Bolwells left without a word, they never said goodbye, and afterwards I went round and looked in the windows. The desolate kitchen, chipped and soiled, drew me back day after day. Without them, without their jangle, it was as if the cottage had died, so still it was, so quiet.

I set about exploring their garden, a place I had never been. I searched about for things to keep, solid things I could own in secret as proof that they had been here and that I had known them. I found myself questioning that emptiness, the first slow steps of the mind, fumbling with their names in psalms of regret.

That empty cottage and ravaged garden, the wayward litter of pram wheels, old batteries, rusty tins, broken bowls, bits of wire that ran through the ground like roots, and all the relics of Jim's inventions, drew me like a magnet.

The ash heap was a fascinating mountain twice my height, unclimbed and perilous, and I hacked my way up its slopes and into its sides to get at the prizes within. Its great dome, smothered with tea leaves and decorated with egg shells, had formed a lovely crust, like a cake, with little runnels made by the rain where I began my exploration. With fingers scavenging like pecking birds I dug out buttons and black spoons, cotton reels, sardine tins (which floated on the water butt like Chinese junks), green bottles, faceless pennies, corks, buckles and pieces of coal which I took shouting to Mother, as if I'd found a jewel.

With bits of a broken wardrobe I built a sort of wigwam next to the pile, and into this I crawled with my hoard, wonderous with solitude and satisfaction. Not long afterwards this garden and cottage became our home, and when the painters finished we moved in.

Two things are memorable about that move next door: we bought our first wireless set, on the hire purchase, at two and sixpence a week; and now we had a telephone – a thing like a black daffodil sprouting out of a box on the wall, which we answered but never otherwise touched. It was because of the telephone that we had moved. The line went only to the big house round the hill, and was to save the Old Man the trouble of walking the fields when he wanted something done in a hurry, which happened usually on Sundays.

When I found out what it was for I stood on a chair shouting into the mouthpiece about my chewed-up sandals and that mad dog, but the Old Man must always have been asleep. Once, after Bob had boxed my ears and Myra had knocked down my wigwam, I lifted the receiver to tell the King about it, but all I heard were strange clicks and swirls, like air flowing through tubes, sounds that seemed to come from behind the moon; so I turned the handle (I was alone) and when a woman's voice spat back at me I fell backwards off the chair, cutting open my head, and never bothered with the thing again.

I was still wearing a turban bandage when the Jameses moved in next door. There were five of them: James and his wife, Poggy and Jessie grown up, and old James the patriarch. Mother called him Kitchener because of his virile moustache and military bearing. He had in fact been a soldier of much experience and many campaigns, with medals won at Spion Kop and the Somme, and when war came again he pinned them on his suit and hobbled off to enlist. On Empire Day and the King's birthday, he'd go to the top of the bank and blow his bugle at sunset, which echoed gravely through the valley. Then he'd light his clay pipe and march down to The Ram to celebrate, and the flag on the clothes prop would stay there for weeks.

Poggy, his grandson, was his half hope to carry the Jameses' banner into the coming affray, for he said that there had not been a James for a hundred years whom the King's enemies had not shot at.

Somehow, though, the blood had lost its fire and flame through several ill-advised unions with squinty eyed, tubercular women, and in Poggy the fire snuffed out. His body was so wasted, so fragile, that his mother feared he might collapse at any time through unavoidable weakness. Ever cheerful and good natured, he used all his slender strength singing: a tender innocent detachment and philosophy which said that there was nothing greater than a day. His favourite song, 'Why Does My Heart Go Boom?', was a natural question considering the state of his health. Once, pumping up a tyre, he collapsed among the sweet peas and it took all the women an hour to revive him.

Jessie, his sister, was the complete opposite.

She alone had tapped the secret source of the Jameses' health and strength, famous in the boxing booths of Wales, and drew it unto herself in a nice stack of smooth hills and hollows that men had been exploring for years. Bob fell at her feet. It mattered not that her hair was dyed or that a hundred lovers had already wrecked themselves over her; where others had blazed a trail he too could surely follow. There might still be gold waiting to be found, and he went after it with a prospector's glinting madness. She was older by several years and half a century wiser, but she took him on anyway and led him away to the woods.

In a few months she transformed him, though he was far too bright to be wholly beguiled. He sampled, then struck her off his list; but it was through her I believe that he learned that there was another world waiting, and one Saturday he went off into Stroud and joined the army. Later, he wandered in whistling and casually delivered the news at tea time. He was only eighteen and Father said that he should have waited; the war would be over by Christmas anyway.

'That's what everybody said *last* Christmas,' Bob said. 'Everybody's joining up. Bej's brother, Ernie Powell – all of 'em.'

Myra wanted to see his uniform and would not believe a word of it until she did; and I thought it meant just that he was going to stand guard outside the piano works and prevent its occupation by the Germans.

Mother took it hard though, bit her lip, went white and silent and absently cut piles of bread, till she broke down and dashed off to the back kitchen to have a good cry.

Old Kitchener came straight round when he heard the news, beat him on the back for ten minutes, and said he wished he was going with him.

Even stone-hearted Jessie was moved, and renewed her interest when he came home on his first leave with his Gloucester badges up, an inch taller and straight as a post. Scarcely had he unbuckled his webbing when she came prowling past our door and drew him away to the dingle with one of her looks. Mother stared sadly at the cold tea and uneaten cake. 'I thought he'd finished with her. And him with nothing in his stomach too!'

Her look said he had gone over the top in face of machine guns.

I tried on his tin hat and lunged after the dog with the bayonet. We gawped through a golden, heroic mist, half afraid to speak to him now. When he pulled Myra's plaits, or twisted my ears, we blushed at the compliment and were proud: already he half seemed like a stranger.

Before he went back from that first ever leave, Mother got out her Brownie, saying that we all had to have our picture taken. We got dressed up like Sunday and went out and stood each side of Bob in the field. Mother looked round for the sun, shading the viewfinder. 'A bit closer. Squeeze right up; that's better. I want to get Amberley behind. Don't move!'

We shuffled our feet for a better grip, squinted and giggled, while Bob stood stiffly between us as if in front of a general.

'Smile,' said Mother, and we pulled our mouths into slits as the shutter snapped. 'Just one more,' she said, struggling with the winder and telling us once again the history of her camera.

'I saved up fifty Hornimans tea coupons for it – fifty!' she told us. 'You can't buy a camera like this for love nor money.' You could actually, but no one said so.

'Ready? Nice big smile now! Good! That's the lot!'

We breathed again and skipped upstairs to change. 'I hope they come out all right,' we heard her say, as she followed us up to pack the camera away in its newspaper. 'I'll waltz along to the chemist tomorrow. Might get them back by Friday.'

We did not realize it then, but this would be the last time we would ever be a whole family; never again would we be united. Bob's leaves were few and grew fewer as the war went on, and there were just frantic unofficial weekends when he came home throwing gravel at the bedroom windows in the middle of the night, reminding us that he was still around. He seldom wrote, and I at least hardly knew him: the gap in our ages separated us forever. He went quickly from my orbit and faded away, known and loved, but a naturally drifting particle like the Bolwells and the Jameses.

On rain-driven nights huddled round the range, Mother would stir the fire and talk about him. 'I wonder where our Bob is tonight,' she'd say, and I would slip at once into cosy regret, trying to remember who he was, for those days of rabbiting were long ago.

'Oh, 'e'll be with 'is pals,' Father would murmur, dozing.

For a while he was at Bedminster, then Borough Walls, not too far away, and hitchhiked home whenever he could. The raids were bad at that time and they worked round the clock digging people out.

He was posted after that and his contact with the village ended. At the end of the war he came back to Stroud, got married, and, except for occasional visits, never came near the hill again.

SCHOOL

The two parts of our village, north and south, were settled round a hill, linked by a lane and footpath. Really they were separate villages, half a mile apart, with the old coach road between, winding by tight elms. We children called this 'Along The Lanes'.

The other, better-known way we called 'Along The Top'. Just a footpath it was, higher than the lane. It began and ended at the council houses, at the north end, where a little iron gate rang like a bell. It echoed gladly in our quiet classrooms, turned our heads up that way to freedom and going home.

We lived in the fields above the south end. In those times villages were self sufficient, though already losing their economic importance; and where once they had supplied the entire needs of its population, ours was an appendage of the town, a convenience in emergency.

Ours was a small village once known by the Romans, who settled here and left their crust underground. Their relics were still being dug up, pavements uncovered, though never in our day. It was steep too; one climbed or descended and level places were few. We boys of course ran the hills and loved them, but the old ones clung on the pitches like beetles going slowly up a window.

The baker, butcher and grocers were still operating if not thriving when we arrived in the mid-thirties, though their days were numbered and the war finished them off. They'd long gone by the time we moved away eleven years later.

The Ram and The Yew Tree supplied gossip, counsel, slander, temporary anaesthesia and the black market in fairly equal amounts. Pubs were male dominated then of course; one scarcely ever saw women in them. They would be abandoned outside on benches, self consciously sipping ginger beer, patient with the men who would leave them there all night.

The street between the pubs was the width of a cart and no one dreamt that it would ever need be wider. Horse troughs at each end were generous bases for thirsty boys and animals. Their flow was thunderous, plunging from leaning walls: sweet, very cold and heavy in one's cupped hands. The water roared from a spring deep in the hill, to cool churns and sun-burned faces. Hard winters turned them massive, pillared with blue icicles, the splashing water quieted by layers of lumpy armour.

The north of the village was different from the south. Open, wider, greener, less cluttered, the contrast lay not so much in its character as in its assembly, which presented the church and school, side by side, with just the road between. If it had less amenities, they were enough, with a sweet shop, baker and The Royal Oak, and they had the virtue of being near the school.

The Y.M.C.A. just up the road from the piano works was in keeping with this more gracious half of the village, and gave us our very first taste of the cinema when, one afternoon, the entire school retired there to watch a film on hygiene. Nits in our hair, black fingernails, scabrous knees and an outbreak of diphtheria at Cainscross gave us this unique hour of Giro the Germ. Though we remained as dirty and medically hazardous as before, the liking for the cinema grabbed some of us alarmingly, and we'd wander off during playtimes to catch the afternoon performance.

The many big, ivy-plastered houses, iron-gated, never gave sign of life except for Navy Weeks or Spitfire Funds. In our dinner hours we boys explored their perimeters, their sanctuaries of silent lawns, clipped hedges, and stone windows. The matter of retrieving a ball from such places was no automatic response, but something we carefully considered, weighed up in sudden committees held in the middle of the road.

'You chucked 'n over so you go an' fetch 'n!'

'I ain't goin' in thur.'

'You be!'

'I ain't an' you can't make I! 'Er'll tell the Boss!'

'Yer windy!'

'I ain't! I bloody ain't!'

'You be. You always be!'

But eventually one of us would screw up enough courage and tip-toe past the gate. There we saw another world, little pockets of elegance, supreme and sovereign. We never knew who lived there, never saw anyone come or go. But we knew without being told that a word from them would have us doing lines till Christmas.

I was not yet five years old when one Monday morning I was taken to the back kitchen, washed with suspicious thoroughness, given a lethally large spoonful of cod liver oil and malt, and told I was going to school. The threat of school (and threat is what it was) was about to be carried out, and I went more or less without resistance.

Nevertheless, I was miserable, said goodbye to the dog as if I would never see him again, took one last look in the silent wood. I won a concession though; said I would be no trouble if Mother took me, and she did.

Down the January fields that first time the sun shone like a fanfare. Hard and flat and wild it blew, to be remembered always. It struck the dew in the long black hedges and moved the white cobwebs strung on the bank, and at the bottom of the slope, mauve shadows lifted the woods into the golden morning.

The school was two wandering miles away in the misty valley, and all the way there Mother tried to make light of it. 'It's only for an hour or two. There, you'll be home before you know!' Myra swung the sandwich bag, doing little pirouettes to show how little she cared, but all the time was ready to grab me if I bolted.

The play yard to which I was delivered was already seething. It was quick and loud and rough, body blobs stretching, breaking and merging with other body blobs, then dividing once more like cells, all part of one fighting animal. That shrieking clamour, the beginning of love and fear, remained to stir and whisper through all the next fifty years . . .

It was a painful beginning, coming from the fields, for crowds were new to me; there had not been as many at Stroud on carnival day.

Mother handed me over to Miss Aplin, the Infants teacher, who took my hand and led me gently away. Snatching a last look at the world I was leaving, I sensed nothing would ever be the same again; and a long despairing look at my Mother going away up the road confirmed it. I wanted to run, but where now would I hide? I wanted to howl my howl, which was like an inner death, but was surprised to find all my rivers dry.

Lines of pudding faces rose and stared as we entered. Miss Aplin looked round the class: 'Mmm. Let me see. Yes, I think we'll put you with Doreen. That'll be nice, won't it, Doreen?'

Doreen smiled enchantingly, and I could not believe it was all because of me. She was the first stranger of my own size I had ever encountered close up, and I gave her a good long look over. I remember she wore a green cardigan and blue dress and had a mop of silky brown hair. Her body was persuasively warm, a distraction gilded with Palmolive.

That morning, and all the mornings in weeks that were years, we made plasticine numbers and chalked letters on our boards. Sometimes Doreen put her arm round my shoulder, whispering softly like a mother. Her hand dangled idly by my cheek, plump and dimpled and a little moist, like a fruit. Her face, very close to mine, had all the power of the unknown, and when she withdrew her arm I felt something leave me, the exact balance of its pleasure.

At some hour or other they came round with milk and straws to suck it through; then we'd crayon on blue paper till dinner time. The school was in uproar for five minutes then went quiet as a tomb, till gradually it filled again with the shapes of voices, boots on gravel, temper and tears.

During the afternoon the smallest of us lay down on little rush mats till playtime. I stared along the worn, dusty boards, through the iron stanchions of the desks at scabby knees, scuffed boots and drooping socks, till eventually I fell asleep and had to be thumped awake.

That afternoon, or one like it, they gave me a jar of water, paint and paper, and I splashed them something so outrageous and puzzling that they thought it must be excellent, and Miss Aplin pinned it on the wall for a week. I remember the silent glances of admiration and resentment, the amazed speculation that I might suddenly become a star, though they need never have worried.

The church clock struck four and they let us go, galloping away into the cold afternoon as if we were finished with it for ever.

At first it all seemed very reasonable; hardly worth the trouble of coming all this way. Yet for all that, and even Doreen's enchanting attentions, I never fitted in. All I did for weeks was to stare wistfully out of the great window at the greater sky beyond, thinking how far away our fields were, wondering how the dog was getting on without me, and whether our Father and Mother might not have moved again before we got home.

Miss Aplin was very patient with me. She would come and play with the chalk on my board. 'See, this is how we do it.' She was meltingly attractive, her touch beautiful and secure; but she never got through. I had little journeys of insanity whenever she leaned over me. She made me an 'A' and asked me to copy it. I looked into her ear, traced the line of her fine jaw, watched her breathing and went dumb. She showed me numbers up to ten, while I studied her eyebrows, the chain round her neck, her silver nails.

'No, don't look at me. See, like this. Oh, dear! . . .'

37

The sense of letters and numbers bounced off me like bullets off armour and left hardly a dent.

'Oh, dear,' said Miss Aplin. 'Oh, dear; oh, dear! . . .'

After a while she left me quite alone, stranded in languid ignorance; except that sometimes she would come and stand behind me and I'd be dizzy with her eau de Cologne. I'd watch the trees and sky, fold my arms and do not another thing till playtime.

'Oh, dear! Oh, dear! . . .'

Our dinner hours in these first strange months were concessions like extra lessons. We were the only children who stayed at school, Myra and I, and that was another difference that set us apart. We spread the bag-tasting sandwiches on the desk and ate them in secluded terror. Silent class, silent meal, with only the ticking clock for company. The tortoise stove crackled and the pike glared from his glass box on the wall. It grinned, and might have died a hundred years ago, but still had a warning in its eyes: watch out for the hook!

Miss Aplin stayed to dinner a few times when the snow was swirling outside. She sipped apples and read *Picture Post* by the stove with her shoes off. In spite of her fascination I never thought of her as anything but Teacher, and teachers were sexless, a separate race and kind, not born like ordinary mortals but made by conjurers and magicians, and issued to schools to tell us what to do and keep us in. They went with the building and had a separate existence, like doctors and policemen.

Their power terrified. For all the smiles, kind words and gentleness with which we infants were favoured, very little softened their awesome authority. Later of course I had to face the fact that they *were* women, and sensation so compounded fear and desire that all punishment henceforth was like love.

Miss Aplin sadly did not long stay after my arrival. She went off and got married and settled in another county. We missed her love for all of a morning and by the afternoon had quite forgotten who she was.

Next day Miss Davage came to take us on.

She was a lovely, well-built Welsh girl who took us over temporarily in addition to Standards One and Two. Being Welsh meant music and she immediately resurrected the school band.

Whose idea it was in the beginning to arm five-year-olds with such lethal instruments as drums, flutes, tambourines, cymbals and triangles we never learned; but they were there to be used and Miss Davage saw to it that we used them.

Nevertheless, these musical afternoons were carefully staggered while the others were out at games, and it was said that our rehearsals could be heard right round the lanes to the bottom road.

The wonder is that we did not all become immediately deaf, or the windows crack and fall out, or the roof shed its slates. We were an ensemble of gnat-like maniacs, buzzing, puffing, drumming and chiming; a swarming torture, sucking blood and turning people mad.

All the while Miss Davage said we were getting better, and getting better meant louder, so the walls shook, flowers toppled from jam jars, pencils danced along the boards.

I had no musical talent even at this level and sank ignominiously down the ranks from four-star drummer to one-star triangle player, and finally out with the no-hopers who just clapped their hands raw and stamped dust clouds across the sharp sunbeams.

Miss Davage broke her hands on the piano trying to keep us together, but her trained fingers jigging over the keys, and the pretty tunes they made, were crushed beneath our thunderous exuberance. What she played we never knew, never heard. Trapped in our own addictive racket, tireless noise but music none, whatever it was we produced in these hourly riots was personally ours, and we dragged it into the light of day like a bucking mustang.

For our health's sake it could not go on – Miss saw us turning mad – and the fortissimo potpourri ended abruptly, the smoking weapons wrenched from our sweating grasp and locked safely back in the cupboard.

While we were bemused and still partly deaf, Miss organized us into a choir. She started us off with the piano, conducting and playing at the same time, which made her arm go numb and stopped her playing the violin. We staggered off into the tune, lost momentum at the first breath, separated into distinguished individual efforts, regrouped again and charged through the chorus. We were hard to start and nearly impossible to stop. Our voices just fell silent one by one, like bursting bubbles, till nothing was left of the song at all.

The only one I can half remember now is about Charlie the Darling.

> *It was on a Sunday morning, quite early in the year,*
> *When Charlie came to our house, that lovely cavalier:*
> *Charlie is my darling, my darling, my darling,*
> *Charlie is my darling, that dashing cavalier.*

Charlie was a bit off duty, flirting instead of fighting, but we took to him like no one else. Once, when we were singing it Miss Davage went bright red – a puzzling embarrassment interesting even to six-year-olds. Our smirking interpretation had caused it, and after that we knew she was a real woman and vulnerable.

After these long singing sessions we were flushed or deathly white, our eyes glittering with mania, our brains turned by the shock and strain of it all. Yet none of us could wait to do it again.

'Can us 'ave another Welsh hymn, Miss?' 'Can us 'ave the band *and* the choir, Miss?' 'What is a caviare, Miss?'

I searched for a friend among that curiously hostile throng and finally settled on Phil Watson who joined us at Easter. He was pale and as transparent as china, with red ears and glasses, and I thought we might hit it off. His father farmed a hundred acres at the end of the village and from our hill we looked down onto his house and barns, half a mile away in the bottom.

Mr Watson did his milk round with yoke and buckets. On the morning doorsteps one would find a jug and fourpence and a saucer to stop the cats getting at the milk. He would start at seven and do the whole village by eleven o'clock. He was a watch; time measured in deliveries door to door. Our worst fear was to meet him at the top of the lane, for the corollary of that was the stick in the Big Room.

He had lost an eye playing football as a lad and the empty socket made him sinister and fierce looking, like a pirate. His good eye ran copiously on frosty mornings, and, half blind, the measures overflowed, jugs tipped up, and snakes of blue milk spilled down the lane in a long series of links top to bottom.

By the age of seven Phil was delivering milk too, on the way to school; two or three cans which hit walls and gates and spilled down his legs, and might be half empty by the time they were delivered. I thought him marvellously clever, a head better than most of us. He mastered everything put in front of him, racing through the lessons and sitting smugly with his arms folded while the rest of us slogged on.

I outdid him only in two things: drawing and poetry. When Miss was absent in Standard One he would lean over the gangway: 'Draw I a cow.' 'Make I a poem.' Spinning his grey exercise book through the air it would crash in front of me like a stricken gull, and I would draw him a monster cow with horns like spears and an udder like an octopus. It filled his farmyard end to end, dwarfing all the sheds and trees, but he never minded a bit.

My star was slow rising, but rise it did, unexpectedly, during anthology, chiefly on account of my well-drilled memory, but also because no one else was all that interested.

'Gerald, would you like to stand up and recite something for us?' It was, of course, a command, not a request, and that first time I gave them *The Doctor*, without realising how much I was destined to occupy their time and skill. I gave my title cough, and hammered it out confidently, as loud and clear as I could.

> *'E comes with mother up the stairs,*
> *And by my bed 'e takes a chair,*
> *And asks in such a twinkling way:*
> *"Ows the invalid today?'*
> *'E sees my tongue an' 'e sees my throat,*
> *And 'e 'as a thing inside 'is coat*
> *With which 'e listens at my chest,*
> *And that is what I like the best.*

It was easy, and I thanked God something was.

Phil was never forthcoming with this sort of thing. He wanted coarser stuff to chew on, to grind up and build again. Adding and subtracting, multiplying and dividing, in this he had few peers. But soft abstruse poetry clogged in his mind like treacle, and one memorable day he dropped himself in it.

Miss asked for a volunteer to recite a bit of poetry and he was the only one to stick up his hand. None knew then or afterwards what made him do it, and he quickly realised what a mistake he'd made. Looking helplessly around at our wondering faces, his ears going redder than ever, he waited for someone to throw him a lifeline before he sank. Finding no comfort in our brutish stares, he coughed and began the ordeal.

'*The Robin*,' he whispered.

'Speak up, Philip; we all want to hear,' said Miss.

He scratched his chest, squinted at the rattling trees, and started again, not much louder than before.

'*The Robin*.' He waited for Miss to interrupt, and when she did not, took a deep breath and began again.

'The north winds do blow an' we shall 'ave snow . . . an' what . . . what will the robin do then, poor thing . . . poor thing . . . um . . . the north winds . . . um . . . an' we shall, we shall . . . um . . .'

'Are you sure you know this one, Philip?' asked Miss Davage, who ceased being neutral and joined the general contempt.

This was his chance to get out. He could have said he had forgotten it and could he do another, or could he do something else – sing a hymn, count to a thousand, anything. Instead he went blindly on, straight for the precipice.

'Can I start again Miss, please?'

'I think you'd better.'

'*The Robin.*' He gave another tiny cough to unblock his memory. 'The north winds do blow an' we shall 'ave snow an' what will the robin do then, poor thing, poor thing . . . poor . . . um.'

Stuck, unable to move, he was totally at our mercy. The walls echoing with laughter and spite froze his tongue and brain, though he continued to struggle feebly.

''E will sit in a barn an' keep hisself warm . . . um . . . warm . . . an' 'ide 'is 'ead . . . um . . . 'ide is blinkin' 'ead . . .'

But Miss Davage had had enough: 'Sit down!'

We never saw anyone so dejected, and through his tears he offered consolation. 'Please Miss, can I do a sum in me 'ead, then? Please can I, Miss?'

'Certainly not!'

Shamed and utterly disgraced, Phil slumped back in the litter of his memory, and we finished him off with a volley of contemptuous sniggers.

At six or seven years of age, Phil had already acquired the natural pessimism of all farmers, and on the way to school in the mornings would reel off a depressing scripture of death and misfortune. The cows had all gone dry with mastitis; the pigs had eaten deadly ivy and were finished; the cart horse was lame and would have to be shot to bits; the hay had gone black and all the corn was in the rats.

His ten-year-old sister, Polly, fell off the granary steps one night and broke an arm and a wrist. ''Er tried to commit sewercide I reckon,' he said gravely. And we fell silent after that, sucking the cold air with open mouths, shaking our heads and pondering the waywardness of girls.

But nothing moved or shook us for very long then. That cosy womb that was the Infants stretched through a whole year and a half, a separate tranquil cell swimming in its own cosmos of plasticine, tasty bodies, dusty boards and lilac. It was the last of innocence, the first of endeavour, and here we looked each other over with mixtures of suspicion and awe, seeing ourselves by turn brutish and kind, quarrelsome and conciliatory, and began the hard business of sorting each other out. We touched strangers for the first time as equals and learned what that meant. We breathed secrets to anyone who would listen, told elaborate stories of what we had, and even more elaborate ones of what we did not have. We began to feel the dark attractive shame of our sexual parts, and to sense its wickedness in the bodies around us.

Now it was that we began our first lustful adventures, brief forays in a desert of expectation where one's thirst began.

Round the back during playtime, comely pink girls, no more than seven or eight, readily lifted their frocks for us, and grinning, sallow-faced boys openly waggled their things, while the rest of us just gawped and grew tight and nervous.

Some girls with flourishing instincts went about as far as they could go. Triss Bevan once took off all her clothes and stood on the lavatory seat, brazen, proud and lovely. She would not do it for everyone she said, but she did it for Phil and Sparrow Groves and me, and we felt as if we had been given medals.

Some like Dina Marsh would drop their knickers a little and, with eyes closed, whirl round like ballerinas, letting their skirts rise just enough for us to see. Then with a contempt we never questioned, they would snatch up their drawers and race away out of sight round the corner, where they'd huddle and glance back angrily.

Others were less forthcoming, though no less provocative; enchantingly and more enduringly teasing in ways that suffocated we boys with a long-aching curiosity. They would stand upside down against a wall and let their dresses fall back over their heads. Dolly-mixture underwear, pink, white and blue, enticed our latent interest, so that things began stirring in the soft caverns of our loins, making us happy and morose.

So, then, on we went in our beginning. Nothing we did or learned was new, yet all was revelation. Our exercise books of these early days had little squares in which we drew numbers and letters, and all day we lay on them inside curled arms, while our lolling tongues searched the chalky air.

We'd hold our bladders till they nearly burst and at last thrust up an arm, fired like a distress rocket. 'Can I go out the back, please Miss?'

Five minutes in the back yard brought back the old ache: Mrs Webb hanging out her washing, the sky filled with trees and fields, dogs barking, cattle still like china, buses in the bottom road.

Happy though they made us, these brief interludes merely caused longer discontent, and one returned to class not refreshed but somehow more rebellious than ever.

It ended, this time of nature rambles, painting, sleeping, singing, numbers and names, in a Christmas party. For a week we shoved our books aside and delirium swept through the Infants. Hands took over from brains as we leaped from learning to doing. 'We're going to make paper chains,' said Miss, and deranged by the sudden switch in routine we started making streamers. These glorious chains, rustling round our desks like sun-splashed serpents, quite made us forget where we were, the time of day, the week, even our names. No one wanted to go home. We just wanted to cut out paper and slap on paint and glue, and some of us would have been content to do it forever.

On the last day the older boys (like men we thought) came and strung these streamers across the room, end to end and side to side, then shoved back the desks to make room for the trestles and boards.

Four o'clock came that day but no one went home. The light faded to blue and black and night boarded all the windows. Two big boys came from Top Class with Mr Magg, the headmaster, to light the gas lamps which popped and hissed, and slowly illuminated the room.

Then all the teachers came in: Mr Magg, Mrs Smyth, Miss Davage and our new Infant teacher, Mrs Sawyer – Sawbones Sawyer who made us yearn for the tender Miss Aplin. They clothed the tables and piled on plates of meat paste sandwiches; sausage rolls and cream cakes appeared for the banquet with jelly and blancmange to follow. But first we had to earn it, and it was surely the middle of the night when we were driven up one end of the room to sing our carols. Thoughts of the coming feast sweetened us as never before, and Miss Davage grew moist-eyed as she drew us carefully into 'Silent Night', 'God Rest Ye Merry Gentlemen' and 'Good King Wenceslas'.

But it was 'Away In A Manger' that did the trick, eclipsed everything we'd ever done and set Christmas over us like a crown. This golden achievement was a gift of the gods for this one time and place, this one performance. Only our names remained, for the better part of us was far away under a star outside that lonely stable.

Haway in a manger, no crib for a babe,
Tha little Lord Jesus a-asleep on the hay;
Tha cattle har lowing, tha baby awakes,
Tha little Lord Jesus no-o cryin' 'e makes.

Breathlessly we spun through the well-known words, broke them down and rebuilt them again in our Gloucester fashion, with the added strength and beauty of the story, the dark night, the coloured streamers, the snow outside, the warmth, our houses waiting. We finished and the carol trailed mistily away over the dark village; and in the wide silence that followed the hissing gaslight was like sighs of admiration.

After that we were let loose and loony. We put on funny hats and sat round the rocking tables. Miss Davage scooped out the jelly, her full jumper touching our shoulders as she leaned down to serve, and she had never been that close before. The natural demands of our stomachs were restrained, and gluttony developed slowly, self-consciously, and only really got going when we saw Pug Dutton secreting the stuff under his jumper. In no time at all we were licking our fingers, washing the lot down with tea poured out of big brown kettles.

From the other classrooms came minor eruptions of anarchy, followed swiftly by cheers or deathly silence.

To each room in turn Mr Magg came and made a short solemn speech, as if he were addressing the House of Commons. He came last to us, and I do not remember what he said, though we all listened intently and gratefully.

With full bellies and our heads ringing with the holiday, we started yawning and falling asleep in the corners. Swaddy Hughes was sick over Doreen, and Pug choked trying to eat a concoction of sugar and tea leaves.

With these emergencies dealt with, they let us put on our overcoats, and we jangled like drunks into the half-dark cloakrooms, grinning at our enemies and punching our friends. At last in the cold pressing night we lit our sparklers in the yard. The spurting glare made familiar faces shapeless and pale, and made the surrounding black hard enough to lean on.

Out of this ragged light parents appeared to collect their own. The lights died in fluttering puffs of sulphur, and in the pitch-black our Mother was just a shape against the stars. She pulled up the collar of my coat and did up the button. 'This night air!' she said.

Father found Myra going home with Audrey Ross, and had a word with Mr Magg out of politeness. We stamped and shivered, bawled goodnight to our friends and half-listened to what was being said.

The last party for years, perhaps ever, said Mr Magg. War. Munich. Mobilization. It meant nothing. I thought the school was closing down and was delighted.

The evacuees swooped on us like migrating birds, all at once and in some numbers.

By now we had moved up to Standard One, just across from the Infants, at whom we now snapped our fingers. In Standard One and Two (we shared the same room, teacher, and stove) was shaped that rough education that developed to the limits of its kind or promptly withered without further effort or comment. Quartered with envy, jealousy, hatred and love, its cauldron coiled with plots and subversion. We were all in this together but none were very close. One's friend of this playtime might be the enemy of the next. All friendships were thin, bare and ruthless, and for the first time you were alone with your own strength and brains.

What harmony we achieved flowered when the evacuees arrived: it was a question of ganging together against them. For a while, at first, we wagged our tails or bared our teeth at them; afterwards, with their city difference, they were attractive, and for a while we collected them like cards, valuing them for their slick newness, till they wore and became just the same as ourselves.

This sudden influx brought practical problems. The trouble was space. Extra desks were found or made by Mr Cardwell, the local carpenter. But it was not enough, and instead of three backsides to a bench, now we were five. Knees touched, elbows crashed, and girls' hair tickled one's face like gnats.

The war came with perfect timing, and gave to learning distraction and distinction. As we fought for elbow room, we'd watch the men outside putting strips of paper like big kisses all over the windows, to prevent splinters. Later they knocked a wall down and dug us an air-raid shelter in the field at the back.

We wore gas masks during lessons and turned hours of arithmetic into snorting carnivals. Miss Davage found herself outclassed in such a circus. 'That'll be quite enough of that, thank you!'

'Can't 'elp it, Miss. It's this *thing*!'

'Can't see *anything*, Miss!'

'Nor I can't!'

'It's good, Miss!'

'Brenda Jackson's fainted again, Miss.'

'I be smothered in ink!'

'Oh, Miss!. . .'

We knew Miss could have killed old Hitler, and as her temper wore thin it brought about our first clash of wills. One day she pounced and dragged me out by the collar, lectured me in front of the whole class. 'You're idle, Gerald Roberts, and you're careless. You're careless because you're idle. You'll stay behind tonight, that's what you'll do!'

I tried to shift the blame onto the Germans, but of course it was no good.

These gas masks were wheels for our personalities too. Some show-offs wore them to school, all during playtime, and even at home weeding the garden. The cry-babies wanted nothing to do with them. They brought notes from their mothers and stamped their feet, yelling on the Bible that they did not mind being gassed in the least so long as they could go home afterwards.

Gas masks finally faded out and air-raid drills became the thing, at least once a week in the early years of the war. Mr Magg would wander into the yard waiting for a friendly aeroplane to pass over, which gave verisimilitude to the emergency; then he'd blow his whistle, three long, hard blasts, and lean on the wall panting, waiting to see what would happen.

Actually, we were fairly well drilled. We'd drop our pens and shuffle noiselessly into the bare cold morning (it was always a morning), following the contours of the building in case we were strafed; then into the field and under it.

It was almost totally dark of course, the duckboards slippery, the raw ragged benches splintery and wet. Water dripped down one's neck and clods of earth broke loose upon us as we lashed out, suffocating. 'There's plenty of air,' said Mr Magg. 'Don't want any nonsense!'

To get our lungs working he made us sing. We were in a burrow so I suppose it was natural that we should begin with 'Run Rabbit Run'. 'Roll Out The Barrel' we bawled like a gang of drunks; the purring 'White Cliffs of Dover' sent Dolly Osborne wailing because she lived there; and 'We'll Meet Again' hung in our throats like a rash promise.

Requests were encouraged, and once I remember we sang 'Keep The

Home Fires Burning', though none of us afterwards could recall a single line of it. The shyest gave out like trumpets and the bullies did nothing but complain. We all enjoyed it, and sternly encouraged the faint-hearted bookworms to do the same, with sharp blows in the ribs.

Finally though, the Germans went away, the All Clear sounded, and we emerged with sodden jackets and frocks and mud-plastered hair, watched by a half dozen heifers whose field it was.

It was back to our desks then, back to shillings and pence, back to composition, spelling, reading out loud and *The Pilgrim's Progress.*

We all had favourites, the things we did best. Sparrow and Phil swallowed sums like butter. Swaddy Hughes and Maggy Thule knew the names of every city and town on the globe – at least they seemed to. They could tell us that Timbuctoo was in Africa and Dij in Rumania. Throw any unbelievable name in the air and they would find a country for it. Their hands would pump up and down and tell us that Kirin was on the Sungari River in Inner Mongolia, and Bd was in Nepal. No one knew how they did it, not even the astonished Miss Davage, for these things were too ripe and wise for our village digestions, and came, we suspected, from their fat, brainy fathers.

History came in a thick red book and was well received, for it meant folded arms and doing nothing for an hour. It was all ancient, a few years before our time – perhaps in grandad's day. Dane speared Saxon; Saxon axed Norman; King Harold and that arrow; King Edward hammering the Scots; King Henry and all those wives. There had been battles not far away at Tewkesbury and Evesham, and a king had been murdered at Berkeley where I was born. The rush and thunder of hooves, the clash and spark of iron, the defeats and victories, the heroism and betrayals, the waste of ancient families, charged through our classroom every Tuesday and Friday. Miss Davage made it live with all the colour and eloquence of the Welsh, till she was breathless and little spots of white came to the corners of her mouth. Her lovely lilting voice presented perfectly the stage of centuries, and we were loathe even for her to catch her breath.

We loved the Trojans; I did anyway. It had happened so long ago and there were only scraps left, but it might have happened yesterday the way she told it.

Battles were in fashion then, their virtue untarnished, unquestioned, and there was not a boy in Standard Two who did not crave to be another Hector, though National Service was the later reality.

These ancient ceremonial wars, Christian, Hopeful and Faithful, the flash of conflict and trials of life, belonged as surely to this classroom as the high perpendicular windows, the tart chrysanthemums, the pink map on the wall, Miss at her lofty desk, the chalk-smeared blackboard, and the lumps of backs curled in rows, like furrows.

We were being measured, and there was no telling which among us would come through, or whether in the end it would matter. We were on the road and the way showed pitfalls which began to reveal our inadequacies. The bright ones were coaxed to the front, the dullards shoved to the back, and the rest of us fitted in somewhere between. Our clothes, smart or patched, started the caste system; our brains completed it. Loud, eager, indifferent, careless, stupid, cunning – we were all these. We began to be cruel and to feel cruelty. When Miss Davage dragged us out we had to swallow the scorn of our equals, the most feeling punishment of all. The bright ones were excessively applauded, the mediocre righteously chivvied, the brainless totally ignored. Some like Tommo Plummer were nearly sightless and had to creep out and squint at the blackboard from a few inches, and spent all day doing nothing else. Those like Lily Barns lost hope early on; gave up trying to spell their names or make sense of numbers, and came each day with little appeasements of flowers and apples, to win a smile from the Teacher and for once to be noticed.

Punishments proliferated in lines up to a hundred and beyond: 'I must not talk in class', 'I must not waste paper', 'I must *work*'. There were heroic ones too, signs of mutinous independence: 'I must not break windows', 'I must not answer back', 'I must not bash girls', 'I must not smoke in class'.

Staying In was a totally humiliating exercise, worse than lines or the cane, for it implied encroaching mental degeneration which had to be isolated before it infected the rest. You were kept in during playtime and, much worse, after school, and I became an habitual Stayer In from now on.

The four o'clock bell and the clamour died in the out-of-doors afternoon, quickly sometimes, or slowly, with boys calling along the lane. Then in total silence I'd huddle again over my book, and the sound of my scratching pen was all.

Alone with the sensuous Miss Davage – the desire of all the older boys! – and here was she and I, touching thighs, squashed at my desk. The loss of freedom and the spite of friends counted more, though, than even her warm pressure on my arm, and usually I did not even get that. 'Don't you go till you've finished,' she'd say. Then, more gently: '*Do* try Gerald.' But I think she knew it was a waste of time.

I would be half dead with numbers, my throat tight with grief, when Mrs Loader the cleaning lady came bumping in with her buckets at six o'clock. 'What, you still here! I should get off home lad!'

She was a large lady with fists like a navvy, and her absolution was full of grace and strength. As I ran out of the yard, boys called to come and play cricket – boys jam-smeared from their tea. But I'd ignore them, running deaf and blind till I was safely in our fields, and never stopped until then.

In Standard Two I fell in love with one of the evacuees. Anne was her name, Sunderland her home. I never knew when she first arrived at our school, but one day I suddenly noticed her among the others, freckled and sun-lit, and she looked at me as if she was meant to.

Puppy soft and Sunday quiet, bright like a flower in stones, no love affair in after years was ever more keenly felt. I was captivated and she knew it, the sure way women do, and never did I wonder why she had chosen me, or why the other lads had not noticed her as I had.

At dinner time we made our separate way to the field and sat by the stream on a little tump, where the rushes put a fence around us. We declared our undying love, which I believed and she did not; though strangely it was years before I realized that. I'd wade out to fetch her little celluloid duck which kept floating off among the marigolds. Sometimes she would follow me, out in the cold water, out on the sun-raked pebbles, her dress tucked into her pants, her yellow hair falling across her face. Distracted by the mud swirling round her feet she seemed wholly self-possessed – with me, yet solitary.

We held hands and to have kissed her would have meant the world; but I never did. We sat close, trailing our feet in the green-tongued weed, and I looked for the pulse in her neck, moving like a thing urgent to be born. She was ever calm and expectant, the bright water reflected in her face, and, enduring my interest patiently, always sought to embolden me.

'Why do we come here?' she asked one day.

'You know.'

'Dave Walby *kissed* Fetty Pearce!' She tossed her head and up went her chin, but the rebuke went wide of my lagging courage.

'She gotta go in a 'ome.'

'Well anyway – he took her up there.' She pointed to the woods in the sky.

'She gotta face like a bucket!'

Then she leaned on me with that hot whisper: 'I seen my dad an' mum kissin'.'

At school we avoided each other in case they found out; but no one did during the whole of those two stricken months. I would watch her skipping in the crowd, yearning for the daily consummation of our secret.

'You know what I am to you and you are to me,' she would say. And trussed by that oft-repeated declaration, there rose in me a strain of seriousness that wished this to last forever.

'Forever' of those days generally ended on Friday afternoons, and this one was no exception. I watched her run out of the school yard that day; she went without a wave or look back and I never saw her again. That weekend her mother came and fetched her home, took her back to Sunderland. I waited for days by the stream, hoping she would come as usual, swinging through the grass waving her ribbon. I said prayers and made promises to all the gods I ever knew, but my wish was never granted. Yet her memory stayed on around that bright flowing water, the wind in the secret reeds like the breathless way she spoke.

After that I rather forgot about love. Anne had gone but school remained, and we endured if not improved.

Bursts of excellence, when one's mind freewheeled, ran with days of doubt, boredom and stark fear, when a vice gripped the mind. Massive apprehension of sudden lethal punishments would come without warning and spread with the virulence of cholera. A terminal hush would descend on the school, when the odd nervous cough was like a trumpet blast in a cathedral. Discipline was heightened by our packed numbers within the walls. Outside, though we were still on a leash, orders and rebukes mattered less, so that events like Armistice Day were embraced like a half holiday.

At morning assembly we were given poppies and a good stirring speech by the headmaster, stiffened with names like the Somme, Flanders, Gallipoli – places known from that other war. They meant little at first, but with repetition became holy, like the Crucifixion and Resurrection.

We'd line up in the wet November light and clatter off in double file to the war memorial half a mile away. Arranging ourselves silently into a thick semi-circle round the cross, caps off, heads bowed, we waited for the church to strike eleven. The strokes fell sombrely over the empty fields, wavering through the mist. We stared at our boots, chewing our lips, as the fog gathered beads in our hair and lashes. Rock still, no one moved a finger, and even the bullies had their eyes closed.

After the minute's silence, 'Oh God Our Help In Ages Past' swelled nobly over the buzzing saw mill in the bottom. Some men, passing by, joined in with their hats in their hands, and women going shopping lingered over by the wall, not singing but watching, as if they would never see us again.

So Armistice Day, Gas Drill and Air-Raid Practice brought the war nicely into focus with that other war of long division, fractions and decimals, where hardly anyone survived. But it was the plane crash that brought us properly into the war. The Home Guard, Salvage Drives and gas masks were accessories of a common purpose. Food rationing and shortages of every kind were strident, immediate ties of a unified effort. The plane crash on the other hand was a decoration which made us exceptional. An Airspeed Oxford it was, a twin-engined trainer, and all the morning it had droned overhead in the mist. Low aeroplanes were common, but this one was very low, and kept drawing our eyes to the window as it circled overhead.

It crashed about midday in the south of the village, in the lane leading up to our fields, and Swaddy rushing back from dinner brought us the sensational news.

We raced away over the fields, Dipper, Sparrow, Pansy and I. It was uphill and we ran all the way. Here and there smoke thickened the mist and the wet air tingled with petrol, but there was no fire. Coming up the last steep bit, open mouthed and gasping, we straggled over to the stile and there gathered in a knot, dumbfounded.

Five or six people were below us in the lane, leaning over a boy of about twenty, lying in a gateway. They had removed his flying helmet (or perhaps it had blown off) and someone had half covered him with a blanket. His pale unmarked face was calm and beautiful, and a breeze stirring his hair a little took away the terrible edge of his quietness. Two men knelt at his side while the others stood around helplessly. A woman was crying with her head resting on the ivy wall. They were hoarse, thin with shock, bewildered.

'Why don't 'em come!'

'Is a gone?' (Whispered.)

'Thought a tried t' say summat – couldn't tell.'

'They'll 'ave t' carry 'im down the 'ill – won't get no ambulance up 'ere.'

Gliding like ghosts and wringing their hands, the lane quickly crowded and mourned. We boys were in the presence of death for the first time; yet only lightly touched I think. This or any other tragedy found no hold in our barren experience, and, whatever it was we felt, we hid.

No one had noticed us staring down through the hedge, till the woman stopped crying and looked up. (It was Miss Lambert, who had all those pet sheep.) She saw us and her hands fled to her mouth.

'Oh, look! Oh, look at them bwhoys! Dear God! Get 'em away somebody!'

She started howling again and a man detached himself, rushing forward and foolishly waving his arms as if he were driving cattle; so we slunk away. Coming down the fields, hands in pockets, we cursed him and talked it over.

'D'you reckon 'e was dead?' asked Dipper. He had blue scabby knees and sniffed loudly after each sentence. Sparrow answered through his scarf. 'I didn't see no blood nor nuffin.'

'I reckon 'e was, you,' said Dipper, sadly.

Thus our sorrow for the dead airman was expunged in these rough observations and few minutes silence.

When we were nearly back at school, Pansy said: 'Did you see that lady?' His eyes blinked at us out of a bundle of clothes. ''Er was cryin' you. I never see a woman cry out a doors before.'

'They be always doin' that,' said Sparrow, who had four sisters grown up and was wise beyond his years in such matters.

Dipper stopped and scratched his festering knees. 'Well I be goin' back tonight any road. Who's comin'?'

'I ain't. I got 'omework,' said Sparrow.

'What about you then, Ger?'

'I ain't comin' all the way back down just for that,' I said.

We looked at Pansy who had his head down, staring at his boots.

''Er was cryin', you; cryin' 'er blinkin' eyes out 'er was,' he said.

Coming home that afternoon a policeman stopped me at the bottom of the lane. 'You can't go up there,' he barked, 'The lane's blocked.

There's bin an accident.' But I was too quick and dodged past him. He started after me but was old and soon gave up. 'I'll 'ave you!' he shouted. 'I know your father!'

The plane had gone in halfway up the lane, narrowly missing Mutton's cottage. The bulk of it lay in his garden, the undercarriage and wings poking through waves of black soil. The wooden fuselage burst among the gardens and orchards, telephone wires hung from broken poles, trees were down, the wreckage deep and difficult to walk through. One engine lay in Gilbert's paddock, being examined by a pony; the other struck the corner of a house and fell on the lawn fifty yards from the impact. Near the worst of it, where a garden gate had stood, a sentry guarded the crash with rifle and bayonet; a cup and saucer was on the wall nearby. Apart from him there was not a soul about, and he did nothing when I snatched bits of wood and metal for my relic box.

I stopped at the gateway where the pilot had died, and never again did we pass that place without saying Amen.

They cleared the debris next day, and only the wrecked gardens and broken walls remained to show what had happened, though a smell of petrol and metal lingered on (and some say lingers still). In the spring the orchards crowded with apple blossom – no one had ever seen it better – and the clean sweet fever of wallflowers made the lane forget. But for years it was possible to find bits of wood and aluminium washed out and lying all down the edges of the hill among the dandelions.

A bit before the plane crash Myra and I started playing truant. To this day I do not know what brought it about, or why that morning should be different from any other, or what led to that rash decision.

Yet it was not even a decision. Until it happened there had been no thought of it. Anyway, our protest – for what else was it? – was too hurtful to examine coldly, and we turned from reasons to practicalities.

Late for school we were that morning, and that had something to do with it. When we saw the empty play yard we stopped as if we had hit a wall. Foolishly, we looked at each other for answers, but I think we already knew what we were going to do. That empty yard meant the Big Room and the stick, without trial or enquiry, so we fled back over the fields and hid in some bushes.

We could not go home: this was commonsense. In any case we would go this afternoon – if we could only think of a good reason to explain away our morning's absence. Of course we never did, and spent the whole day in the bushes, unspeaking and for the most part utterly miserable and fearful.

When the clock struck four we crept out like criminals and made our way back up the fields, taking care to arrive home at the usual time. We had to force down the bread and butter. Mother felt my forehead and thought I might be coming down with a chill. We were both so quiet and half witted that she said that what we both needed was a good dose of syrup of figs, which was promised for Friday night, with a good hot bath by the fire.

Through the evening we waited for a knock at the door, for there would be murder and scandal when we were found out. And of course if we could find no excuse for the morning, how much more difficult to explain away a whole day.

We talked it over on our way to school next morning.

'Let's just say we were sick in bed; sick day and night let's say.' This was Myra's offering, wobbling on crutches. It was flat and too well rehearsed, used over and over whenever the circus or fair came to Stroud. We wanted something snappy and original to make them gasp with surprise, but nothing came to mind.

'We could say our Mam kept us 'ome cos of the wet,' I suggested. Myra gave that one her heavyweight frown. 'Don't be daft!' she said. We raked through chapters of improbable emergencies, from mad bulls (we'd need at least a dozen) to German parachutists and medically unknown viruses which vanished in a night.

As we mulled over these still-born pleas, our legs slowed with our wits, until both finally ceased to function, and when nine o'clock struck we were still far from school – another day in the bushes.

Conscience made us observe the rigid school routine. At half past ten – playtime – we allowed ourselves ten minutes to talk and go to the lavatory; otherwise we were silent, or if we spoke it was furtively, as if we might be overheard. At twelve o'clock the church bells reached us in the woods, the signal for sandwiches and restoring circulation, ever watchful, like a couple of old lags on the run.

At first we were lucky with the weather. It was autumn and the sun smote the red leaves with shoots of translucent light, so that in the wood's silence we were half charmed with colour and solitude.

On the third day it rained however, but even then we were not deterred. A bower we knew of would do. Part hedge, part tree, matted all over with clematis and tiled with leaves and fern, it was quite waterproof, like an upside down coracle. Getting to it through the long grass whipped our legs red; but inside was crisp and dry, and here we curled up like badgers all through the day.

The cold was wretched, and every ten minutes we'd creep out under the dripping boughs to rub our limbs and kick our feet back into life.

We had spelling games: spell artillery; spell geranium; spell conscience. At the end we added up the points: Myra won as usual. I led her on to poetry to even things up: 'Oh to be in England'; 'Into my heart an air that kills'; 'I wandered lonely as a cloud'.

Tired of this, we made up stories of places far away in summer before schools were invented. We drew the shapes of lands and peopled them with tribes, calling them Nakimars, Tuskies and Vorshers. We gave them kings and queens and princes, made them heroic or brittle, and left them behind in the wood at four o'clock.

Yet there was misery in every thought, in every game. We knew it could not go on but had no will to end it; till Myra at last made up her mind that truancy was no fun any more.

'I'm goin' t' tell our Mam tonight,' she said; and so we dragged ourselves home, wet through, and told her what we had been doing these last few days.

We gulped out our story close up to the range, our eyes with the little green flames wobbling over the coals. 'Oh, I know all about that,' said Mother after a long silence. 'The school attendance officer has been here.'

It was like saying we were going to be hanged.

Mr Warrat, the school attendance officer, was as smooth as silk, his manner superficial and overbearing. His strained-back raven hair was equally polished. He was a neat dresser too and careful where he put his feet, like a cat. He hated our stony play yard and drove his Morris right to the edge of the veranda to keep his shoes clean; honking his horn and waiting for one of us to open his door.

In front of Mr Magg he was sometimes pompous, often obsequious, and stared at we children as a viper stares at its prey. Indeed there was much of the smoothness of the serpent in him, and much of the venom.

Our return to school after three days in the woods was a warming experience in every way, and grew a good deal warmer as the day wore on. We waited, each in our separate classroom, each in our separate dread, for the punishment we knew we could expect. When exactly the blade would fall neither of us knew, and as noon approached I at least began nourishing the hope that we had been miraculously pardoned. But just before dinner we were sent for, and in the corridor outside the Big Room we each received four strokes of the stick.

All the school knew what was going on, rather like a prison when an execution is due, and when I returned to class, all eyes were upon me – some mocking, a few anxious, all more or less curious. There had not been a caning for a year, and no girl had been caned for a lot longer than that. No one could ever remember a brother and sister double event before, and during the dinner hour we found ourselves celebrities, much in demand, like survivors of a purge.

For our part we were prepared to let it go at that, but not Mr Warrat. That was not at all his way. He had us out a dozen times in the following weeks. He'd look down through his steel-rimmed glasses in fair imitation of Himmler, waving a tobacco-stained finger and fussing with his head cold which he always had.

'You bay be sure I shad forget this,' he said, 'I've never heard of such goids on. I hope you've leard your lesson!' We had, and timorously said so. At that he stiffened and grew loud. 'I should thig so too! Disgraceful!' We were dismissed with a flick of the hand as he slid away to his car.

The truant episode made an odd unexplained stain on our school days and was less forgivable because we did it in one lump, and not over a period of sly half days.

Myra left school in 1943 and after that I went on alone. They would have no more trouble with me, and though the harness was irritable I bore its restriction without further defiance. What resentment remained was spilled and lost in the riches of those times, where we knew not, in our school goal, that we would ever again have such freedom.

In that freedom were the fads and fancies that rose among we boys without known origins or seasons, but which were suddenly discharged in solid passions which lasted a week or two and as quickly disappeared.

Marbles rattling in our pockets were an instant challenge, the bitter struggles fought out all over the yard inside circles of knees. Red of blood, green of emerald, blue of sea, mauve or black striped – we rolled them through our miserly fingers like jewels, brief symbols of one's wealth, when a pocketful set one apart, and losing them made one vengeful or suicidal.

Pages from our exercise books made striped gliders which landed on the roof and blocked the drains. Most were limited in range and ceiling, but Dipper's strong arm and a freakish gust put several in the churchyard.

Conkers came round regularly, like birthdays and Christmas, a heritage passed on to each generation. Someone would pull a couple from his pocket and show them to our scowling envy. It was the starter's flag, and going home we'd spend hours under the chestnut trees in loud rituals of greed, for the biggest, brightest and hardest, and came away only when our pockets were ripping and the mangled grass piled with husks. We bored holes in them with a meat skewer for the string, and claimed, bare-faced, scores of fifty and a hundred.

These temporary fashions, though, were off-shoots, side shows to the sturdier stuff which went on all the time. One thinks of those playtimes now as one continuous bloody riot, and no one over the age of ten was excluded. To give it a name we called it British Bulldog, with one team attacking the back yard, the other defending. The struggles were unbelievably frantic and violent, the noise from our twenty throats reaching the very edges of the village, where it sounded like distant thunderous surf. Those attacking had either to force the door or scale the wall, to get into the yard and win; and we attacked and defended in turn.

Prisoners were treated with the usual observance: held down and a piece of coke drawn painfully up the nape of the neck, which made them howl, turn treason, or offer bribes of *Dandys* and *Beanos*. If we had too many to deal with, we let them off with a Chinese burn and their promise of something from next month's sweet ration.

One day, after several attempts, we captured Tatty Hollis. He had got us all into trouble at one time or another and now he was for it. He was bigger and stronger than most of us and it was all we could do to hold him down for the torture. When finally we overpowered him he became explicit.

'You buggers! You wait Hockey – bloody evacuees! You wait you buggers!' Coughing and choking, he threw punches at our legs till gradually he sank under our combined weight, and Heap Wolmer and the Londoner Hockey finally choked him senseless with his tie. 'You wait,' he croaked. 'You just bloody wait! Our Murv'll kill the lot on you 'e will! You wait 'n see if 'e bloody don't!'

His desperation fuelled revenge: 'Give 'n some more, Heap,' we bawled, for Heap was a natural psychopath, thin and gangling and always ready to spill someone's gore.

When Tatty's eyes were glazed over and sticking out like pigeon's eggs, we let him go, writhing at our feet, struggling to loosen the tie round his windpipe. We yelled our battle chant, threatened and mocked, savages to our boots.

We went back 10,000 years to revive in these twenty-minute wars the embryonic passage of our blood, the sure dawn of our beginning. The little restraint we had so far acquired was thrown away in an instant. We reverted at once to our good belligerent marrow, and the girls cheering from the walls confirmed the need of it. Blood-smeared noses and cracked knuckles were bestowed and accepted, ancient symbols of brave controversy. Once I was knocked clean out and came to alone behind the coke pile, the play yard empty. No one noticed my absence in class and I stayed there in a half dream till four o'clock.

We grew older and stronger if not wiser or cleverer, and our ages seemed more important than all else. We Standard Five and Six boys were given half the playground to ourselves as proof of our peerless caste. The flag pole stood athwart the boundary of the yard's two halves, and in passing it we moved a step closer to our work in field or factory.

With this honour came more freedom, and we went into Stroud once a week for woodwork. It was only half a day to be sure, but we made it reckless, like a holiday, talking to strangers on the bus, flirting with the conductresses, running through Woolworths and walking in the road.

Five of us went, and two boys came in from Edge, making seven in all. For three hours every week we planed and chiseled, sawed and hammered, nailed and glued, with a devotion to wood and sawdust that would never go beyond those walls. The dust settled on us like cloth and we were up to our knees in shavings. We sneezed, cut our hands, and sometimes made things good enough to take home to our startled parents. Dipper found a talent, and his ambition quickly grew. While we were struggling with our pipe racks and book-ends he made a chair, carved the back for good measure, and walked home with it along the main road.

The rest put up with it, knew in that easy way that this was not for us. Mr Simpson knew it too, that sad, grey-haired bone of a teacher, badly ailing and no stronger than one of the pieces of battening he so carefully hoarded behind his table. He'd lost the battle with boys years ago, though the ones like Dipper still gave him hope. He sat a lot or shuffled painfully among the benches, holding his rupture and erupting violently whenever he found our hands as empty as our heads. He was kind, never kept us in, always lied to give us good reports; and when he died there was no more woodwork then or ever.

At twelve o'clock, or long before, we were out and running up the alley way, straight for the chip shop – our out-of-doors, out-of-the-paper dinner for sixpence.

We sat upstairs on the bus, always the back seat, enveloped in a relish of vinegar. We screwed up the paper and kicked it under the seat in front, and dropped old bus tickets onto the people outside.

Uncaring, unhurried, we came back to school along the bottom road, level with bedrooms, above factory roofs, below garden walls. Flashing commons, tall chimneys and boiling woods made us think of the long warm evening ahead.

Our twopence brought us to the piano works and we came leisurely up the hill, laughing, for we would work unsupervised in the garden all the afternoon.

In this way we reached a peak, having touched the limits of the village school, and without remembering when we went into long trousers.

Although we had shared the years with them, only now did we start viewing the girls differently; the ones we had scalded and scorned because they could never kick a ball straight and were useless at cricket. The braids were gone, the hair cut and shaped, their smiles suddenly tempting and dangerous. They were less brash now, had acquired all of a sudden a sense of preservation and timidity; they kept away from brawls and guarded their bodies like temples. Their eyes might condemn us, but the hearts and names they scratched for us along the lane told silently of love.

Dinner times we roamed the village, Dipper, Sparrow, Pansy and I. We bought loaves at Garroways, sweet and straight from the oven. Tearing them apart, feasting in the lane, was like a declaration of our turgid spirits.

Our wanderings always took us to the churchyard. Funerals were special and mystical, a sort of lost-life distraction which temporarily drained everyone. We were kept in for funerals; we never had a playtime when one was on. It was a tradition that the school went dumb and blind for an hour, so all we could do was extend our senses. We'd hear the cortège arrive, the sound of feet on gravel, and the iron gate swinging. Then came the low, lapping tunes of the organ, and the singing, like punctuation: an end and a beginning.

Later, in the dinner hour, we'd go and have a look at the grave out of curiosity. The heavily scented lilies drew us quietly to the heave of flowers. What deep reason lay in our observance of this long-established habit never reached our conscious selves. Most of the time we never even knew who was buried there. But some impulse tried to make us understand the sum of this small mound. We, of course, were immortal; yet for some it seemed there was this end, and flowers, and clay.

We lingered among the graves, reading out the names, and when something in us had been satisfied, left, one by one, running hard up the road to feel our hearts pumping.

In our dinner-time roving, different from former times because of the urges now within us, we sought the means of our probation, bold plans that might, like removing apples from trees, bear little risk, for some were not far off our grasp if we had the nerve. It usually involved a girl or girls; sometimes trespassing or petty larceny. Mostly our minds cooled as swiftly as they heated, and although we rebuked the fainthearts who let us down, we were thankful for their caution all the same.

So until another time, another crime, we had to make do with tried and tested hazards like Allens Pond. We skimmed stones over it, lay on its bank catching sticklebacks, shared bread with the swan, shouted and heard the water echoing.

In the dead of winter we came as well, when the wind tearing in the elms made talking useless. We'd creep onto the ice, bawling and daring. Once we were measuring ourselves for it when Dave Walby came by, he who had ruined Fetty Pearce. 'Go on then,' he yelled. 'I bin further out than that. Right out in the middle I bin!' He hung over the fence blowing into his large blue hands, looking lustfully around the pond. 'I ain't scared,' he said finally, and pushed past us onto the ice. We followed tentatively, the ice shivering and squeaking, the black water waiting below.

'Yer scared the lot on yer!'

Right out in the middle he was now, and started jumping up and down. 'Yer scared, that's what! Yer scared stiff an' it's a foot thick I bet!'

But it was not, and at that moment it crashed open with leads running out like a great star; and we dived for the bank as he plunged in and disappeared.

We gasped; he was gone. Then we broke out laughing as he reappeared black with slime and mewing like a seal. 'Help I! Help I!' And somehow, on our bellies, we dragged him clear and lighted a fire for him in the copse. 'Our mam'll kill I 'er will!' he groaned. He chattered, beat his arms round his naked body, curled over to stop from freezing. Strength glowed from his hair-patched body as he twisted near the fire.

His clothes steamed on the brambles, and when we had looked enough someone lent him a coat. We left him squatting by the smoking sticks like a forest Indian, moaning with the cold, there to remain all the afternoon.

Just below the Pond was the Rifle Range, but how it got that name no one knew. It was merely a dip in the bank and no range at all. Yet it was a perpetually sinister craze, a cup of danger with a black shed at one end guarded on all flanks by fatal nettles as thick as fingers.

The worst of our gang punishment was the Rifle Range. Was it that lonely locked shed or the brooding trees, like clusters of whispering witches, cloaked and bending forward with arms outstretched? Or was it just the morbid seclusion? – or because no one would ever tell what went on there?

So far as I know no one ever solved its lethal reputation, and it remained an unknown and cherished fear, one of many we drew along with us in those days to keep our inferiors in their place.

Top Class, to which we came at last, gave us much time to dwell on these diversions, for we did practically nothing all day. Standard Five and Six was supposed to round us off, smooth our rough grain usefully for our future work. But in fact our education, over which we had clambered like obstacles set in our path, virtually ceased altogether when we entered Top Class, and the reason for this lay in the extraordinary character of our headmaster.

By turn frightening and comic, Mr Magg kept us on edge all day long. He was part leader, part clown. There was some mystery about him and none knew what it was or how to cope with it. Standing at the window, watching the council houses, he kept those loud secrets all to himself. He told meaningless jokes and we laughed like drunks; he roared as if he meant to kill us; he involved us in idiosyncratic pastimes which crawled from his skull and leapt on us like devils. Hours of quiet, then he would pounce.

'Is there anything on my jacket, Phil? See, round the back?'
'No sir.'
'Are you sure? Look hard, boy.'

'No sir.'
'Have a good look!'
'Can't see anything sir.'
'Well brush it off, there's a good chap!'
He had us all at it. A new boy or girl coming up would faint when asked to remove a non-existent spot from the headmaster's backside; and we loved it.

On high summer days, when all the doors and windows were open, he would suddenly stiffen, and we all knew what was coming.

'Listen!'

We froze.

'Listen! Sounds like a wasp!' We listened but knew it was pointless.

'Can't hear nothin' sir,' someone would say, but already we were reaching for our rulers.

'Yes, there it is again! It's a wasp all right! Get after him boys!'

Crashing through the desks, our rulers slashing like sabres, we kept it going for all we were worth. Today, Swaddy led the attack.

'I think I see 'im, sir!'

'Get after him! Don't want anything to do with his sort!'

The Boss was standing now, conducting the charge like a colonel of infantry as we barked out reports from every direction.

'It's in the window, sir!'

'No, sir! 'E's over 'ere by the door, sir!'

'No, sir! Please sir, 'e's under my desk, sir!'

'Give him a good un,' yelled the Boss.

'I nearly 'ad 'im then, sir!'

'Give him what for, Dave! Keep after the blighter. Where's he gone? Where's that fella with the football jersey! Can you see him, Pete?'

We tried hard but never could keep it up, and finally even our enthusiasm cooled.

'Think 'e went out, sir.'

'Give him a good un!'

'Think 'e's gone, sir.'

'Get after him!'

''E's gone, sir.'

'Eh? Gone? *Gone?* Well why didn't you say so! Good! Well get back to your work! Stop wasting time!'

The wasp idea had always to come from him. Sometimes we'd try it ourselves. 'Think I hear a wasp, sir!' But Boss Magg would never be drawn like that. He'd look at the boy as if he had gone mad, slowly repeating the words. 'A wasp? Heard a *wasp* d'you say?'

'Think so, sir.'

'Rubbish! Not the sort of day for 'em. Get on with your work unless you want the stick!'

Stunned and very foolish, the boy would look round for someone to back him up, but of course we never did, and our concerted treachery retreated behind sniffs and coughs.

We observed his queer rules and oddities unquestioningly and it never occurred to us to do anything else, for in spite of it he was all-powerful and aloof, like an old lion.

Still, for all that he was human; he had his favourites and stuck to them loyally. Boys summoned grandly and sent on errands round the village, or asked to fill ink wells, give out books, wind clocks, fill coke buckets. At Christmas he even warmed to me a little and forgot about the truant episode when asking about a duck or cockerel.

A few days before Christmas I would trudge down the frosty fields with a bird banging over my shoulder, like an ancient pilgrim bearing gifts to a caliph: to please and appease.

He stood over our schooldays like a law, judging us for our brains if not our hearts. His great desk was between the stove and the piano, next to a picture of Neville Chamberlain, at which he would stare for hours on end when he was tired of the council houses.

Anyway, it was here in his class, under his thumb if not always under his eyes, that the scrapings of an education, fed drop by drop through the years, finally stopped and set, shaping us in ways that might endure to the grave.

Our blood was running and grown-up things tugged us free of books. Doreen was in a shop, Dipper at the piano works, Sparrow at grammar school. Samson and Swaddy took the last days off but still got a visit from Mr Warrat and their names put in a book. No one grinned when they left and no one wept either. Though we wanted freedom there was a sudden reluctance, going out into a blank space where all had to be built afresh.

Schooldays were closing and one by one we left. We older boys commanded like Caesars, unable to believe that we had made the long journey all in one piece; and all those Weekly Tests had left not a mark on us. We were primed and shaped, our preferences ready formed, and few of them had anything to do with school.

For all my pent-up desire to be gone, that last day still held surprises. Along The Top others whose names I would never know, whose faces I did not even recognise, ran past me now as I had once run past others, years ago. On that day I was early and strolling, and never more would I strut with such ease. I suppose it was meant to be that on that last morning I should be alone. Phil had gone. He should have been leaving with me this Easter, but in fact had not returned after Christmas, when his father put him to work. I had seen him once or twice since, coming down the street with the horse and cart. He sat sideways on the shafts like an old hand, with a flat workman's cap over one eye, plastered in muck. He had quickly grown to his life's work, and school was already half forgotten.

'Ain't you left yet then?' he asked.

'No. Soon though.'

We were a bit uncomfortable I remember, and the difference now lay along that road to school. The horse swished and stamped and Phil flicked the reins.

'Well, I best get goin'. So long.'

I savoured every yard of that last walk to school, like a prisoner between prisons, and the early sun was at its best and brightest, like that very first morning.

The clock struck four more deliberately, more finally than it had ever done. It came shivering down the long thread of years, each stroke illuminating an epic; and then I was on my feet, my paint box in my pocket, out at last into the golden sun of all my afternoons.

Out of the yard, over the fields, and I lay down by the shining stream. I lay watching the clouds, the chestnut trees, the bank, the church spire, all timeless in the sun.

The weathercock winked, the clock struck my first quarter hour unbound, and in a puzzle I rose and started home through woods and fields that I knew had changed forever.

One night we were pulled awake by an explosion. The common and beech wood lay between, but it was unmistakably a bomb. The windows rattled, the dog howled, and Father got up and searched the garden with the lantern.

A mile away, on Selsley Hill, the missile blew out a fifteen-foot crater, and next day we went over to look at it.

No one had ever seen anything like it, except the old soldiers of the First War. Hundreds came to look at the hole. We smiled and nodded; satisfaction and pleasure was everywhere evident. We hummed and hawed and puffed out our chests and no one ever dreamt of complaining.

This accidental compliment by the Luftwaffe was like surviving a total air offensive. We enjoyed it, boasted of it, and The New Inn just down the road did a roaring trade. It put a seal on our war effort; it was a worthy scar proudly exhibited and thoroughly approved of. All our army, navy and airforce drives, the waste paper, aluminium, rubber, and wool collections, the flag-fluttering boundless camaraderie stemmed from this time, this bomb.

The Germans were overhead, the common had been bombed, and suddenly the Home Guard were everywhere. Every Sunday morning they used our fields for practice.

For all I know they may well have drilled with broom handles and pitch-forks in that first headlong rush to defend our village. But when they got going, when I first met up with them, they definitely looked the part: battledresses pressed as if for parade, polished leather belts and gaiters, Springfield rifles and virgin bayonets – what were my tin soldiers compared with these?

They were pot-bellied and middle aged; some white haired, others, one or two, no more than youngsters. They staggered up the lane and fell in by the gate. Most had not seen these high fields since their courting days, and now drew on that scant knowledge for cover, ambush and deployment, for the hill had not changed her dress in half a century.

Unfortunately, their old bodies were no match for their new duty and half an hour round these banks found them wasted and spent, with little inclination to do anything but lie down and defend trees and hedges. Only the youngest could hope to storm these slopes, bayonets fixed, and capture the hayrick astride the Long Ground ridge, a make-do enemy target.

They made two teams, Red and Blue, pledging their strength for a week in full battle order, with backpack, respirator, steel helmet and rifle, as they launched themselves at our barns.

Camouflage of course was no problem, the nets of their helmets so heavily forested that their faces were invisible, and several together looked like a bush sliding sideways down the slope. They had no bullets, their rifles were empty, but even so their games seemed intensely real to me, even if the execution of them was eccentric and haphazard. If their attacks were inclined to wither with cramp, dizziness, tachycardia and old age, their defence at least was rock solid.

Ambush was their speciality, the thing best suited to inclination and physique. Eight or nine men would lay a trap, with a man out watching. Like war in general, accident played a more or less crucial part, and all means to victory were fair.

One morning I met Blue Section coming down the drive. 'Hey, you lookin' for that other lot?' I asked. 'Well, I seen 'em comin' round First 'Oles.'

After that I was well in, for they wiped out Red Section to a man. I hung around and they let me stay. I ran home to fill their water bottles, took messages to their wives in the village, was sent each week to the back door of The Ram: 'Please, Mr Latham, Mr Dwyer said can 'e 'ave ten Star please?'

I knew most of them by sight if not by name, and being civilians they never knew how much they should put on with their khaki. Once or twice they told me to go home, saying it was dangerous, but I always went back.

They were right about the danger though, and once I nearly blundered into trouble. I was late that morning; they had assembled at the top of the lane and vanished into the fields. They might be anywhere and it was no good trying to find them.

On the way home, distantly, I heard the crump of explosions; several strung together, but muffled. I turned that way through the long copse, and came out at the top of the dingle. More percussions, very near now, drew me to the lip of a hollow where smoke zig-zagged away in the troubled air. There was a biting smell of lyddite around the hollow, which was a natural pit in the hillside with almost vertical sides, fringed with fir trees leaning in. At its entrance was a breastwork of sandbags, newly erected, about five feet high; and from this cover they were throwing Mills bombs. They had not seen me come up, and before I could shout, a steel head appeared and an arm came over, like a bowler delivering a full toss, and something black hurled towards me. I dropped into the grass just as it exploded. The tufts hissed along the edges of the hollow, and white shards torn from the trees sprinkled down onto my back, smelling of turpentine. Another blast and another followed quickly, and after the third I heard nothing. The trees moved in the wind without a sound, and for minutes there was only my hard breathing and pumping blood, as if I were buried. Seemingly there was a brief lull, and in that moment I wriggled away backwards and took to my heels. My feet hammering down the path thudded on my brain, like someone at a door with their fists, till the locked-up sensation finally went away.

It was not long afterwards that Colonel Vaughan, their commander, left his car unattended in the drive. It was unlocked and on the back seat lay a Webley revolver and box of grenades. It was more temptation than I had ever known or could resist. The revolver was loaded and very heavy. I weighed the grenades, one in each hand, like a juggler about to perform. The rings were bright, the pins quite free and untaped. I took up the Webley with both hands and without a thought, fired at the gate post twelve feet away, blowing a strip off the corner. The jolt wrenched it from my grasp into the mud, and when I had wiped it off, I returned it as new to the seat, then ran. I was nine years old and of such things are a mother's nightmares made.

They dropped out of trees, crawled in the grass, slid off hayricks, these Sunday soldiers; you might find them anywhere. Once, Mother was throwing away potato peelings and found one under our privet hedge. He seemed not much older than Bob, and asked for water, the time, warmth, and companionship; and we took him in like a stray cat and gave him hot tea. It turned out that he had been one of the painters who had decorated our cottage, and when he'd downed three cups of tea, Mother got him to do over the pantry ceiling which was flaking again. Afterwards we put him back outside under the bush.

They were too few in number (perhaps twenty at a good turnout) and the hill too wide and wooded, so that if one of them became detached there was little hope of him ever finding the others, except by chance. When that happened the man usually went home and dug his garden.

Others, more conscientious, stayed where they were until ordered to stand down.

It was four o'clock one afternoon when we found Harry Wickman holding out at Top Barns. His comrades had long since gone home to their Sunday dinners, and might even now be in shirt sleeves and slippers, by their fires. That made not a jot of difference to Harry: he refused to leave his post, and I was sent up with a bottle of tea to keep him going. He was the village roadman, swept it from end to end, always came on time, never left early. 'If I can't be trusted wi' me time I ain't no use t' God nor man,' he used to say. On this occasion he guzzled the tea, wiped his mouth with the back of his hand, and said: 'I ain't leavin' till I'm told to, an' that's that!' He was still there after dark and we had to phone the colonel to come and fetch him.

The exercises went on for months, and at the end of the day they'd converge in packets on the banks, light cigarettes, sling their rifles and saunter home. The battle was over till next Sunday, the farm safe for another week.

Quite suddenly they stopped coming but I never remembered when, and neither saw nor heard anything of the Home Guard after that. Some of the young men went into the army and one or two of the old ones died. Anyway, the tide was turning and we knew they would never be needed.

But of course the war went on, Sundays were still there, and now there was a gap to be filled. That's how I met Jack and Bert, my long-loving inseparable companions. They were silent about their origins and I never then or afterwards enquired too deeply of their coming, just accepted that there was perfect balance between us, and wondered at their devotion to me. They came and went at my fancy, were summarily dismissed without complaint, and reappeared again whenever I wished.

The three of us carried on where the Home Guard left off, defending our woods and fields. Our three in one started as a company and ended as an army. We rose from privates to generals, and a peeled nut stick under the arm made the difference. I made a sort of uniform for myself from an old raincoat, and stuck on red tabs and general's badges and fancied I looked like a Commander-in-Chief. An afternoon at the Ritz would do the trick. Where others saw only the grass-matted slopes ruffled by wind and patched by cloud, I (or rather we) saw a smoking battlefield, battalions on the march, heard the clamour of guns, saw bursts of bomb and shell, the meadows rich with crosses.

These faithful friends, Jack and Bert, these comrades of the mind, figments of my curious loneliness, finally vanished, never to return, when I left school. No doubt they are still there, bound to those sacred acres, haunting each wood and hollow, searching for the one person who could give them back their lives.

However real they were to me, of course they always gave way when boys came up from the village, which was not often. In some ways this was never as satisfying, for real boys have minds of their own and are apt to leave you flat. Yet imagination, even the most flagrant and exotic as mine then was, was no substitute for pals.

A boy, solitary like myself, lived on the common, and once or twice we'd meet in the fields. His name was Alfy Cook and his father was a prisoner of war. Sunday was our day, too, when the hill was quiet and the train chugging down the valley seemed unusually loud and near.

The scheme that day was the best we ever had. We would go to Aston Down aerodrome and have a look at the planes. We never told anyone where we were going, and it was a long way. Surely, too, we never meant to complete the journey, and continually looked for distractions.

The first was the donkey by the railway station. He had turned his back on his bare paddock by the brook, and hung over the wire looking sadly at the fresh grass along the edges of the road (which Harry Wickman would dig up tomorrow). We pulled an armful and heaved it over the fence. The donkey fussed the succulent tufts, and while he slowly chewed we played with his muddy ears, through the wire. He was very old. There were people in the village drawing pensions who remembered him there when they were children, and warned that he belonged to a gipsy who would throw lime into the eyes of anyone who touched him. Smokey Curran and Bej had both been nearly blinded when they were surprised riding him round the field. They'd been dragged off, beaten up and nearly killed for it – so we were told. We wanted none of that, and the coming train was a legitimate excuse to leave him.

We raced to the level-crossing gates to look at the two coaches and seven passengers, rigid as wood behind the windows. Steam hissed, a little hoot, and away it clanked to Stroud, leaving black smoke in the road.

It drifted behind us along the way and up the hill, where we stopped to thread our gaze over the village and up to our starting point in the fields. We were parched and already tired with the idea, though dare not say so. Instead we got interested in a gulley running away among brambles into an old quarry: an abrupt limestone face pitted with sinister caves. It was promising and so we went along it, but wire at the bottom and piles of fallen rock made us cautious.

Locals called this place, humorously, Smugglers' Caves, and the stories I had heard from Bej made it the site of every dark crime save rape – and even that was hinted at. The brambles and nettles made it ordinary however; but Bej's story-telling, and Bob's and Colin's, made the place scary enough to stay.

We found nothing, saw nothing: no dead bodies, no one captive, no contraband, no car tracks, no spent bullet cases or blood, nor anything of interest. Only some butt ends, and a piece of a girl's frock caught on the barbed wire.

We threw rocks at the quarry face and watched tiny avalanches of stone sprinkle across the caves' dark mouths, and we halloed loudly to hear our voices catch among the rocks.

The signposts had gone because of the war and there were five roads on the common. The way was obvious though and we put on speed now that the day was advancing and a mist coming down. We started running, to get it over and done with. Our hobnails broke loudly round the walls and sounded like a dozen clattering ponies.

We had never walked so far from home and the spur of adventure had become blunt hours ago, but a combined stubbornness kept us ticking over till at last we were outside the main gate of the airfield. A tall, white-faced policeman stamped by the wall and watched us go by. We abandoned hope of just walking straight in. There was nothing flying, nothing taking off or landing, and we considered what to do, for it was unthinkable, half-witted, just to turn round and go home.

The mist was thicker now and the gate slid out of sight behind us. We halted and listened, but only for a moment; then flung ourselves over the wall, running hard, and in five minutes were crawling on hands and knees through a hedge. Ahead of us, printed in the shifting mist, were the shapes of several planes, and in a minute we ran our hands along the sleek wing of a Spitfire. We found ourselves among fifteen or twenty aircraft parked in a field by the aerodrome. I climbed on the wing of a Hurricane and the hood slid back without any trouble. I looked swiftly round and jumped in. A panel of instruments faced me: artificial horizon, air speed, fuel pressure, boost, turn and bank, firing button. It reeked of petrol and rubber and perhaps had been in the shooting. It made strange noises that machines made after hard work; though this machine had not been up for days. Beads of mist ran steadily down the perspex and pattered softly from the wings.

Alfy was in another Hurricane to my right, invisible except for the top of his head. Now and then he drew himself up, looking round; but the rolling fog made us safe, if we were quiet.

Once, he forgot himself and bawled: 'I wonner 'ow many miles they've done?' and clapped his hand over his mouth as he said it. But the mist, nearly as thick as a blanket now, strangled the outcry, and though we strained our ears to breaking point no one came to look.

We sucked the milk of a whole wonderous hour in those mighty machines of war, careless of time, untroubled and unmolested. Imagination lay us on a world above cloud, sun-lit in the silent vapour.

'We best get goin' don't you reckon?' said a voice. I heard it across miles, a disturbing human distress call. It wavered and repeated itself insistently, dragged at me till at last I touched down. I peered over the side. 'What?' I said.

'It ain't arf gettin' dark,' said Alfy quietly.

The fog was sponging up the last daylight and hunger scratched at our bellies like cats in a bag. We clambered out and slid off the wings; aching with dreams but with our boots on the grass.

'Which way?' said Alfy.

I pointed. Through a hedge and over a wall and we found ourselves in the middle of the runway. We stopped running, for our nails thundered on the tarmac, and went tip-toe across; but the fog served us well. Once across we ran again, headlong and blind, our ears loud with wind, our mouths filled with air.

Then something loomed and I crashed into it, rolling along the wet grass, winded. I looked and saw a policeman standing over me. He already had Alfy by the collar, and dragged me to my feet.

'Up you get!' He looked down severely. 'I bin searchin' for you young buggers ever since I saw you hop over the wall.'

He tightened his grip and hurried us along to the guard house where a sergeant was putting up the blackout boards.

'Look what I got 'ere, Sid!'

Flushed from his afternoon nap by the fire, tunic unbuttoned, the sergeant eyed us suspiciously. The office was stifling, but we shivered and begged for mercy: 'We ain't done nothin'. We ain't stole nothin' either, 'onest!' I said. We had done nothing and stolen nothing, but I knew we were guilty.

'What d'you make of 'em?' said the sergeant at last.

'A couple of saboteurs I shouldn't wonder. Best shoot the little buggers,' said the first policeman. The Lee Enfield in the corner reinforced the threat. There was no telling what they might not do in war time.

'We ain't sabashooters! We ain't done nothin,' I said; but I knew we were doomed.

'If you 'urt I you'll know all about it!' said Alfy with a quite unexpected menace, a resistance that warmed like the sun.

'You'll get some lip from our mam you will,' he added. Folding his arms he stared at them defiantly.

The two policemen gaped at each other at this awkward turnabout and decided to make us a cup of tea. They brought out some sandwiches and biscuits and we ate the lot with our knees scorching by the fire. Afterwards, like uncles, they took us down to the road and packed us off home. Sid's voice followed us in the fog: 'You come back 'ere again and we *will* shoot you!' We heard them chuckling and their boots go away behind.

It should not have ended like that, arrested, in the hands of the police. And now it was all over we grew bad tempered and weak legged, and all sorts of pains reminded us of the potatoes and gravy we had missed at dinner time.

Alfy had had enough of me and aeroplanes and policemen, and wished he had never left the common.

'I ain't comin' no more,' he said. 'I got earache.'

'It weren't my fault. Come on, let's 'urry up 'ome!'

'My feet do 'urt!'

'Well, an' mine do.'

'I ain't comin' next time!'

'Come by meself then!'

'Nor I ain't doin' what you want no more!'

'Don't then. I ain't bothered.'

We slunk along in silence, each of us separate in the pitch-black night. Father was at the door when we arrived home, the light from the back kitchen thrown square at the fog. He had on his overcoat and had been looking for us by the lakes. He was decisive: 'Off to bed! Yer Mother's off 'er 'ead with worry.'

73

'I thought you were drowned,' said Mother sadly, and she set about frying eggs to hide her feelings. Always she thought I would end in the lake, or break my neck falling out of a tree, or be taken away and murdered, and had scribbled down all my physical peculiarities over the mantelpiece, ready for the coroner: tiny build, birth mark on right ankle, mole on left shoulder, crooked front tooth. She had copied these things neatly onto a piece of paper and it lay waiting on the table for the police. Her relief at seeing me still alive and wheezing was so great that she did not attempt to intercede on my behalf, and after my egg I was sent to bed as promised.

Alfy came off better: no bed for him, and no father to enforce it. Myra took him home to his house on the common and he told his mother that he had been in a Hurricane fighter plane and been arrested by the police for it. She boxed his ears for telling lies and let it go at that.

World war was exciting, at this distance, and we lumped it with our games, added it to the idle hours out of school, away from home. The distractions were old but capable of limitless variation. The war did not change them so much as enrich our vocabulary: spies, Germans, machine guns, tanks, Japs, sabotage, bombers. So, war was never a separate game but a variant of our semi-criminal pastimes. It inflated ordinary activities to national survival. Growing up, growing older, was a vague assimilation of parental hints, moving up a class at school, increased height and an enclosing sexual sweetness; but we kept these games going till we started work.

At times we felt as strong as men and an omnipotent recklessness let us tackle anything. The mansion a couple of miles away among woods and lakes was an appropriate target for our pent-up steam, and the silent night would make it better still. Indeed, it had to be the night, for it was the forbidding dark hours we craved most when we were in these moods. To be out in the black night – that in itself made all we did extraordinary.

One weekend in summer three of us took over the shepherd's hut under the hedge in the clover field. It had a stove and bunks and a lantern and a small window which we covered with a sack after dark. There was a frying pan, kettle and mugs and we scrounged rations from our mothers and set up home.

My companions for the weekend were Samson Collins and Spud Dalby. We waited for the moon, and set off through the misty fields.

We knew all the creepy tales connected with the mansion, empty these hundred years: stories of a weeping nun who prowled the woods looking for her lover, a local man with savage inside him, who killed her by the lake and afterwards blew out his brains. The headless horseman, who galloped the drive and disappeared without a sound into the deepest mere, was never seen except at Christmas, so we had nothing to fear from him. Most menacing of all was the evil dwarf, said to bring ill fortune or death on anyone who saw him. And as if all this were not enough, lights had been seen there nights, flashing like signals while the Germans were overhead.

The Nailsworth police had been round the village asking questions. They even came up to the farm and solemnly requested proof of our identity. Our cowshed lights were often left on and might sway and wink through the broken windows: could it be that? They thought not, they said. Father suggested the mansion, according to rumour. 'Ah, can't be there,' said the constable, 'That place has been empty donkey's years.' They never even checked it out, so tonight we would do their work for them.

Soon we were at the wood and started down a wide track ribbed by the moon. It was late, later I think than any of us had ever been out, and we hurried along under the sparse trees through which the stars clustered brilliantly.

We faked courage to conceal fear – a fester common to all woods at night. The air was colder than in the fields, and, around, wild blind dramas of rustling leaves and cracking twigs kept us on edge. Paw, snout and claw shared the night with us, and we went cautiously, very alert, heads snapping round and eyes bulging at the faintest sound.

Nerves or unexpected exertion set Spud backfiring, full ripe bursts which made him hold his bottom. 'I wanna go,' he gasped.

We fell on our knees, sniggering, holding our noses.

'I'll shit meself,' he warned.

''E's boastin',' said Samson dryly.

Spud ran on behind, cursing us and groaning. He would have left us and returned to the hut, but lacked the pluck to go back through the wood alone.

The path led on cunningly. No good now looking over our shoulders, for the wood had closed in and only the dazzling sky, in the trees, reassured us.

In ten minutes or so the track narrowed at a bend and round it the massive parapets and chimneys of the mansion loomed dramatically among the lighted shapes of the trees. A gloom, blacker even than the undergrowth, stretched in our way, and we stopped abruptly.

'We be there! Now for it,' said Samson quietly, and we dashed into that dark patch, through it down a slope.

We came out into a wide grassy area sheeted in light, and stopped to catch our breath, staring at the towering front of the building and its hard, hanging shadows. High on the buttresses hideous gargoyles snarled down, tongues thrusting out, and fifty wrecked windows smoking with spooks gazed blindly on the lakes. The whole place menaced us.

We clustered together like chickens and it was some minutes before we spoke; then it was not speech at all but half-strangled alarm.

'What we goin' to do?'

'Nothin'. Just look round.'

'Scared? I ain't scared!'

'How far we come then?'

'You go fust; I can't see proper.'

'Don't push, dope!'

'Keep quiet!'

Our bladders let us down, and when we saw Samson fumbling with his buttons, we joined in, turning so that our backs touched. We sprayed the grass, relaxed, and looked about wondering what to do.

There were five lakes and the nearest, down the slope by the house, had an ornamental causeway, decorated and splendid once but now decaying and sinking into the reeds. We ran down to look.

The water was dull steel in the bright midnight and we could easily see its full length, the teeming growth along its banks throwing pitchy shadows far out into the water. So wide and long was its arrangement that we seemed to stand on the shore of a great loch. I threw out a stone and the ripples broke the smooth surface in perfect moon-flecked circles, which slowly widened and came rocking the lillies where we stood.

We reached for our Woodbines, lounging on the parapet. ''Ow deep is it, d'you reckon?' asked Spud. No one answered. We sucked our fags, stifled coughs and listened to the hooting owls.

'Hey, 'member when they 'ad that do down 'ere?' said Samson quietly. We remembered. A few years ago it was, just before the war. A sort of gala and fete with demonstrations by the civil defence and fire brigade. For ten minutes we talked of it in whispers.

They built a large wooden hut that day in the park, stuffed it with old tyres and timber, soaked the lot in paraffin and set it all alight. In a moment the pump broke down and the hut roared to a furnace, driving the crowd screaming to the bracken; and when the sparks lit that we dispersed and gathered again round the house where we watched the hut collapse in showers of sparks.

Meanwhile, the civil defence fixed up ropes and pulleys at the highest window and started rescuing people from it. Volunteers they were called, but they had actually been press-ganged by smooth-talking officials who promised them publicity in the *Stroud News*.

Polite applause greeted the safe arrival of the first two; then it all went wrong. A pulley jammed, and the fat man at the end of the rope threatened to plummet into the crowd. 'Get back!' someone shouted. 'Look at 'n swingin'!'

We moved back in a wave and for the next half hour he stayed there swinging helplessly in space; just now and again we'd glance over our ice creams, as he struggled like a fish on a hook. There was some dangerous talk of cutting the rope and catching him in a blanket; but no one was well enough insured to stand under him, and just when it was more or less decided to leave him there, the pulley jerked, the rope twanged and freed itself, and they lowered him unconscious through a bottom window. St John Ambulance rushed forward with smelling salts and slapped him till he opened his eyes. Later they took him semi-conscious to a tent, where he lay staring into space muttering, 'Clare! Clare!'

While this was going on they greased the pulley wheels and began again. A very pretty young woman was next, swindled into this by her friends. They swung her out and very gently began to lower her down when the pulley jammed again. Unfortunately no one had thought to check the harness, strained apart by the fat man, and she began slipping through.

The crowd drew its breath and moved forward, a tide of faces looking up. She dangled twenty feet in the air, her dress creeping up, building in folds under her breasts. We fell silent. The gutted hut spat and flared, wreaths of purple smoke rolled into the stifling afternoon, the brigade laboured at their pump.

No one cared about that now; we smelled disaster and wanted a front seat. A tin-hatted civil defence man who seemed to be in charge stood under the girl giving slow, thoughtful advice. 'Hold on . . . ah, yes . . .

hold on if you can. Er, hold on tight, that's the thing. Just . . . well, just hold on.' But the poor girl merely whimpered and looked down on our swaying throng as if it were the last scene on earth.

Orders were shouted but no one listened, and finally civil defence took off his helmet, wiped the inside of it, and came over to join the crowd. 'It's the straps,' he said. We nodded agreement and passed it on to those standing behind.

The hut was burned down, the fire pump was broken, the fat man was raving, and there was this girl half naked on the end of a rope. It was too much for the crowd. Some started fighting, others wandered languidly to the woods, half a dozen jumped in the lake. On the rest there settled a half savage expectancy, like an open-air execution, where one went not merely to look but to participate.

The silken legs danced in the sky and we ravaged them. We bit into our ice cream till it hurt. Jaws went slack, shoulders hunched; narrow glances waited a signal to start looting, raping and murdering, and we each marked a victim. We moved forwards, backwards, rocked and chanted, offering sacrifices to fire and smoke and water.

They got her down of course, unharmed, though pale and weepy and not the least bit pleased that she had been the star of the whole show.

It was Spud who saw the light first – a sudden glare in the crumpled black area where the stables were. We stared again but saw nothing. 'You be seein' things,' said Samson. But Spud crouched, like a spaniel sighting a bird, and we turned and looked, and there was the light; it seemed to move and then was gone.

We raced blindly up the slope, then stopped to listen. There was no sound save the light wind in the high pine trees. We touched each other for safety, blowing hard from the dash uphill. Samson whispered he was going inside; a rash decision instantly regretted. The doors were nailed, so it would have to be a window, and they were high.

We went quietly. 'Bunk I up,' he whispered. 'I wanna 'ave a look fust.'

We got under him and heaved him up to the ledge. Sour earth and mildew pricked our courage, and when we looked straight up the house appeared to lean and move against the teeming stars.

We trembled with his weight as Samson cautiously poked his head over the sill, and the black bowels of a lower room, perhaps meant for a drawing room, opened up before him like a gulf. 'Can't see nothin',' he breathed. We groaned as he stirred, trying to get higher.

Just then it was that the door opened away on our right; and we dropped Samson in a heap. Stuck in the attitude of shop-window dummies we were immediately, fearfully, alert. Our blood ran away, our breathing stopped, our hearts ceased pumping, every organ turned in an instant to an extra ear.

As always we took our cue from Samson, the biggest and bravest of us. His hair stood up like a cockscomb, as if his skull had shrunk, and when he took to his heels so did we.

Plunging after him down the track we attained speeds that none of us had ever before achieved, and would never ever repeat no matter how hard we tried. With the briefest contact our feet hurled us forward at such velocity that our eyes burned and watered with friction. Twenty yards in front, Samson rushed headlong down the woodland path. The moon flicked on him and for a fraction of time held him, as it were, unmoving in powerful stride.

I knew he must have seen something and that I at least, the smallest of our party, would be overtaken by whatever it was pursuing us. That I should never again see the light of day, or kiss girls, or thieve in Collet's orchard, were not conscious considerations, though they must have done their bit, for I caught and passed Spud easily.

Panic laid into us like a whip; boys never ran like this in all history. Soon my feet became quite sensationless; a numbness spread into my legs as the nerves died one by one, and there was just my head rushing through the night. We lost a year along that moon-drenched track, speeding like javelins to catch our naked minds streaking ahead to safety.

We shot out of the wood, out and over the stubble field easing to a gallop. By this time our leader was back at the hut with the door locked and bolted, and when at last Spud and I arrived we had to rave at him to let us in.

We guzzled water and panted for ten minutes. It was Spud who spoke first. 'What was it, you? I didn't see nothin'.' He was red and wet and looked ready to burst from his fat skin.

'Somebody was standin' there! – standin' right out in the open! I seen 'im; I bloody seen 'im as clear as day!' Samson fired his fright with another drink of water. 'I seen 'im! 'E was standin' lookin' at us! Bugger, what a shock!'

'I bet it was the dwarf; I bet it bloody was, you!' I said.

We were hoarse with air and night and fear, and when I mentioned the dwarf we went round eyed, waiting for the curse to drop us in a heap. Spud's lips quivered, and I knew he was thinking of his mother and brother and his father who worked a team of horses at the saw mill. 'I be off 'ome,' he said.

Samson half laughed. 'Don't be bloody daft. 'Tis the middle of the night.' He paused and lowered his voice. 'Anyway, 'e might 'ave followed us.'

He checked the bolts again and stood against the door listening. We watched each other for the first signs of fresh panic, each ready with his share. The scheme had been mine and Spud's reproachful glare needed soothing.

'It'll be all right. Our Dad'll be up with the tractor in the mornin'.' I said. 'We be safe enough.' Without another word we sat on the bunks and took off our shoes. Spud thought we had found a nest of spies and started guessing the reward and spending it. Better a spy with a gun than a dwarf who could finish you with a look.

After that there were just grunts and mumbles as we curled down on the straw mattresses. Little fluttering sounds in the stove pipe were comforting; we scratched and belched and turned over to the wall. The last I heard was Spud: 'I don't 'alf wanna go,' he said.

Next morning we all woke up together with the sound of voices outside. We pulled back the sack from the window and saw the landgirls going up the field to Top Barns. We flung open the door and the sun struck the back of the hut. We washed in the trough in the hedge, boiled water, and fried sausages, and spent all day playing cricket on the common. Whatever it was we had seen or heard that night never outstayed that day, and we seldom spoke of it again.

But the lights went on flashing at the mansion, and the rumours grew so that the police finally had to go and investigate. They found a man and woman living in part of it. They had been bombed out of their home in Coventry they said, and had wandered the roads looking for somewhere to live. In so remote a place they thought nothing of the blackout and went on showing lights right throughout the war. The police were satisfied about them, but for the rest of us they were a source of suspicion to the end.

They vanished in 1944 and nothing more was heard of them.

The planes in the skies were the nearest we ever came to the war. They were no more than a sideshow of course in the Cotswolds, yet death swooped here as suddenly as on some far away battlefield. One plane had come down in the village; but that was not the end of it.

The sky was full of engines, the background to all our days and nights. Some planes were so low that we dashed out to make sure the chimney was still there. Some were visibly holed and oil streaked, miles from their base, looking for any convenient airfield. They limped along with dead engines and vanished over Amberley.

But mostly they just passed over; high or low, they were a common sound around the hill and often we never even bothered to look up.

The fighters came from Aston Down. They'd sit on the blue air of the valley like sharks in the deep, come silently, swiftly, over and gone before the noise hit. They flew around us all day long sometimes: young men beating their breasts at a still distant enemy. Then it was a slow, regular barrage, with five minutes or less between bursts of massive thunder. They were low round the woods, or very high and sun-lit, diving silently till their engines punched the banks: one felt the blow on the ear when they were this low.

A good, fine day would bring them up; singly, but usually in pairs, dog-fighting over the hill. Today it was fine and hot; the sky looked like ice. Two Hurricanes (Alfy's and mine?) chased through the blue; raced up and down the valley to Nailsworth. They stopped the haymaking and men leaned on their pitch-forks to watch. It was nothing out of the ordinary; yet there was something about these two that held one's attention – like a man on a high-wire over a gorge. I think we already felt fear.

They came back along the valley and up over the woods, ten feet clear and nearly invisible, climbing steeply to a thousand feet. They curved in air, on one wing, catching the sun, and plunged over the farm very low. They repeated the whole thing twice more, with low sweeps over the hay fields.

It was nearly combat, with sharp dives and rolls and the margin for error grew smaller by the minute. One went the length of Selsley Common and returned thin-edged, over the beechwood. He swept over low, and climbing a little, looked for his partner; just then swooping up the valley towards the farm. Its brown shape vanished momentarily in the confused colours of the woods, then streaked above them, climbing and turning. Clearly they had lost sight of each other, and their engines welled into a single massive roar. In an instant they were very close, yet it seemed still safe. Then one twitched and it was done: the port wing of one sliced cleanly through the other, just behind the cockpit, cutting it in half; and in a breath the sky was empty.

We were in the garden at the time, and Mother gasped and ran away under the apple tree, smothering her face.

'Oh, my God, Those poor boys!'

She shivered, though it was stifling under the wall, and Myra came and touched her thin shoulders, as we stared bewildered at the thread of dark smoke rising in the still air at the corner of the wood.

We watched its slow progress mark the point of collision at 400 feet, then turned to our Mother, asking if they had crashed; but of course we knew they had. She turned away, sobbing. 'They've gone to their doom!' She went in and cried on the bed all the afternoon.

One crashed in Watson's field, with the pilot by the wall, dead in the cockpit. The other spun out of control onto the railway embankment. They found the pilot's body among the haycocks.

~~🕊~~ FATHER ~~🕊~~

Father was born in 1898 at Woodford in Gloucestershire, one of six children. His father and mother I saw only once that I remember, and my fragmentary recollection of that single visit is of a barrel-shaped grampy with tight waistcoat and gold watch chain, and a stick-thin granny in a floor length dress and black button shoes. They lived at Swanley then, in their little humped cottage which had somehow forced its way up through the rose bushes and seemed not much taller.

The garden that day drowned in sunshine; a misty light lay over it, flashing with insects and flowers. The heat and dazzle never passed beyond the rag mat inside the door though, never cleaved the cool interior or rearranged the mingled odours of soot, onions, paraffin and bacon. The whole place exuded long life and content.

Grandfather, who had the full forehead and frightening promise of genius, abandoned intellect for pleasure and wasted most of his life at Berkeley Castle, looking after the horses and playing cricket.

Somehow, through a lucky bequest, shrewdness or favouritism (there were endless arguments about it), he bought a small shop selling sweets and tobacco: to that he added free advice to the lovelorn, predicted the weather and the outcome of the test matches with miraculous prescience, and pronounced on the virtues of hard work and thrift. The shop stayed open twenty-four hours a day, made a sack of money, and kept them comfortably off to the end of their days.

He drummed into the boys that they must use their heads if they wanted to get on, but none of them ever did. He told them that it was the only way up the ladder, but the boys had no such lofty ambitions and all were doomed to labour in field or foundry for as long as their health lasted.

Tim died of drink trying to forget about work and the Somme, and Ted dropped dead of his heart after a row with his wife. Farm and factory, shop and mill claimed the rest, and like so many of that generation they were to spend their lives chased by poverty, as natural and irremediable as a birthmark.

Father started work at twelve years of age, thereafter attending school only when he was dragged there, or when they were giving things away

83

at Easter and Christmas. On Saturdays he would set off at dawn with a thick piece of bread and a pluck of fatty pork, wrapped in cloth, and be gone all day cattle driving.

One of the longest journeys, he told us, was from Berkeley to Kingscote, through Dursley. The animals trampled gardens, splashed doors, broke windows, knocked down walls, and always went fastest down the wrong streets. Screaming women snatched up their youngsters; dogs barked, snapped, and followed for miles; men stood defensively in front of their shops, bawling revenge or calling for the magistrates.

He never stopped running or shouting or fending off abuse. He ate as he ran, bread in one hand, stick in the other, drinking from the wayside streams, stumbling home long after dark more dead than alive with sixpence earned for his mother; for grandfather saw to it that the housekeeping never went above a guinea a week.

At fourteen he left school and went with Farmer Curnock full time. Cattle driving was still his main work and would be for years. That and crow scaring and picking up stones was the natural apprenticeship to the land in those days, and on Mondays he drove stock twelve miles up the white stone road to Gloucester market.

It was on one of these journeys that he met my Mother, a slender pinch of a girl with hair flowing out behind like a damp veil. That day she was riding her bicycle round and round the patch of green outside her home. The bullocks blundered in, trampled the flower beds, ate the hedge and knocked her down. Her mother came out and clouted his ear, and that should have settled it. But every week thereafter he got a smile and a wave from the girl; and their meetings were thus over the width of the road, though the distance was closing between them. Although it never went much beyond this for several years, she had touched his heart fatally, and he had already made up his mind that one day he would marry her.

He was called up in 1916 and went into the Royal Horse Artillery. In Flanders they made him a battery runner. Gassed at Ypres, he was sent home sick, and met my Mother again. When he returned to the front they started writing to each other. She sent him a lock of hair tied with ribbon; and he had his arm tattooed with two hands clasped over a heart, and the words 'Albert and Nancy – Hearts Entwined'. Her letters and lock of hair were still in his box when he died over half a century later.

They married in 1921, at Thornbury, soon after he left the army, and went to live in a cottage rented from her father. Bob was born a year later.

Then things began to go wrong. His in-laws half a mile round the lanes had something to do with it. There was nothing wrong with them except the bone problem of over-expectation. Mother became difficult and unpredictable, went listless and quiet for days on end, forgot Father's meals and worried over everything. Loud shouting matches left them both stunned, as if they had found a horror in themselves. She was often in tears. He thought money lay at the root of it, and begged round for all the work he could get, to put an extra couple of shillings on the table Saturday nights. None of it did any good.

One day, ill and grieving over nothing that she could explain, she put Bob in the pram and went home. Father fetched her back. Her mother started coming round – an irrepressible malice who could drop you with one look. Left to themselves they would have come through all right, but now it was open warfare between the two families, arguments and fist fights all round the lanes, and at dawn they'd hold a roll call to see who was missing.

It came to a head dramatically. Two of her brothers, George and Percy, sat in The Greyhound all one Sunday night, gazing hard at their beer, as if therein lay the solution. Their reason was well-oiled and freewheeling as they pondered these family things, wondering what they ought to do about them. They chased the problem with ale till it filled them; each pint drowning caution, rousing passion and anger.

At last they staggered out into the dark, growling that this business had gone on long enough and had better be settled once and for all; that they would fetch their sister back home and drive the Robertses out of the village, and no one had better stand in their way.

It was late when they got to the cottage, and they banged the door with their fists, shouting they wanted Albert, that they meant business. Mother got up and came to the bedroom window, leaning out. She told them to go away, clear off. They barked they had come to fetch her home, and told her to pack her bags. She tried softening their temper with humour, as she had many times before when they were in drink. This time though they were too far gone and, roaring threats, stamped off to the woodshed to fetch an axe.

Somehow or other Father managed to sleep through this, but now she shook him awake, and helped him dress in the candlelight. They cursed bloody murder outside, the door started to splinter, and the quiet lane was suddenly in hideous uproar. With Bob in her arms, Mother screamed at her brothers to go away, leave them alone; but the axe bit into the door harder than ever and nothing would stop them now. She beseeched Father to get out quickly, while there was still time, and not come back until they had sobered up and come to their senses; otherwise anything might happen.

He looked at her anxious face, tormented and deathly white. 'Ah, all right then,' he said. 'But tomorrow it'll be my turn!'

He squeezed her hand and leapt the back fence into the field. She watched him go away up the slope, unhurriedly in the moonlight, as if he were setting off for a day's work. When he got to the railway line he disappeared. She did not know then of course that it would be many long years before they would ever meet again.

He walked up the line between the shining rails, his past dying behind him with the moon. One feels how easy that break must have been at that moment, how each weary step, taking him farther and farther from home, seemed like a stretching of the links that held him. Somewhere in the night the connection broke, and then came the dawn wind, and light, and by then he was in Gloucester.

The streets were still and empty, so he made his way to the park and lay down on a bench and slept. When he woke the city was warm and alive, and he made for Southgate where there was a café. He knew the owner from his army days, borrowed a razor, and the bacon and eggs were free. Afterwards he wandered down to the cattle market.

During the night he formed a makeshift plan and remembered a man who might be useful to him. He spent hours round the pens and at midday tracked him down in The Crown, and straight away asked him if that job was still going. Yes, the farmer said, he was still looking for someone, someone on hand, someone to live in: was he interested then? Father said he thought it sounded just the thing, so they shook hands and had a drink on the bargain. With what money he had he bought soap and a towel, climbed into the lorry and went back with the farmer to Stow-on-the-Wold.

No one knew then, no one knows now, all the reasons for that dramatic rupture. His determined movements after he left the cottage have the taint of premeditation, yet he could scarcely have forseen the course of that Sunday night's events, let alone plan for them, and nothing in after years ever gave us a hint.

Nevertheless, he surely never intended staying away so long, and it was meant – at first anyway – as a gesture, a raised finger, an interlude that would give everyone time to back off and calm down.

In the event he stayed at Stow many years, and in the end returned only by the merest chance.

These years of course passed differently for both. Father settled quickly into his new life as if it had all been planned. The farmer and his wife treated him like a son. He ate at their table and slept in a room over the barn. They thought him a single man and he never gave himself away. He wrote regularly to his mother and for years she kept his secret loyally, would indeed have kept it forever. No one else knew what had become of him, for she used to meet the postman in the lane so that no one should know of his letters. Rumour had him murdered, gone back to the army, drowned in the Severn; and the village talked of nothing else for months.

How easy and futile that break had been only came to him later. He bought a bicycle and on Sunday afternoons rode miles round the roads of Oxfordshire; he had never before known such freedom. He put on weight and grew a moustache and let the harrowing guilt evaporate in the shining of new things. There was just the unhealing bruise of lonely remembered moments in the long nights of winter, or when a girl's voice made him turn quickly in hope and rage.

It was very different for Mother, among those she knew and all of them knowing and talking. The police looked into it but there was nothing they could do and told her to get in touch with the Salvation Army. After six months of worry she gave up the search, accepted at last the loss of him; though something of him always lingered, whispering like the wind once anger and fear had passed.

Unable to support herself, she went back home. A year passed, then another; she shut her mind against ever seeing him again, though surely the hope was always there, crouching, springing up with every knock at the door, every footstep in the lane.

When they were all in bed, and she alone in the kitchen, she fancied she heard his boots scrape on the flagstones outside. It was only night sounds, but she would search the orchard with the lantern, and come in and lie across the table, listening, till dawn at last touched the curtains.

At other times she was numb and hard, practical and matter of fact, convinced he was dead and gone and what was the use.

They might indeed have stayed separated evermore had not the farmer decided to emigrate. He asked Father to come with him; there was a great future in Canada, and land was cheap; it was a chance of a lifetime. Father thought about it, though I'm sure never seriously for he knew that if ever he left England he would never come back, and suddenly realized that what he wanted most of all was to go home.

Word spread rapidly round the lanes that Albert Roberts was back from the dead, and Mother knew within hours; yet there was no immediate reconciliation, no hurrying to put things right. Any haste now might trip them up, so they took their time about it while both families held their breath.

One day Father came down the lane and saw the boy playing in the orchard. Bob was nearly eight now, and came to the gate when Father called, though it was a week or two before he knew who this man was.

Watching from the curtains, bedevilled with nerves yet wonderously curious, Mother thought she'd die with shock when she saw him that first time, leaning over the gate. When they tried to push her out through the door she ran upstairs. Then, later, she told Bob who this man was, and next time Father came Bob tugged his sleeve and brought him up the path. Father stood at the door, sunburned, already a little grey. 'Hullo, Nance,' he said. Seven or eight years had been a heavy price to pay for both of them, and the relief at this first meeting was like the abrupt termination of a life sentence.

One imagines her smoothing her frock and playing with her bun, a charm of delights and dreads. 'Hullo, Alby!'

There they stood in the Old Mill kitchen and tears and handshakes closed the years of parting. Cider flowed, plans were hatched and Bob, the link of the two, was squeezed, patted and passed round the room. 'Your dad's 'ome! There, there! 'E's 'ome!'

Their cottage was still empty, and the three of them went back there a few days later, the door still marked from that fateful night.

He got his old job back, at Curnock's, and took up his load once more. In the evenings, bit by bit, she drew the story out of him. Had there been other women along the way? 'No, no women,' he said. 'I thought you were dead or gone off with someone else,' she murmured. It was years before she was convinced that there had not been another woman behind it, and it disappointed her.

Father used to cycle to work along the lane by the railway track. On one of those mornings patchy fog drifted about, and all round the black trees reached out from the swirling wraiths. Father and the express train were always so regularly on time that they passed each other every morning more or less in the same place, between the elm clump and the bend. But this morning the train was late. He stopped and looked up and down the line through a gap in the hedge. The mist closed in again as he stared down the empty track, and he got back on his bicycle, standing on the pedals up the stiff slope. He heard the motorcycle coming and pulled well over, but it slowed down and stopped. He recognised the goggles and gloves.

'Howbe, Art! What's up then? Bike givin' trouble?'

'Ain't you 'eard! The bloody train's crashed!'

'What! Where?'

'Charfield. I'm off t' 'ave a look!'

Art Tilson opened up his Raleigh and wobbled off into the mist, hunched over the tank. Alone between the dripping hedges, Father listened to the exhaust cracking round the road, and, in the returning silence, far away, heard the clamour of fire bells breaking faintly through the woods. Then he swung his bicycle round and pedalled hard for the station, three miles away.

Long before he got there, in the growing light, he saw the boiling black clouds with flames winking in them. A thin thread of voices, terror driven on the air, surged and ebbed and grew louder.

The express missed all the signals set at danger and crashed into two goods trains, smashing them into a pyramid in a narrow cutting under a road bridge. One of the coaches hung on the parapet, with the doors off and people dead in the road. It burned all day. Water jets turned to steam, tar boiled on the road, the stones of the bridge stayed hot for days. All were helpless in the smoke and heat. They knew it was hopeless but some men forced their way through, pulling at burning timbers in heat like an oven, and were downed and staggered away choking. From this time Father's fingernails stopped growing. Joking, he would say that it was because he had to scratch and scrape for a living, but it was undoubtedly shock.

Three trains wrecked, fifteen people dead, and he'd talk about it now and then. We used to climb onto his knee and make him tell us of the day the mail train crashed in the fog at Charfield, and of the two little children whose bodies were found in the wreckage but never claimed. 'They buried 'em in the cemetery,' he told us, 'and to this day no one knows who they were or where they were going alone so early in the morning. But they do say that a strange woman dressed all in black often visits their grave, and weeps over it.'

Whenever Father spoke of the Crash we always thought he meant the trains under the bridge, at Charfield, when what he actually meant was the Depression. For years the two tangled in confusion so that I believed the one had caused the other and made Father leave the land, which he did at the worst possible time.

He went into a foundry, at Dursley, for an extra five shillings a week; but soon regretted the move. The foundry closed six months later, and it was touch and go for the next five years.

He kept going by rearing pigs and repairing motorcycles, filling in at haymaking, potato planting and apple picking. He dreamed of pounds but scraped shillings, and every man for miles was doing the same. Mother patched and mended, scoured the roads for firewood and blackberries and kept them going on cabbage and pig's trotters. Myra was there now, out under the apple tree in her pram, cuddling the cat like a toy, and even the apples crashing like bombs never woke her up.

Father got up at five, and straight out he'd go to check the rabbit wires in the half-light fields. At seven he'd set out looking for work. He cycled miles, was often gone all day, and at midnight he'd roll into his hollow bed, embracing sleep like a child embracing its mother, and sad to let her go.

They say he changed a little, became more defensive, more withdrawn. His kindliness and reticence was often mistaken for meekness. He was entirely without guile and, assuming innocence in others, was easily taken in. Because he was tender to their probes he kept to himself; and when he could not, humoured their big mouths and laughed quietly, so that they never guessed that their boasting fell on deaf ears.

He read little, spoke only of day things, and never gave advice (though received plenty). He had dark areas that rarely opened, but, when they did, unexpectedly showed that he knew things and had weighed up the world. His feelings grew coarse to guard his soft heart and, sometimes, he might seem indifferent and hard. Partly this was his health of course, which was never good after France, and his chest was always bad.

He was a man of hands rather than head, and liked engines. He was untrained, and learning took hours of lantern light and late hours in the shed next to the pigs. Mother would turn over in the middle of the night and find his place empty and cold. She would sit up, startled; then hearing the hammer below would sink again to her penny sleep.

Blue with the cold and as black as a sweep, he would come in to breakfast telling of the night's troubles. 'Seized right up 'e was; I 'ad t' cut the bolts t' get 'im free'd off. Red wi' rust them cylinders were. Wonder if 'e'd part wi' ten bob?'

It was hand to mouth then. Days lost their names, the weeks their sacred beginnings and endings; the natural parcels of time slipped away. Work and rest came with the supply of energy, or lack of it, directed by necessity. And my arrival added to their problems. Now it was me in the pram with the cat, and Myra had to put up with it.

It was a bitter day, pouring with rain, when he set off for Mudgedown to see about a job. He arrived wet through, his teeth chattering with cold, and the job had gone anyway. But for once he was lucky and they took him inside out of the rain. Was he prepared to move, they asked. A brother wanted a general farmworker up there in the hills near Stroud – arable and fat stock. There was a good cottage going with it.

That was our way back and he grabbed it. Clock time, a wage; proper day, proper night. So we went from flat, misty fields and tree-roofed lanes to rolling hills and surging woods shaking with the gales; and Father came back to his chains, the weeks again were what they had been, with Saturday afternoons off, cake for tea, Sundays to doze, and a pint at The Ram when he had the money.

His new boss (the Old Man we called him) was what was then known as a gentleman farmer. It meant money if not ease; meant that the farm was a sideline, a second interest. He had factories in Dursley (Father had worked at the foundry) and his engines were masterpieces sold round the world. He soared, I remember, in that spotless pre-eminence then reserved for gentlemen and ladies, lords and squires: part of the natural order of things, and there were no trouble-makers to tell us differently. He and his lady were mostly invisible, but sometimes came by the cottage on their chestnut hunters, stiffly, unseeing, and very remote; or they'd walk the banks with their silent children and yapping dogs, and we trembled lest they should come close and speak, for, if they did, how should we answer and be understood? They were a bit down from the King and Queen, and here we were, on their land, in their cottage and under their power.

For all that, they needed us, and although they were distant no one wanted it any other way. There were horrific spasms, as if winter and summer had changed ends, when the instinctive barriers of men and master were torn down and the Old Man came striding into the harvest field, threw down his jacket, rolled up his sleeves and climbed onto the tractor. Such outrageous behaviour was like a doctor getting into bed with his patient to share his pains – unthinkable. The fun died like a switch, the swearing stopped, conversation grew square-edged, and work went up 500 per cent. Pipes stayed unlit, the cider grew warm among the stooks, and backs bent till they broke.

When finally the Old Man had had enough and returned to the big house to rest, the men quickly gathered in a knot, passing the cider jar, suddenly very talkative as if after a disaster.

It was on one of these lightning visits that Bolwell and the Old Man broke into an open quarrel. No one knew what it was about but Bolwell, at the end of his tether, knocked the Old Man through the hedge in lieu of notice, and the next day Father was foreman. There was a four shilling increase which came in handy, and now he had full charge of the tractor as well.

Father and the tractor blend in the senses and stubbornly refuse to part. Where you found one you would also find the other. They carried the same fumes – a cocktail of oil and paraffin and hot metal. The blasting day-long noise not only made him hard of hearing but tore the very clothes from his back. His jackets aged, the fabric sagged and lost colour, the seams tore open, and stains appeared round the pockets like black glass.

The tractor, a Standard Fordson, blue with orange wheels when it had paint, carried the farm on its back, for horses had their limits on these banks. It ran on paraffin and was a devil to start. Getting it going on cold mornings was hard on patience and very fatiguing. To start, a bucket of hot water went into the radiator and the plugs were warmed on the hob; then Father swung the handle till his arms dropped off. After that he'd come in cursing and down a pot of tea. Slowly, like a mangled boxer getting off his stool with the fight still to be won, he went back out for the next round. The second attempt, more desperate with every minute, was always too much for Father's gas-corroded lungs, and soon he would start coughing, as if his head would burst, jerking about like a doll and sagging exhausted over the radiator. Sweat dripped from his chin but he had to get it started, though it put him on his knees when his chest was bad.

There were beautiful times too, as wonderful as any in memory, when it fired straight off, thundering tremendously inside the shed.

The two of them ran through the hours with ferocious endurance:

eighty most weeks, and a hundred, sometimes, in the long double summers of wartime. It is how I remember him best: Father and the tractor preserved in the spinning seasons, with their separate colours and furniture. I see the brown weather of the ploughing, the polished furrows like walnut wood, white gulls stirring in the sooty sky, hedges gone to nothing, wild woods filling with leaves, the razor wind in the east, and Father in his old blue coat leaning sideways on the mudguard, watching the wheel along the line.

Every hour he would stop under the hedge and shut down the engine. Steam would come out round the radiator cap, and he'd drop the blind so that the fan could suck more air. Carefully, he would take off his gloves and move his fingers about, rubbing the frozen sinews in hands drawn in like claws. Up close to the hot manifold, he'd light up a cigarette, for in spite of his chest the pleasure of tobacco drugged the biting cold and made it bearable. Then he'd move his marker fifty yards down the field, tying the fluttering rag high on an ash sapling. Back on the tractor he would adjust the sack, tied to the seat with binder twine, pull his coat across his throat, bang his gloves tight, and set off across the stubble till the day turned dark. Unhitching the plough at the headland, he followed the track home from memory as the winter night closed in.

Mowing in the flame of summer was more than just a rotation of jobs and weather, a reversal of nature, it was Father's cure, his convalescence and restoration; for in spite of the long extra hours it tired him less than the cold, sweeping down from the common. The fields, green and thick, were ours again for months, the valley a blue mist end to end.

I would be sent out into the field with a bottle of cold tea, the first job coming in from school. With his head thrown right back and his Adam's apple working like a rachet, he guzzled in a terror of thirst. We'd watch Myra search the silky mow for moondaisies, poppies and campion, which made our kitchen a wilderness of limp flowers, moths and beetles.

When Father came in from work we looked him over to read his day, and by practice knew almost which field he came from. He entered with his eyes well down, as if part of him was still out there and wished to be. He never spoke until after his meal, and then it was like an overspill of worry, addressed to no one in particular.

'We're right down on paraffin.' 'Wonder when 'e's comin' fer them calves? Can't keep 'em penned much longer.' 'I should 'ave finished that three-cornered piece, but old Frank come a-hinderin'.'

After the delivery of these choice items he fell sound asleep in the chair and snored till it was time to go to bed. Round about him rose the flavours of field and barn: hay, meal, sheep, dung, sweat, grass and tobacco; additions to underlying oil. His jacket, slung on the back of the chair, was a daily bulletin. Flecked with cow hairs, it sagged with nails, knives, pliers, wire, solder and little flat tins sealed with insulating tape. I was eight before I could lift it and even then I had to use both hands.

He slept a lot, tired out; and was most tired at threshing time. He came in blacker than a miner, with little bobs of dirt in the corners of his red eyes. Beans were the worst, and dirtiest; but barley awns worked right through to the skin, and he'd tear off his clothes in the back kitchen as if he were burning. As he piled it in a heap we stood ready with the cat: mice trapped in his clothes never lived long. Rats were exceptional, and crushed at once through the cloth as soon as they arrived. Mice were sport (except with the landgirls), but rats were feared because of their bite.

After he had washed he would reach for the Owbridges and drink half a bottle straight off. Next morning, when the dust had started bronchitis, he coughed himself awake. He coughed for an hour in the kitchen. He went out into rain and biting cold, still coughing. Our milking cow answered him from the yard, and went readily to her stall. But as soon as I was old enough I saved him that chore.

Father never easily made friends, but for this one brief time he let down his guard and brought all sorts of people up to the farm. Mother was suspicious about some of them. 'He's just out for what he can get, anybody can see that,' she used to say. No doubt she was right, but Father chose to ignore the warning. The regrets came later.

Mother gave them all nicknames, labels as varied as they were unflattering. The Noise was one, and he was a regular. A tall curly-headed scrounger with thick black eyebrows and sly eyes. He had hands like shovels and an unrepentant mouth which never quite opened. He never knocked at the door, but drew attention to himself by whistling 'Dolly Grey', dropping spanners, or tapping out a tune on the mudguard of the tractor as if it were a big base drum. He came, he said, to see if there was anything 'doing', any casual work. He had a crushing mortgage and earned only three pounds a week as a farrier. If there was no work Father gave him a bag of oats as interest on his willingness; though in the end the interest far exceeded the capital. 'He's been up four times this week,' said Mother, who took note of such things. But Father let him get away with it. "E's a good worker, old Brian, one of the best,' and no one could argue with that. Good reliable help was hard to come by when the war was on.

The Dandy, though, had never worked in his life; had no need so long as he could talk. Words poured out of him and drowned you so that you would do anything to get away. His facile tongue was all the muscle he ever needed, and he exercised it, sometimes, as a commercial traveller. He came in his shining Wolseley every Sunday morning at eleven o'clock. With his green bow tie, red handkerchief, brown and white shoes and whisky-blue nose, he was our unfunny clown.

'Mornin' Elbert! Delightful frost.' (What did he know or care of frozen water pipes, chopping out water troughs or getting that damned tractor started.) He'd clear his throat, fuss with his tie and talk about the war, shortages, his car, his ailing wife, his job, clothes, teeth – anything but the real reason for his visit. He would keep it up for half an hour and we all pretended to listen. As he was leaving (the car door open, one foot inside), he at last showed his hand.

'Oh, Elbert. Suppose you haven't got a bit for my birds? Only a bit mind. Don't want to cadge or anything. Daphne loves an egg.' Sighing loudly, looking round the yard, his eyes always came to rest on the granary.

'Shall have to get rid of 'em I suppose. Just can't get the grub, that's the trouble. Blasted war! Cocked everything up. Just a bucket full – anything at all. Sorry to ask and all that. Damned business. Half a sack would do.'

At each visit his hens grew weaker, thinner and he knew it was only a matter of time before he would have to knock them all in the head. Pretty soon he was coming twice a week.

'Only two eggs yesterday and Daphne needs the protein. The doctor said that without it . . .' He shook his head and looked at the floor and there was nearly a tear in his eye. 'Can't get the grub, that's the damned trouble. Tried everywhere. It's the blasted war. Only a bit, Elbert; don't want to cadge. A hundredweight would fix me up.'

His hens, if ever they existed, went from bad to worse, and had nothing better than kitchen scraps. For the Dandy had a ready market for these sacks of oats, though we only heard of it years later. He spent the proceeds on his mistress who lived at Cirencester, for some fool was giving him ten pounds a bag.

The Driver was different. All he wanted was someone to teach him to drive a tractor; not that there was much to learn. He had a passion for tractors as some men have for horses. All things mechanical fascinated him, but he loved tractors the most. In gratitude he brought us baskets of fruit and had us down to meet his wife. Not that any of this was necessary – Father would have given him the tractor if he had asked.

The trouble was, the Driver was an idiot with machines and should never have been allowed near anything faster than a wheelbarrow. That first time on our tractor he reshaped the farm: holes appeared in hedges, walls suddenly had gaps where none had been before, gates broke in two, bushes were flattened – and he could never remember hitting any of them.

He had a lethal preference for top gear and never understood that you had to stop to change up or down; not at all like a car. In the end Father told him to give it up; his wife told him to give it up; all the village told him to give it up. But he just laughed, not in the least concerned with two or three major accidents a week.

He went tractor driving for Fowler but lasted only a couple of months; then the War Ag. took him on. Wherever he went, wherever he worked, he carried a double-barrelled shotgun; carried it with him on the tractor, loaded. He'd stand up and fire, at rabbits or rooks, it mattered not: it made the job interesting he said, and those who foresaw tragedy were soon proved right.

One day near Tetbury he was rolling corn, got his wheel on a low wall and went completely over down a bank. They found him crushed under the wheel. He had apparently fired at something and forgot what he was doing until it was too late; there was an empty cartridge in the chamber. He was known to stop while he aimed, but on this occasion had not done so.

Another gun man of a different type was Inspector Hobart; and how Father ever got to know him is something of a mystery. But he was a regular visitor at one time, and, with his two-two rifle, telescopic sight and silencer, could wipe out a field of rabbits in an hour. Afterwards he would drag them back to his car in relays and go off and sell them to hotels round Stroud.

He had a big shining round red face and high blood pressure. Our banks threatened his life and brought on violent nose bleeds. He would come dripping to our back kitchen, blowing like a buffalo, his shirt crimson from collar to belt. When we first saw him staggering to the door we thought he was shot. He held his head under the tap till the bleeding stopped, then changed his shirt, for he was always well prepared. An enormous man, over six feet and eighteen stone, he filled our kitchen uncomfortably. Never had we been so familiar with a policeman and his comparatively high rank was oppressive. When he spoke to us children we mumbled like idiots and avoided his eyes; guilt rose in our faces and we waited in suspense for the jingle of the handcuffs.

He was a careless policeman, too, especially with poisons, and loathed foxes more than villains. Once, unknown to us, he put strychnine in a dozen eggs and dropped them casually round the banks, killing a sheep dog we were training.

All sorts of things he'd leave behind – watch, wallet or bloody shirt – and these I would take to Stroud Police Station on woodwork days. He looked twice the size in uniform, and a great arc of buttons rose up as I entered his office. I could never look at him directly, and always addressed his belt, level with my head. I'd throw the things on his desk and bolt, stammering like a half-wit and going red for those wretched things done and got away with ever in my mind.

So these friends of Father's came and went; we relished them for their sharp difference but blessed their infrequency too. Whatever they meant to Father, to us they were merely curiosities, chips of the outside, shapes of village and town and other lives. As far as we were concerned they were strangers and remained so always. When they came into our kitchen a peculiar chill came with them and the air turned as sour as vinegar. Nervous and watchful as we were, it seemed a natural response to strangers.

Yet ignore them we could not, and stayed, listening, watching the way they stood and what they did with their hands. When they bent down, pressing a sixpence into our fingers, we'd go pink and look at their teeth, blue chins, and white partings. And when they were gone we were relieved, the room strange and drained, as if they had taken part of it with them, till it slowly filled again with ourselves.

Then Mother sang in relief, and Father coughed to relax: well-loved invocations to exorcise their stain and make our kitchen home again; sounds that threw folds about us, an expected counterpoint to repose.

In fact Father's chesty cough, jarring like a toy drum day and night, was a steady solo performance, rising sharply in volume after October. He had bronchitis and pleurisy every winter now, and the banks kept him prisoner months at a time. His hair curled like string out of his cap and touched his collar like thatch. When at last he was well he came home from the barber close-cropped and looking like a boy.

The bare, wind-loving hill, thrusting in mist and pelting rain, took its toll of Father through the years. He would never see a doctor, unless critical. There was nothing they could do, he said. They just gave you pills that never worked, and made you feel ashamed to be ill.

We had to fetch the doctor once though. He collapsed one morning in the rick yard: chest pains, fever, depression and a cough that had no bottom. Doctor Blake came out from Nailsworth. He was old, smoked like a stove pipe and had a chest far worse than Father's, but out of these tangled symptoms he diagnosed influenza and incipient pneumonia, and advised against eggs and onions. A pan of hot water kept the air moist and after a week he regained his senses. Straight away he got up and came downstairs, very drawn, with his hair on end and eyes very rich in their black sockets, crawling from chair to chair. He went back to work a week later, though he could barely walk, and reminded us again of the swift dangers awaiting those who stayed in bed too long.

What it did was to make him see that his time on the hill was over. Other things worried him too: the broken walls, hedges climbing over the sheds, fences sagging or non-existent – and he wondered what the Old Man would make of it when he came home. No good telling *him* about the labour shortage. He was a good boss but Father thought the Army would turn him. He would stare at the fire and all these things would rumble out in the open.

'There'll be changes when 'e comes back from the army. It'll be all spit 'n polish; do this 'n do that.' We knew he was right, but Mother had hopes.

'Oh, it mightn't be all that bad. You used to get on with him.'

Nevertheless, we started taking *The Farmer and Stockbreeder* as insurance, going carefully through the situations vacant.

'We've gotta get somewhere where it's flat. Never ever thought my chest would pack up like this.' He pencilled round the jobs like a gambler throwing dice, full of hope but with little expectation. A farm bailiff on 500 acres at Wantage; farm foreman, large arable farm with good cottage at Swindon; tractor driver at Frampton – he circled them all. Mother wrote the letters, dozens of them, and he came in at dinner time looking for the replies. He never bothered much about the money; it was the actual situation, the lie of the land, that was important.

'No more climbing up and down banks, I ain't got the wind for 't.'
Spreading his map on the kitchen table he studied it like a general.
He wrote to a place near Gloucester I remember, but worried in case it
might be perched on a hill. 'I'll ask Brunsdon's chap when 'e comes fer
them bullocks. 'E'll know.'

But we never had a reply from Gloucester, and instead went to
Chelworth, a village in another county. It was only tractor driving, but
he never minded that. We were not long there and moved half a dozen
times in quick succession, trudging up and down the Cotswolds trying
to find another anchor, though we never really did.

He rose at five as usual, but was no match now for the hours as once
he had been, and drew himself thinly through his days in the fields. The
young brawn easily outdid his faked rallies of strength, and anyway he
was nearly past such deception now.

In the end we moved to Marsden and were there six years; years
clouded with sudden serious illness, and only Myra stayed fit and well.
After, we went to Leckhampton, to eighty acres and an inside lavatory
and mains water. This latter triumph had been long coming, but
vanished swiftly and never returned during his lifetime. To get this job
at all he knocked five years off his age; to get his next job he knocked
off another five. Age and a bad chest had broken him, but no one could
tell just by looking; so to be sure he posed younger then he was, but ten
years is a lot. He ended his working life at South Cerney: gardening,
feeding calves, milking a cow, and leisurely came to his retirement.

Somehow or other he saved enough to buy an old bicycle, and rode
round the lanes on summer evenings as once he had all those years ago
at Stow. Now and then he found enough wind to ride across the hills to
the Bristol Road, where his sister Florrie lived, the last of his family.

In these last years I often took him back, back to the common, the hill,
the woods that we still called ours. And he would complain often that
there was no colour in the fields any more.

'I used t' like t' see a bit of charlock in the corn, and a poppy or two.'
Leaning on a gate he would blend best with the past, trying to find in
these fields all the years that were gone.

LADS AND LANDGIRLS

In the bitter spring of 1941 we moved over the fields to the farm cottage where we lived for the next six years.

The Old Man was away in the army, his children all at boarding schools, and his lady had fled to Bisley where she sanguinely awaited the German Army. The big house was empty, the blank windows never so blind, till the County Council later took it over for war orphans. The woods were distant now (whereas before we had stepped from our door into them) and we were blocked in by top cowsheds, bottom cowsheds, stables, granary, tractor shed and barns. Just the kitchen window, looking over the hollow, showed up the valley as far as Nailsworth.

It was about this time that the dog disappeared. He was in the village that morning with some soldiers, but we never saw him again. There were undercurrents with his going and I sometimes sensed that it had not been mere chance, but I never got to the bottom of it. Mother dwelt on it for years, disquieted and darkly suspicious. I believe she thought Father knew more about it than he pretended.

Though sheltered by the barns the farm cottage was very cold. Mother said it was the coldest place we had ever been in, colder even than Stock Hills, unknown to me, but a lasting measure of polar conditions that were never forgotten and which they had been lucky to survive.

For the first fortnight we never took off our overcoats and fought like wolves for a place by the range. We were irresistibly frozen; the wind filled all the curtains like sails, sliced at our legs under the doors, took away our breath climbing the stairs.

Our bedrooms were far arctic places of eternal night which, in winter anyway, we never consciously saw. The marble washstand seemed a natural block of ice which you might chip bits off and suck, and our iron beds, groaning like ships against a berg, threatened to fall to pieces under us. The floor cloth touched our bare feet like fire, and in bed with the blankets over our heads, we curled into balls and listened for the padding of bears.

We fought back with everything we had and kept the range going day and night – till the chimney caught light in the early hours and ever afterwards Mother poured a bucket of water on the grate at bedtime.

We stuffed potato sacks under the doors, paper in the cracks round the windows, and waited for the sun to come crawling back along the cowshed roof.

On the other hand we had a telephone again (only to be answered), and, most wonderful of all, electric light, generated by our own plant tucked between the barn and stables, where it rumbled all day and night charging its hundred batteries.

Other glories were the tilting greengage garden and tree-filled hollow beyond, a natural cleft in the hill, south facing and very steep, filled with eighty or ninety pear trees – sharp quinces that dried one's mouth like sand and went to Yate for perry making.

Sweet pears for the house and harvest field were just over the garden wall, and every September the hollow filled with a sort of sugary musk, top to bottom, a buzzing, darting cauldron of juicy vapours which soaked the farm in a cidery essence.

A thin stream trickled out of the bank, winding through the trees. Loud at the top, quiet at the bottom, it vanished in marsh and kingcups. I'd sit in a tree over the swamp watching the calves drinking below. The nut tree shade cast black nets among them and dragonflies bobbed in the ladders of green light.

This mint of crisis, this bough, this cattle-reeking sun-lit copse, was a place of contemplation. Dangling my legs above mud and water, head staggering with confusion, fifty things passing through it at once, always left the same startling debris: Miss Davage in white shorts, the football boots I'd been cheated of, the circus tickets stolen from my desk, how one lie made five, the treachery of boys, Jenny's delectable chest. I began writing it down in a book, these things of love and hate, never knowing whether it was because I wished to be rid of their impact or for fear that I might forget them.

I came here every day after school, till the year was cold, the wood desolate; or simply till the time came for me to work around the farm. On my birthday Father weighed me on the corn scales and marked my height on the wagon-house door, and when I was ten I was set to work.

He sent me to Frank, who said he would have me on approval and packed me off to fetch hay for the carthorses. Frank was really the foundation of the farm. Others came and went but he stayed on forever. He did largely as he pleased and now, because he was terribly old, was pleased less and less. I liked the way his cap moved round his head with the sun, and how summer always came with his old yellow boater. Nature took her cue from his straw hat and it always stayed fine when he wore it. It became a forecast for haymaking and harvest and a hint to pitch my tent in the hollow. He was well fashioned for the hills, short legged and wide, with a great white moustache hanging from his mouth like frost. His large stomach was all his dignity, a wide leather belt looping under it like a truss. Gaiters and boots, welded together with muck, salt the memory of him, as does his odd speech, the result of a horse accident years ago, making him unintelligible to all except his little wife. He never shared our skimmed conversations in the barns and fields and I would sit with him all day on the cart and only grunts would pass between us. The landgirls teased him and held his throaty rumbles as threats of love or lust. 'Ooh, Frank! What would your wife say if she heard you talk like that!'

Generally he worked by himself with Boxer the grey cart-horse. He'd whack the beast, growling at him to go faster, but Boxer never minded the joke. Frank cursed him all day long but the massive hooves never quickened once. It was a tacit understanding they had. One was old, the other idle, so they made a natural team. Both could be bad tempered, and one approached Boxer respectfully before eight o'clock in the morning. When he flattened his ears and turned his backside, only a madman would have ignored the warning.

Once it nearly led to tragedy. They stalked each other for half an hour, round and round the bushes in the half light. Frank had no real hope of catching him when he was like this and persisted far too long. Boxer snatched the halter out of his hand, trampled it in the mud and kicked the bucket of oats down the bank. Frank came down, waving at Father who was working in the rick yard, and he went up.

Instead of one target Boxer now had two and he turned savagely on them both. With teeth gleaming and ears down flat he made a sudden lunge, reared over them, drove them back into a corner where a high fence and wall trapped them. Only the walnut tree saved them as he charged. They dived for it together as the great hooves closed in and lashed out, stripping a yard of bark. He came at them three times like that, ripping strips off the tree with his rear hooves, while Father and Frank cowered round the other side. With one last flourish, bucking left and right he thundered away down the drive, till the grating stopped him at the edge of the common, for he was always too lazy to jump it. Later he came innocently home, wrenching grass all down the edges of the drive, delighted at having pinched half a day out of the cart.

Peggy was his field mate, a torrid worker, nervous and lathered and far too racy for old Frank. She often came home alone, spilling her load over a hundred acres as she dashed headlong from a low aircraft or a bird rising off the clover.

So for Frank it was Boxer or nothing. Though he complained that Boxer was the worst horse he had ever had anything to do with, and constantly advised the knacker, he'd wink at his old pal when he said it.

At five o'clock, easy with his pipe by the stable door, he'd stare at the dying day, wondering how much longer he could drive his tired frame up these banks. Rich tobacco smoke and stable gas drifted through the yard at the end of each day, signals for the sun to slide through the trees and the stars to come out.

No one knew how long Frank had worked on the hill and he could never remember. He seemed always to have been here, ageless, growing old like a great tree that is never noticed until it is no longer there, and then afterwards one knew how well it had filled the space around.

When the war started Pally and Young Un had gone into the army, Mutton and Doddy had retired. Then it had been just Father and Frank for months, till three ailing soldiers came to help with the haymaking and harvest. They moved into our old cottage under the wood, ready for fresh air and hard work to get them fit again.

They were an odd trio, all from different units, just thrown together for this one summer. Ralph came from the north, a lean, slightly stooping gentleman in uniform; very quiet, very religious. He would sit on the rick-yard gate and tell me about the Scriptures. 'Never take the Lord's name in vain, my boy, and pray like the devil,' he used to say. If the simile sounded odd I got his meaning, and promised hard things to repay his interest – for why should he bother with me at all?

He was not our idea of a soldier, but made more impression on us than the others, and to please him Myra started saying her prayers morning and night – intense muted appeals with her head buried in the mattress; whereas I merely looked up through the window and flung mine at the assembled stars.

Corporal Marsh was their nominal superior and he and Ralph never got on. It had nothing to do with the stripes and seemed no more than a laboured resentment by the man of action for the clerk at headquarters, for the corporal had been pulled apart at Dunkirk and smoked out the fever of that catastrophe with sixty cigarettes a day. He hid his shattered nerves with forced bravado, but we knew. His troubles had at least been bravely earned; all Ralph could offer was double pneumonia.

The third was Paddy, a little Irishman of antiquity who should never have been in the army at all. He swore richly in great colourful, forbidden words which I had only just begun to understand. From this khaki-clad man the words took on fatal black-and-yellow stripes of danger; wicked words that I could never say out loud, but whispered alone in the fields to register their warming effects, like brandy. The very foulest of them darted to one's crotch – a new, shameful sensation.

Paddy cursed everything: the army, the war, women, weather, his friends and his luck (he had been run over by an armoured car). All things living and underground he scorched with a profanity hot and strong enough to dissolve stone. Ralph and Paddy fought for my soul like God and the devil. Two hours with Ralph made my marrow near pure; but all would be undone in five peppery minutes with Paddy, who'd scatter my new innocence till there was nothing left of it, and I would wander back indoors neither good nor bad but just the same as I had been before.

Ralph and the corporal never left the farm, nor had they any wish to. They had tea with us every Saturday afternoon, easy among the muddles of our kitchen, glad to be fussed over by a woman again. They peeled apples and podded peas and gave us Scribona swiss rolls, saved from their rations, and let us eat the lot.

A quiet teatime was not to Paddy's taste. He would go down to the village looking for girls, and on Sundays trudged through the wet fields to the Catholic church. He sang as loud as he swore, though never so expertly, and his hour-long confessions were self proclaimed.

He was the most unsettled of the three, and perpetually anxious about his wife in Londonderry. 'Sure she niver writes,' he told us, 'and I've half a mind not to go back.' His little eyes were almost silver, watery, with restless shades passing through them. 'Tell me now, which would be the greater sin – to leave her flat, or go home and clout her fer not answering me letters?'

At the end of harvest a three-tonner came and took them back to the war. We had been expecting it. 'When the last sheaf is ricked they'll be gone, you mark my words,' said Father, and they were.

Tom and Colin came a week or two later, on loan to us from the War Ag., and it is with these two that memory lingers longest. Not that I saw them all that often; weeks would go by without a sight of either. But our encounters when they did occur were bright extensions of my education, introductions to original senses and hungers that had nothing to do with books.

For Tom could neither read nor write, and Colin hardly every bothered. But they showed me how one could make do with one's self; how little one should ask of life, and how little to expect.

Tom was so pickled with weather and ale that he was nearly invisible in a brown field, like a bent tree-stump. His cap, black with years and grease, plastered one side of his head, and a little slit at the back made it fit better. He never took it off to show his bare skull, except at bait time when he put his teeth in it. Swallowing his dinner in lumps, he chewed tenderly for the sake of exercise, and what was too tough he threw at the cats.

He was by inclination a satyr, and though in no way wise, often repeated the utterances of Silenus, declaring that it would have been better for him never to have been born at all.

Barely fifty, grudgingly single, his thoughts constantly centred around women, and curdled obscenely when the moon was full.

A lagging shyness kept him celibate, though in fact women were his life's delight, his desperation, his yet unsatisfied vice. Women passing in the street, or on a bus, clinging inches away, were torments that never eased; a bone timidity held him back, put them beyond his reach, beyond everything.

These women of course were mostly strangers, figures of generality, and none closer than a three-penny bus ride. So when the landgirls arrived and he had to work with them shoulder to shoulder, he knowing their names and they knowing his, seeing their shapes heaving near his trembling arms, he roared to white heat like a dynamo out of control and as quickly burned out. It seemed to finish his carnal desires completely. His lust still flared now and then, but no longer were they the great sunbursts they once had been. All his overt desires for women collapsed after a month with Jenny and Grace. He would still listen to Colin's adventures with the prostitutes of Bristol and London, but no longer requested the salacious details of the dark delights savoured in the blackout between raids. Anyway, London and Bristol were foreign parts to Tom, for in all his life he had never been further than Gloucester where once, near the park, he struck up a passing friendship with a wild, dark-haired girl called Joan, who was selling flowers in the street. To his amazement she liked him and he took her to tea in King's Square. They got on so well that she agreed to meet him later and go to the pictures. *Wuthering Heights* was showing at the Palace.

At the Cross in the dark and rain he waited for hours; he waited till ten o'clock at night but she never came. His bus long gone, he set off to walk the ten miles back to Stroud, wet to the skin and desperate with his fate. When he got in his mother leathered him, though she was no bigger than a sparrow and he like an ox.

This partial success was the dinner of his mind for years, but the luck that brought it about deserted him forever after, though he prowled Gloucester for a year trying to find her. Leg weary with all the women he had followed, thrashed by years of disappointment, he kept his head down when the landgirls were about and never even looked up to say good morning. Colin tried to get him off with Grace. ''Er'll do fer you,' he told him. ''Er's impressed with you, I can tell.' Tom wanted to believe it of course, wanted to believe that every kindly smile held the seeds of his name, but it was no use – and anyway he was raving with Jenny, as we all were.

In matters of the heart, at least, Colin was Tom's opposite. He had learned a lot about women when working with the fairs. The girls had run him ragged then, and in the end he had given up the fairground and taken to the land. Latterly though he had had no luck at all. 'It's all these damned uniforms. A bloke like I don't get no chance up against a smart soldier.'

He had a sailor cousin who had deserted and was being hidden by his sweetheart in an attic in Stroud. Colin borrowed his uniform and went round the pubs at night. He always knew what to say to the girls to get them up behind the church, but without the uniform it was hard work and expensive. Mostly now he paid for his bed pleasure and biked a hundred miles to London to nibble danger, buy a woman and afterwards sleep it off on a bench by the Embankment. He survived the bombs and the ladies of Notting Hill and for days afterwards came to work on the bus. 'Me legs 're blasted stiff an' I can 'ardly stand upright.' Wincing with pain and rubbing his thighs he would ask us if we had an old penny or two for the bus home, because he was broke again.

He never seemed to eat and worked all day on Gold Flake, rolling the wet stub round his mouth till it scorched his lips. He had the lean, hard look that often goes with endurance, but was flawed by a mind too easily moved by the unexpected and unexplained. Thunder and lightning, always very loud and violent over the banks, sent him racing for cover with his hands over his head. A primordial demon took hold of his innards, turning him hysterical and speechless during a bad storm. He would dash wildly about from hedge to barn, wailing like a child, or stagger half dead about the open field with the rain streaming off his chin, howling to be spared.

The day the old oak tree was struck by lightning he nearly went out of his mind. The old tree, leafless now, had been shade and shelter through three hundred years, the lone survivor of an old copse long since gone. It took a full bolt of lightning and flew into strips, the smoking earth curling back from its roots like petals. The charge passed through the ground and sparked off the water pipes in the cowshed where Colin was hiding. Not touched, not injured in the least, he collapsed with fright by the meal bins and came to in Grace's lap. Dazzled by the streaming sun, and seeing only a lambent shroud of dust and light, he thought he must be dead and in the hands of an angel. Groaning, he looked and saw Frank staring down at him, mangling words: 'He 'usn't urt, you. 'A be a-moovin' 'is bloody yud!'

It might have had tender shoots that silly little incident; anyway Mother thought so. She said she had seen Colin looking at Grace in a certain way; they were a match those two. For nut-brown Grace, a child of the outdoors if ever there was one, was really something of a catch. With a rosy red heart for men, she could match their strength no matter how long or hard the day. There was nothing frivolous about her though, nothing superficial, no icing on the cake. She knew she was not beautiful and never pretended otherwise; men had never pressed her and never would. But she was all quietness and shy smiles that a man might lock up and keep inside himself for years, if he took the trouble.

She wanted to be loved and married, and her mind skipped round it daily. The cinema was for weeping and so were white dresses and Easter. In an odd way Mother got really taken up with it. 'Colin's getting off,' she'd say. 'I wonder where they'll live? They could have our old cottage now the soldiers have gone. Nice and handy!'

But the thunderbolt never turned into cupid's dart in spite of all Mother's wishes, and the whole thing fizzled out after a week or two. For Jenny was there casting shadows over every girl for miles and propelling males of all ages to such breathless heights that their minds were never afterwards quite the same.

It took me years to recover, if I ever did.

She was just twenty when she came to us that spring, and she was very beautiful. It was a cloudy beauty though, as beauty often is, and had such depths that men went dumb. They were overawed, their advances foolish and timorous (poor coin with any woman, especially this one). Their natural infatuation scarcely ever reached hope; for what hope could they possibly have with one so lovely, and able to have any man she wanted. Yet there were brutes, strong and nerveless, who sensed a hunger she thought safely hidden, and went after her not begging but demanding, and found victory easy.

For years she was the measure all women had to match, and even now in some ways I regard her so. Her character was lovely too, and what weaknesses came to be revealed were merely storms of nature, though it was years before I understood that.

She was my first love, my first disillusion, both as awful as the other because they had the same source in vanity. I languished like a sick thing with these deadly coils about me and the pain of the fangs was exquisite. Anne had been a child, but this was a woman and I was old enough now to know the difference. I followed her about the farm like a dog, lame with love and half winded with imagining. I took hay out of her hair, just to touch her, and sipped whole cups of misery watching her dust bits of straw from her bosom. I was teased by her body and she noticed me watching. Her little brown hand flicking away specks of mud and grass had a life all its own, while a sort of expectancy overcame her, a vacant curiosity and amusement kindled by my intense interest.

On the cart when she was only inches and ten years from me, I touched with mind, felt with words; subtle connections elaborately planned days in advance. When others were there, though I was just as intense, I'd be dry and deaf and silent in case they guessed the love I had inside me. We loaded hay together, mucked out sheds, unfroze water tanks, stooked corn, picked up stones, cut thistles, spread dung, chopped mangles and crushed oats. Did anyone know how crazy I was, how dazed and battered, except she? And surely she must have known, for I was with her all the time; and being near her was all the love I knew.

Fear and envy touched my pulse when men looked at her, especially strangers, casual labourers. Of Colin and Tom I had no fear; they were too familiar and no more dangerous to my love than brothers. It was the sly unknown men which bothered me. I made myself ill by eating berries that I knew were poisonous, and when she came and asked Mother how I was, I was more certain than ever that she felt the same as I.

The trouble was, she was already engaged to be married. Once, he came up to see her, a Flight Sergeant with one tour of operations over and half-way through a second. Tall, blonde and pale, smudged by tiredness, and gaunt with the echo of daily perils, he looked far older than his twenty-five years. I took him up to her in the field where she was hoeing beet. She straightened up as we approached, astonished, then nervous. He stepped forward, trying to embrace her, but she pulled away fumbling and blushing. Shyness, I thought, but it may have been something more. I left them holding hands in the middle of the field, she looking at the ground as he spoke urgently of his leave plans.

What did I know then of the secret undercurrents women endured, resisted or gave way to, of the tiger appetites of men, of struggles with implacable flesh demands beyond their scope of reason or will to resist . . .

A gang of foresters working by the mansion clearing scrub and planting spruce used our fields as a short cut to the main road. There were five of them, prison material so people said. Hard-boned and unshaven, with shirts open down to their belts or none on at all, they seemed fit enough for trouble. They came from somewhere far away, displaced foreigners brooding with the violence of mountains, vast steppes and forests like inland seas; and when they came through the village people hurried indoors lest they beg something from them, and watched them pass by from their windows.

I met them nearly every day coming home from school, and one fateful day they were sprawled in the grass among the humps, smoking and arguing in their broken English, the common language of their several tongues.

The thicket roared with birds and grasshoppers, and blue butterflies flicked like sparks among the brambles in the pressing heat. The path through the trees was sweet with bark and leaf on days like this. The searching sun held one's face through a mist of green and spilled brightly about the dim woodland.

Beyond the thicket where the brown path went round the dog roses I met Jenny, and she stopped to tease me in the cherished way that I fancied she reserved for me alone.

She smiled down from the sky. 'Had the cane today?' she asked. 'Chased the girls?'

Struck dumb by a power that she alone possessed, I shrugged and said they were not worth the bother.

'Oh, it might be fun,' she said sweetly.

Staring hard into the tangled bushes, hiding my heart in its fortress of thorns, I let her voice run over me like water and drown my stricken ears.

'I'm going to the flicks tonight,' I heard her say. 'George Formby. I might click.'

Daggers of jealousy, and I recoiled like a snail, trying to smile.

'Yea', 'e's good,' was all I could think to say. Then, as always, she laughed that laugh which said she was only joking and that she was mine and always would be.

'Well, must go. Bye.'

I watched her swing along the track round the hedge out of sight, her image lingering in imagination where in the distance the tall grass made a mist near the bend. And as I stared through the empty field, feeling the sun on my bare head, watching the bees crawl in the flowers, there came through the air, out of nowhere, a soft menace like a lit fuse, and I was suddenly hard with dread, bewitched by bushes and trees and the sun's blasting heat. In moments the innocence of the fields stopped and the hill itself seemed to close right up, like some flowers do before a storm, as if this place and time had been set aside for a crime.

For no reason at all, but in a soul-driven panic, I ran down the field after her, though for evermore I wished I had not. I ran hard and because she lingered going through the thicket I soon had her in sight: but I was too late.

The foresters were still there. They fell silent as she approached from under the trees. Two sat up and words passed between them. She saw this and her stride faltered. Doubt or fear should have made her retrace her steps and take another path; not this hesitation, not this helpless reluctance, as if she had blundered into a web and already knew that it was useless to struggle.

Anyway, she did not stop, quite, and after the first surprise quickened her pace, looking hard at the ground.

One, the biggest, with grizzly hair, rose out of the grass and stood in her way like a bear. There was an easy set to him as if he knew what he was about, and when she made to go round him he stepped wide and grabbed her wrist. Laughing, he swung her a little round and threw out broken words of love. Jenny strained back, at first angry then distressed, looking sharply around at the others, who avoided her eyes and stabbed nervous glances about the woods. I heard her say something, and his

110

gruff laughter thundered startlingly about the dingle. Then a moment later he jerked her in and kissed her.

Something was about to happen, and the madness spread to me. White-faced and fearful though I was, it drew me on, sliding from tree to bush till I was only yards away, well concealed. I was close enough now to see her fear; I saw her plead with him. I saw his growing confidence and determination.

He still held her arm and she was bending away from him at full stretch, when very deliberately he pulled back and slapped her. Crying with shock and pain, straining in his grip, she nursed her face, staring in horror. Once more, growling, he slapped her again, very hard, and she fell against him whimpering; then slowly he drew her head round and kissed her again, roughly.

When he released her at last she was sobbing, and whether by experience or brute scent he knew the signal. When he lifted her up she did not resist him, and he carried her swiftly into a dip while the others, who all along had remained passive, rose up and followed, taught as bow strings and ravenous.

Crawling close, suffocated with a dread that I only half understood, I edged round a mound to see into the little saucer of ground where they were. She was on her back struggling feebly, head rocking from side to side, pleading and discharging the heat and terror of his flesh on hers.

The bear was kissing her, rubbing his rough face over hers, pulling at her clothes, ripping them off and throwing them wildly about.

Pressed hard in the grass her breath quickened on the plate of his filthy words, and when she was naked he got on top of her.

Fear and fascination held me bloodless as once it had when I put my hand by chance near an adder. Dirty school talk had not prepared me for this. Till now I thought that whatever happened between men and women was an organized thing with formal rules, behind walls, with a bed, in great secrecy. I had not thought it an appetite, a hunger, rising up and being satisfied while the sun looked on . . .

His barrel breath swept over the buzz of insects in the weight of the summer's afternoon, and at last, flushed and dripping after a final convulsion, he rolled away from her. She turned a little to one side then, away from their eyes, but when another scrambled forward and touched her shoulder, not gently, she fell back moaning, and let him come.

With what senses I still possessed (it seemed a dream) I wondered why she had not broken free or shouted, the village was close by. I thought

I should start an alarm, fetch someone. But I feared these men; most of all I feared her knowing I was there. Anyway, now it was too late, the horror was there and I was stone and rooted.

With yellow grins, drooling, sunburned, they spent themselves; some quickly, others at length, till they had all done with her. The last one, a red-haired freak with a crooked back, played with her a bit afterwards; then stood up and pissed on her.

This final thing was like the crash of a bullet, and I screwed my hands so tightly that the imprint of my nails left blue marks across the palms. Yet, too, this was nearly like relief, like someone finding himself not mortally hurt after all, and I had a compulsion to laugh out loud, while I shook with a heat I had never before known.

Red Hair did himself up and, very casually, and without looking back, lumbered away down the track, calling unintelligibly to his companions clattering far ahead down the lane.

Five minutes more she lay perfectly still, except for tiny movements of hand or foot, recovering ever so slowly in the flattened grass, her things strewn by her on the stalks. At last though she sat up, flushed as if waking from a deep sleep, and looking round became aware of the near footpath and her shimmering nakedness.

Twice she fell back full length, but at last she sat up again, plucking grass and wiping the mess from her thighs and stomach; then, very reluctantly, without a sound, she began gathering her things and pulling them on.

Hours had built and toppled since it had all begun and the shadows were washing out from under the trees. Tight with feelings which I suppose had been creeping up my nerves for years, I slid backwards into cover, with a rage hammering inside me. I found the path and senselessly began running, faster and faster for all I was worth, to unwind.

Then, hours later, totally spent and weaker than I had ever felt in my life, I came up the bank in the dark and, finding my cheeks wet, thought it must be the wind.

THE HILL

The hill, that part we called ours, was 500 acres of steep fields, mysterious woods and silent hollows, between the village and the common.

Some of the fields had names: the Park, Long Ground, Home Ground and Bird Ground are a few that I remember. Beech, silver birch and oak dressed the slopes and Scotch fir trimmed the banks and dingles.

The hill was generous, not merely abstractly or beautifully but in practical ways, almost perhaps as compensation for excesses of mud, rain and snow. At blackberrying Mother would hand us the basket lined with brown paper. 'Not too many mind or they'll squash.'

We knew where all the best brambles were, well away from paths. Langorously we filled the hamper to just above the paper: all the rest was reproachless gluttony in the fruit-scented heat of the bracken. This enterprise would take all the afternoon with hardly a word spoken, and, quenched, we'd dawdle home through the hot nut wood.

The blackberries, nuts, sloes and pears of the hollows were our exclusive bounty, a privilege, we thought, bestowed with the hill; ours without question or argument, though we were often robbed by the villagers long before we could lay hands on them.

The mushrooms were different though, harder to find, and only Father knew just where. They thrust in the grass out of warm September night and looked like scattered shingles. Cold as the dew and soft as a dog's ear, the matted sod held them fast like snares. Father brought them home in his cap and laid them on the table very carefully while we looked. His eyes were very bright and full of morning. The Sunday ahead with nothing to do, the free mushrooms smelling of the fields, were gifts Father never took for granted; a combination rare and felonious which made him chuckle as if it were undiscovered mischief.

The mushrooms he cooked himself, an odd arrangement which seemed to have been settled at the wedding ceremony, for Mother never interfered. He shared them with Myra and I, and they plopped onto our breakfast plates, oil black and shiny, a strange paternal offering from which Mother was excluded.

Puff balls littered the slopes like soft brown skulls. You could eat these too, when picked young, though the old ones were fit only for football and their dust gave us rashes and coughs.

Our den (our 'On Our Own') was in the bluebells, very lonely and quiet. Myra lit it with primroses, wedging the jars in the fern-lagged walls, singing tuneless made-up songs and fussing invisible children. But separate we stayed in our thriving innocence, this our copy of home and family: she sitting on a flat stone at the entrance to the bower, and I in my low bough, secret in the gilded green of the quiet trees . . .

The hill's character was very old, shaped by man and horse and tearing winds. Clover paths hewn by boots, and deep cart tracks printed by iron wheels, had a strange permanence in some of the rough unused fields. I'd wander in the shimmering quaker grass nearly as tall as me, captured there for hours as if by the will of the ground beneath me. Bee orchids and rock roses we took for granted in places like this, decorated and set aside, too valuable for use.

The Park was like this, and, with its foot in the village, all who came passed through its climbing length. Half of it was a beech wood, deep with leaves and fallen branches. It had packed the hillside through all the tragic centuries, an unapproachable bastion, held up like a shield to protect the fields beyond. All its sounds taunted us: leaves scuttled, tree trunks changed shape every morning and night, and the silence around it might end so abruptly that one's jaw flew open and locked. It was tremendously steep, and each May the crowns of the trees sealed it over, the light was shut out, and nothing grew beneath except stars of anemones and wild garlic, which swamped our cottage in antiseptic.

The footpath made the Park public, though few used it. It was a place of loneliness, of wild brown grass and old stone walls. It seemed to have the power to give itself alone to each separate traveller, for through all the years we hardly ever met anyone there. Yet one knew they came of course, by the trodden grass and dead flowers, and felt where the silence had closed again behind them.

Nor did we ever see other children here. We heard them though, heard their distant cries stretching faintly through its lonely length to our back door; but when we ran down there was never anyone there, though we heard them still, with the same distant clarity, like the closing sounds of a dream.

The looming stump by the path, the black fir trees like hooded men, the unseen wood ants in their boiling mounds, made the Park an eerie place with night coming on. It faced us abruptly coming out of the lane and seemed to be waiting for us. With its back to the sun and the dark filling the dells, here it was that our hill night began. It came thickly across the banks till only Top Barns and the windmill touched the last gusts of the day, and all the hill, massive in the darkness of our homeward path, pressed hard on the cold plan of the stars. Then one felt one's way through the soles of one's boots, by the snagging greenery, by the chill on one's face. The dark indeed assisted on the banks; at least I always felt it did. Light of day showed the steepness and distance still to go; visible challenges to anyone over forty, and of course our parents were.

The move over the fields to the farm made the Long Ground our other way home and we rarely used the Park afterwards. Parts of it were very steep, open, windswept – a terror in winter. The lashing rain and half light made a silent breakfast, as if there were some foreboding. Mother would stare out over the rick yard, commentator on its swirling riot. Laughing at Grace, down on all fours in the mud, she scalded us soundly for doing the same. But for old Frank she had only pity, pinned to the gate like a bat, his black oilskins cracking like pistol shots in the gale, for he seemed destined to die there of exposure unless we rescued him.

The wind jabbed, hooked, pounded; thumped in a dozen directions at once; squeezed out the last of your breath. Round the buildings you hung tightly to the walls and fences, with a sharp eye out for stuff flying at your head. On the open banks it knocked you flat and surged over you like water.

Snow of course was different and luxurious; esteemed for making the ugly beautiful, and the beautiful, more beautiful still. There was no colour then save bare white and black and we used it quickly for the day, or week, or for as long as it lasted.

They began, these blank brief days, with our bedrooms white and soundless; then Mother was there ripping down the blackout. 'It's a white world!' she'd cry. She had about her that rapture reserved for unusual and joyful occasions. She would not have announced the king more reverently than she did these snow-filled mornings. There was no thought now of anything but the outside. Had the drifts been up to the roof it would not have much mattered, and sometimes it seemed as if they were. We sucked porridge and drew on our wellingtons in one smooth ballet movement. Measled with Dunlop patches, the soles lethally smooth, we hoped they'd see us out a couple more winters.

The porridge was scalding. 'Take it from the sides,' said Mother. The rich Jersey milk had been in the cow five minutes ago, and we stirred in spoonfuls of Mother's black-market sugar.

Father had put the chains on the tractor and now came in for his third pot of tea. He stared through the window and his look said murder. 'It'll rain before the day's out; sure to,' he said. His cough said the rest, but we never understood; nor did we like his predictions of rain – the swift corrosion of our virgin hill or the filth it left behind. So we looked at Mother for the expected denial and she rarely let us down. 'More snow I'd say. The sky's full of it.'

This certain forecast was sanctification, Mother's blend of piquancy and mercy which defeated Father and kept the snow on the hill for weeks.

At half past eight we leapt out into the sandpaper wind. All night long its shrieking had carved motionless waves and elegant balconies all along the hedges; put long thick ridges of drift over the banks. Snow flurries blustering like a matador's cape turned our faces thin and yellow. The turbulent air burned like pepper, and in our melting gaze swam frozen colours rising over the empty sun. Rabbits and birds and badgers had been before us, but the first human tracks were ours, for Frank came by a different path and the others came over the common.

Mother always claimed she felt better for the white weather. To some extent this was true, though the boast was half humorous, to amaze and confound, and she scorned the blazing sun for much the same reason. Nevertheless, she found it body-breaking carrying shopping up through the drifts twice a week.

Coming home from school we'd find her separate tracks, a little lower on the slope than ours, where it was smooth and not too deep. Every fifteen yards little craters betrayed her fatigue, where she had set down her bags and rubbed her white fingers; and the little pillows of tumbled snow showed where she had fallen. We looked for these tracks like returning explorers, silently and for the comfort they gave.

Once or twice we children were caught out in hard storms. One occasion I especially remember started with a bitter morning, a flake or two of snow at playtime, at dinner time half a blizzard. It blew hard all the afternoon and from our desks we watched the drift pile against the churchyard wall.

At four o'clock we hurled out of school, a ragged red-eared pack pulling on coats and scarves. We threw back our heads to catch the wet flakes on our tongues; then attended to necessary custom.

Snowballing was a masculine affair; the girls had little part in it, except for a fierce shot to rouse a boy they fancied. They had no aim to speak of and their tactic was to thrust snow down one's neck from behind. They had no hand in those brief bitter battles where it was every man for himself. The air blistered with missiles, our coats sprouted white bumps, and bits of shrapnel melted round our collars.

''Ere Heap; try this un fer size!' Wallop! Outrageous laughter cracked like whips, except from the gangling Heap, who as usual had no coat and was digging ice out of his ear with trembling fingers.

'You sods!'

He charged furiously, revenge twisting his long chalky face. Stooping, he gave a little hop, aimed and fired. Little Tommo let out a yell and dropped in a black shapeless bundle, an act of submission quickly learned in the playground. Respite, threats and treachery were its real purpose however; but Tommo was feeble, we all knew that.

'You wait! I'll get you back fer that! It weren't me you 'opeless bloody dope!'

Squinting, he grovelled in the snow for his wire glasses; Elastoplast and string held them together and he was blind without them. He got to his feet cursing, fumbling with the ear pieces, when another shot hit him hard in the neck, and he half turned, covering his head.

'Lay off you, Heap! Bloody bully!'

Our cruel herd instinct sniffed blood. Here was an outcast, someone weaker than ourselves, and we shamelessly ganged up on our pal, pelting him for all we were worth, till he sank again on his knees, whimpering. Caked and bareheaded, cap and glasses gone, his face emptied, reddened, and tears seeped from his tight eyes.

One by one we dropped the next salvo and blew into our hands.

''E's cryin' you.'

'Well 'e started it.'

'No 'e didn't. 'Twas Heap.'

'Well anyway, 'e chucked one at I fust,' said Heap defensively, and we all knew that justified murder.

Backing away, we avoided each other's eyes and someone said: 'I be goin' 'ome.'

As we shuffled off, Margaret Thule, that soft heart who nursed all the small boys, came running up and helped Tommo to his feet.

'You gurt blasted bullies!' she yelled. The accurate summary, so boldly proclaimed, made us account for ourselves promptly.

'Well 'e started it . . .'

'Oy! 'E damned well got what 'e asked for!'

Myra was waiting by the council houses and we set off over the fields. The stream at the bottom of the slope, where I had courted Anne, was thick and slow, as black as tar. We lingered a bit on the stepping stone, watching the thick snowflakes touch the water. The river gave no sound, no light. The live blue thing of summer, reckless down its coloured banks, keeper of the rare mousetail and bogbean, crept now through its winter to Allen's pond, unseen, unsought till spring time.

Uphill it was from this point, and the clock struck half past four behind us as we arrived at Collett's orchard, the scene of last summer's raids. Through the plum trees, up Whiting's fierce bank, and by the time we got to the Park the day was nearly done.

We set off through the cut leading to the copse in drifts half our height. Suffocating gusts seemed to smother us in feathers, and we walked backwards into the shelter of the wood.

The sudden gloom surprised the eye and the rank air of roots and leaves chilled us to the bone. We looked up with some concern where the strident wind surged like an engine through the tree tops. It roared and purred and clashed like a machine, and sucked and blew and choked. A branch gave way, like the flat of a rule struck hard on a desk, and a sharper sound followed as it peeled and swung in the convulsion. The dark track was bare of snow and along it we ran, blind and breathless, till we reached the gate at the end.

In the Long Ground the storm leaped on us again. It pulled and pushed and knocked us flat, half buried us too, froze us, made us empty-headed. It stopped us on the ridge, which was no surprise. The snow blew down, blew up, pressed like a pillow over nose and eyes and we fell half strangled into a drift while the wind piled more on top of us. Lying stunned in a white walled cave, shrieking for breath, we began crawling towards the hay rick, which was invisible in the blizzard but somewhere over there.

There was something ahead, and when I grabbed at it it moved: we found ourselves among the sheep. We hooked our frozen fingers in their wool and pulled through them bit by bit, while they remained dumb and quiescent, bemused, but without fear of us or the storm. We fell into the wire and crawled through, then wedged ourselves tightly under the rick, piled up a wall of snow against the blast, and settled down behind it.

Now and then a sheep called her thin high note of distress, but the gale, so violent, muted the cry; made it seem very far away. Cold was the enemy, but the sheep would not freeze like us; and when quite soon our overcoats were no longer warm we shivered and pulled the rick round us for comfort. The hay was old and peppery and made my chest tight, but we forced a hole and wedged ourselves in it, knees up under our chins, hands deep in our pockets. I wheezed, Myra sneezed, sometimes a sheep bleated: forty-two living things squeezed round a hay rick on top of a bank with the night shut down and a white gale howling on us. We glimpsed the stars when the clouds broke; it seemed like two nights in one – one on top of the other. So we looked, waiting for the stars to come, thinking of the red hot range and blazing buttered toast not half a mile away.

Frozen we were and hungry, but hay gas worried us mostly. At school we had all heard the story of the tramp who went to sleep in Fowler's rick and died there of the fumes. No one knew he was there, till the hay knife went through him next spring. The thought of that great blade cleaving our mummified carcasses would have kept us awake a month. 'Remember that old tramp!' was Myra's ceaseless alarm, racking like a bell warning of rocks in a lashing sea. 'Our Mam'll be off 'er 'ead with worry,' she said, and on came the frown and lip biting, those two accompaniments of disasters large and small, which through all my formative years I always found rather frightening. Although it was too dark to see her face I knew they were there. 'We'll be goners if we get fallin' asleep,' she said. And she kept hammering my arm in case I nodded off, a rough and ready measure against refrigeration. So I started doing sums in my head, a subject at which I was hopeless. Every time she thumped me I lost my place and had to start over again. I added and subtracted, divided and multiplied: none of it worked out to an answer.

Somewhere along the raging evening our parents finally missed us. Mother rang every police station for twenty miles and Father set out in the dark.

In the meantime the smothering air, wind and cold lulled us very quiet: the first lethal embrace of exposure. Myra stopped punching me and I settled down to sleep. I was warm now and suddenly happy, and the thunderous wind no longer menaced but soothed and enticed. Happier I grew, under the hay, till Myra's elbow crashed into my ribs. 'Look!' she said. 'The moon's coming up.'

Roused on the dizzy ledge of a startling world where numbers grew legs and arms, I hit her back and told her to shut up: the dream fascinated, filled each foundering sense one by one. I saw the numbers uncurl; they were really only straight lines after all, a row of sticks nine together, and the rude '0' at the end looked like a girl.

Another rib-cracker shot me wide awake and I saw the tumbling night as wild as ever. I remember something about the moon, and there was a soft light through the drift. The sky was livid and full of snowflakes, yet the glow filled and gathered into a burning centre above the snow. The sheep knew before us that it was Father's lantern and called huskily till he stopped. When we hulloed the light changed direction and came over. Then we saw the bottom of Father's old blue overcoat, and, above, his outline smudged by night and swirl. He pulled through the flock, held the lantern well up and forced apart the strands of wire while we crawled through. 'Our Gerald's gone funny doin' sums,' said Myra. That was her frugal summary of the whole episode and no further explanation was ever required.

It seemed then to stop blowing, the wind to soften and veer, and the snow fell straight in a ragged veil, hissing on the glass of the lantern. The going was very hard and deep and it took an hour to reach the cowsheds. Half frozen, covered in drift, we staggered in dazzled by the light. The night, blizzard, and cold lay conquered outside and Mother seemed scarcely able to believe we were alive.

'You poor mites! Get it all off! What were you thinking of out in this! You should have stayed at school.'

This astonished us; it seemed a wholly unjustified proposition too, merely to escape death in the snow. 'No fear!' said Myra. 'No fear!' said I, but my chest was a time bomb ready to go off without warning, and mother's look said she could already hear it ticking.

'I shall have him in bed again. Up and down the stairs all blessed day! I shall be worn out with him, I know I shall!'

She talked to the stove, saucepan, mantelpiece as she heated up the milk and Myra started biting her lip, repentant, as if she herself had caused the blizzard. They looked at me as if I were already done for and that there was little time left in which to order the flowers.

Mother poured out mugs of boiling milk with medieval faith: 'It's a food,' she said. 'It'll drive it out.' This merely depressed me further; for all my bronchial attacks began with those remarks, then hot milk, followed by the doctor, quinine medicine and a week in bed.

I said I was sure I'd be all right, but Mother knew differently. 'You ought to have had more sense, the pair of you, coming home in this! You might have got down!' And 'getting down' we knew was certain death whatever the weather, whatever the season. The wind blew you flat and night finished you off: country people were used to it and kept ten pounds in a drawer ready for the funeral.

However, for the present we had survived, and Mother dragged us up to bed with our bottles. Still muttering of hospitals and doctors she left us and went off to empty the tea pot over the coals – a voodoo rite which prevented the house catching fire in the night.

I pulled the blankets about me, buried myself beneath them ready for those dancing numbers. I coughed once or twice to test my chest; it still seemed all in one piece, so I called softly across the landing: 'Wasn't it good! Just like Captain Scott!' But Myra was already snoring, and the patter on the window said it was snowing harder than ever.

The Long Ground was our way in and out for six of the eleven years we were on the hill. Below it was Second Holes and in the thin green runs mapping the rough grass we set out rabbit wires. The snares had to be properly made, set obliquely to the track, wide one end, narrow the other. Trapped rabbits were better than those downed by Father's twelve bore, when the lead shot turned the flesh purple and broke one's teeth at dinner.

Myra and I spent hours looking round the wires, watching the clouds slide above the tilting hill. It was a place to nourish ills, hatch plots, plan subversion. One day we lit a fire behind a high bush. We had stolen matches in our pockets, and potatoes and half the butter ration, and said we were never going back again. From now on we would live the rough life, feed ourselves, wear skins and live in the towering woods. The row indoors had rekindled our Eolithic spirit, and deranged by rules, laws and temper, we determined the blaze should be worthy of our new freedom.

The colossal pile of timber dragged from the wood ignited at a touch, and the abundant heat and flames, shouting liberty, scarcely heard the quieter cry of folly. Sin thrived with the fire's tall fingers, and when some tufts took light we accepted that even this low-level revolution had its price. The flames licked and wriggled and leaped in the dead grass and we stamped them till our legs were black and our socks burned off. Then up it soared for Dog Copse at the top of the bank – and the barns beyond were all wooden. In half an hour it would burn down; in an hour we would be in the cells.

Ten acres burned; trees and bushes and half the copse went up in smoke. Yet there were no questions at home, no accusations or recriminations: we were exonerated without a trial. The wind had changed and on had come a drizzle, the miracle that saved the barns. Yet it was scarcely drizzle: a wet mist rather crawled over the slope, till there was nothing but smouldering tufts and gouts of ash tossing in the freakish gusts.

They saw it at Nailsworth and Minchinhampton, a great moth of smoke clinging to the hill; it seemed the whole farm was blazing. Yet the police and fire brigade, on war alert, never moved a wheel, and we were thankful. The fire touched the flanks of the Long Ground, but the saddle was untouched and from its crest the hill looked unmarked.

The Park and the Long Ground were our highways to the world, though that world was only the village and Stroud. Indeed, the memory of the place is clearest of all in their highs and hollows. Other places claimed us at haymaking, harvest, and potato picking, but they never built stories for us, never dragged so surely at the heart, never whispered goodbye or hullo. The fire on Second Holes blew its ravening breath in every direction save theirs. It burned Dog Copse, sped to Dower Wood, climbed the ash trees and holed the brambles – even scarred a half-dozen pear trees in the hollow; but these it let go by, the two ways out, the two paths home.

The hill also made us monastic, covetous for isolation, jealous of our space. All strangers were regarded with suspicion – I suppose unreasonably so, though the war contributed to that. They came with field glasses and sketch pads, singly or in pairs, and miles from the footpath. None were local. Passing through, bombed out or on leave, they deserved all our attention and got it.

Myra and I followed like half-crazed Sioux. Hiding in the thick cover we shouted at the top of our lungs, a sort of war-cry and warning which rumbled round the bottom as if the hill itself threw in with us. Few could withstand these unseen assaults and quickly decamped.

But some were hardier, or deaf, and actually brought sandwiches to make a day of it. I fired arrows at these (peeled hazel tipped with vengeance out of a proper yew bow), an impotent gesture lost in the wind but a significant aid to determination.

When we felt extraordinary, inflated by a weekend or holiday, we employed more subtle methods to rid our land of these foreigners. We approached our victims from below so that they would see us and grow curious. We came slowly, prodding the ground with sticks, flourishing a sack. It seemed that we came on them by chance, and we feigned surprise, smiling innocently. Then we let them have it.

'We be adder catchin'. Seen any? There be dozens an' dozens up these banks usually. We sometimes get a sackbag full, don't us Myra?' Myra nodded sweetly, scalding my exaggeration. 'Well, a dozen anyway. We send 'em to the zoo,' she added serenely. A thin smile and wide eyes showed our victim in distress, and few ever questioned the sense of it. With reason abandoned our poison took hold and we quickly took our leave. 'Well we gotta be goin' 'ome now. S' long.'

We'd start up the bank lifting every leaf and stone, while our dupe tip-toed to safety. Even if they pretended to take no notice, enough doubt remained to spoil their day, and we never minded a draw.

We encountered these outsiders round tumps and bushes, in woods and fields; no-namers we called them and none were innocent. Those coming out of the Park towards the common we ignored. It was the ones who walked aimlessly about or stood on walls without moving hour upon hour, and seemed to be talking to themselves or to the trees, that bothered us. In the main they all looked alike: middle aged, tweeds and walking sticks, usually alone but sometimes in pairs. Unless directly challenged they never spoke and often not then. If they noticed us at all they'd simply nod or stare right through us. The couples had no rapport, at least none that we could see, circling each other in curious orbits, immutably linked but always separate. When at last they departed it was reluctantly and aimlessly, as if they had nowhere to go, anchored as to a thread and pulled away against their will into the wild woods, for that is where they all disappeared.

When on a Sunday (they loved weekends) one of us ran indoors gasping that a stranger was coming, it was like saying a lion was loose. Mother would go pale and hold her chest, then start rolling pastry to calm herself. She used an old lemonade bottle half filled with water, a trick of the trade she said. She put all her weight into it and the dough spread raggedly over the kitchen table, till it was as thin as tissue paper and broke up; then she'd scrape it again into a ball and start over, blowing the hair out of her eyes muttering: 'Who the devil can it be? Who the devil is it . . .?'

If Father was having a pre-lunch nap in the chair, we'd tip him out, yelling the emergency. When brain and limbs unscrambled he'd slam on his cap and follow us into the yard. Spies and parachutists were ever present in my head: 'Take the gun, Father. 'E's got a damned gurt stick mind!'

Later, having checked all the locks and bolts of distant barns, Father would return to the kitchen to be de-briefed. ''E made off towards the common. Looked like a toff. Snagged 'is jacket proper gettin' into the drive.'

'Serve 'im right,' said Myra, and how well she spoke for us all.

Combined operations over, Mother's breathing returned to normal. She tucked in her hair once more and what was left of panic and pastry got made into an apple tart. But just to be on the safe side she'd send me back along the paddock on sentry duty.

Sitting on the wall, watching the banks, I would measure the time to dinner by the tank train going up the valley. It did not seem at all an odd thing to be doing, for this was private land, and before the war the Old Man had done much the same thing on horseback.

Things were stolen from the barns, so could these people have been the innocent nature lovers they seemed to be? In the dark of winter we several times heard footsteps in the yard, and once or twice voices. Switching out the lights, Mother would leap at the doors and test the bolts; then in the fire's glow we gathered in a knot, like sheep roused by wolves on the prowl. 'Oh, I wish your Father would hurry up! The pubs shut hours ago!' I was barely eight years old and began wondering what would happen to us if he did not come home . . . waylaid, beaten senseless, murdered!

These prowlers (the word itself was sinister) always came when we were alone, and Mother had a theory, probably sound, that someone waited in The Ram for Father to come in, then slipped out to plunder our sheds. Sacks of corn, trusses of hay, and tools went missing on these nights, or sometimes nothing at all, which was worse. Twice we heard someone come up to the window, as if listening, and our eyes locked in dread; yet we were too frightened to look out in case we came face to face with a grinning lunatic. 'It ain't the Ripper is it, Mam?' I asked one night. 'Bless you, no,' she whispered. 'He's fully employed in London.' It was fifty years since he had been, but there was no logic on nights like these.

So the Ripper was discounted and we never found out who it was, though we had our suspicions, or rather Mother did. She spent several days snooping round the village asking questions and writing things down on a pad like a detective. She finally settled on poor old Mr P who had nearly cracked under interrogation, and afterwards, through guilt or fear, always gave her a 'funny look'.

I expect the seasons on the hill were no different than elsewhere, yet they always seemed more abundant. By comparison the village hardly changed at all, and the long year trailed through it, an unobserved margin to our own full land.

Eight hundred feet of elevation, our tilt to sun and wind, drew our separate spring into life like a glass of quickly filling wine. It came on April afternoons so that it was there coming home from school: a spreading, surging life breathing from the hedges. The young hawthorn we called bread and cheese; its taste was wholesome, a compulsive ritual solemnly observed by all we boys, like a folk sacrament. The new wind polished the ivy, the banks were lush and cowslipped, and the buttercups in the meadows looked like drips of the passing sun.

With heads bent to the driving gale rushing up the Long Ground, we made for the cold daffodil grove owned by the wealthy Mrs Gerrar; and home we came at tea time with arms of squeaking sheaves, our guiltless faces glowing in the yellow lustre.

Our commando raids to Mrs Gerrar's started the spring properly. All the months between June and February had so smoothly merged one with another that they left no violent imprint. No season but spring had so great a contrast, and we had all but forgotten that trees could make leaves, till the encircling woods grew fat in a single windy night and half the village disappeared beneath them.

There was a delicate order to it, each scent by turn foremost in our awareness: green earth, nettles, sheep – especially sheep, for the bleating of lambs traced all the warm winds after March.

A row of cherry trees in the old rick yard threw their colour among the barns, and the pecking hens all day long had blossom in their feathers. Cherry trees, pear trees: their scattered petals found even the kitchen table and the covers of the beds. For spring was not constrained to rick yard, hollow and garden, not when Mother had no further use for windows and doors. The first time the sun found the wagon house entrance our cottage lost its winter seclusion. Air rushed through in torrents. It sucked one in and blew one out and on the stairs it hit you both ways at once. This was Mother's overture to the Long Days, and next came the singing, the crooning. Gracie Field's songs were the ones she liked best and she knew them all by heart. She imitated her so well and for so long that she finally unconsciously adopted that style. 'I'm just as good as any of them on the wireless,' she'd say, and meant it. Only Miss Fields and Vera Lynn were better. She sang to the wireless, but more often it was a solo effort, a spontaneous overflow of happiness and sorrow which found her heart and ours. They were popular songs, some going right back to the Boer war, which she first heard sung in the pubs as a child. She warbled through the housework, chanting like a rebel; but occasionally a fire overtook her completely, her pale face flushed, her eyes were gay, and the song took on a performance. An audience of starlings on the cowshed roof or the calves milling by the yard gate was all she needed to set her off. It was a release that sprang out of winter and made long lanes through all our hill summers.

The spring brought other things, too; no less loved though most were abstract and workaday. Father's old blue overcoat went back on the nail; the cat crept outdoors and slept on the steps till October; and coming home from school was to lemon curd instead of stew, rhubarb tart instead of suet pudding.

Summer was the other side of this: the hill changed subtly, secretly, in different lights and shadows. Also came thistledown blown past the windows, we warm and sleeveless, the lambs full grown, the mowing deep and dark enough for love, the corn gone dusty dry, the nights hot and quiet and full of lightning.

Landgirls and men vanished in the fields and one would walk a mile to find them. The tractor purring all day long behind the woods was a sound we never heard at any other time, except on still cold days in December. The long days and swelling heat brought a snuff of horses, the jangle of chains, jackets on walls, wasps in the orchard, empty sheds, swallows in the rafters, a haze over Stroud and Father in the fields till Sunday.

I was about ten when I started work on the farm, evenings, weekends and during school holidays. I received no wages, except pocket money. Only at potato picking, when it was government sanctioned, did I take home a wage, thirty shillings for the week: good pay then, for boys.

However, money counted less than the freedom from words and numbers; though some boys with chronic backache deserted after the first day, renouncing both freedom and wages without regret. Potato picking was easy work but unremitting: one stooped and stayed stooped till dinner time. Wages or no, there was not the easy earnestness of hot days in the grass, haymaking and harvesting, with brown men and women with whom one became enchanted or mistrustful, and in whom one beheld bewitching superficies and lurid temptations.

After school I'd run and find them. Today they were in the field of no name, the one that went from the Cottage Ground to the common, sloping and very steep near the bottom. The rick was half made, the air exhausted and heavy with hot oil from the Lister engine. They were the other side of the rick, curled on the grass with their dinner bags. It was tea time.

The sweet heat rising from the ground and the clatter of machines – these simple things: why should they remain? The fields I mowed then with my Father: were they ever so big? the haystacks ever so large or so high? The men too: were they ever so lustful, so strong? the women so provocative, so pretty, so absolutely wrecking? In the ways of innocence they were, and that first confine within the heart, which changes never, has let them safely endure for all these years.

Frank was half asleep under the stack, his dry fingers knotted over his high belly. The landgirls lay on their backs, conspicuously isolated, too serenely still not to be self-conscious. Colin stared that way, and now turned and carefully rolled a cigarette along his wet lips. Recumbent women stirred the itch relieved on Saturday nights. This was only Tuesday, but for him there would be relief of sorts; for Tom there never would be. His painful gaze harpooned Jenny's enchanting bosom, and he twitched with a torture never to be relieved or pardoned. The girls had laid down in his full view, deliberately, not caring that the fun was theirs. And with a hard expression he turned away and beheld one of his mother's massive sandwiches, dragged from the bottom of his bag. 'Spam!' he said quietly. The meat sailed down the field, and content just with bread and butter he slipped the crusts sideways into his mouth and pummelled them till they were purée. Then very tenderly he ran his tongue round his gums and replaced his teeth.

''Ave you come t' work or mess about?' he asked, as I dropped down at his side. 'I ain't in no mood fer messin' mind,' he said. He waved a massive brown fist under my nose with a good honest look; but I knew his gall was only temporary, part of his digestion, and the girls lying down made him wretched.

I distracted him by asking about Gloucester. I loved him to tell it just to hear the others groan. Gloucester was Tom's passion, an ideal of something never realized. It was failure and success and he cherished both, glorified it, never let us forget it. He rubbed his dark chin as if contemplating his weekend shave, while he tried to remember the beginning.

'Ay, I've banged about a bit in me time, that I 'ave,' he said. Eyes half closed he stared away over the space of Selsley Hill. 'Ah, I've 'ad some fun bwhoy. I bin t' all the picture houses in Gloucester; more'n once mind. Lots of times. An' all round the market. Mostly that was work of course.' He jerked his head proudly. 'I 'ad me dinner in Bon Marche once. I 'ad zoop, a good roast an' a nice sweet for afters. They do you all right in there. Course that's when me suit was new. That's a new suit sort of place that is.'

He emptied his dinner bag and threw all that was left under the rick for the foxes, as he recalled for the hundredth time his great love.

'Lord it rained goin' 'ome. Teemed it did, an' cold. I got in a shed an' took off all me clothes, wrung 'em out 'oping it would lift a bit, but of course it didn't. So I thought I best get on. I was perished. When I come to I couldn't find me damned shoes. All me matches was wet an' I was done. I never found 'em; never did. Walked all the way 'ome in me socks.'

The blitz was coming and he feared it. The few bombs we'd had were nothing: he expected the village to be flattened.

'An' you wait,' he said, 'they'll be after them factories at Brockworth again; you wait'n see if I 'int right! Them burrage balloons wunt stop 'em.' We could see the balloons now, very distant and sun-capped above the mist. He stretched a huge finger towards the common. 'Look what 'appened over yonder. A bit t' the left an' they'd 'ave 'it the bloody inn!' His eyes roamed in the many pints he'd downed there, watching the men play skittles outside. He made a cigarette in his clumsy fingers, licked the end, and the smoke drifted sluggishly in the dead air.

He drank the last of his cold tea and put the bottle away; then teased his haversack, flicking a quick devouring gaze over the girls. He stared at the ground as he went on: 'Ah, Gloucester wants some beatin' you. I saw a black man once with one of them flower pot 'ats on, an' all the little boys was a-runnin' up the strit behind 'n. Course they'd never sin one; come to that neither 'ad I. Then you 'ad all them blokes singin' about the roads; singin' their 'eads off they was. They've all gone now, most of 'em, but there was dozens an' dozens at one time. A lot was Welsh an' 'ad good voices. Singin' for their dinner they was an' somewhere t' doss down. Course the war finished all that.'

He went on and on in his sing-song way and always remembered something different, such had been the impact of his thirty visits. Gloucester was the County Council, Assize Court and the river Severn. He knew every street like a native. His morsel of expectation never rose above it and one day even that would be abandoned.

Withal it was some achievement, those thirty visits, when people in our village died there without having gone farther than Nailsworth in the whole of their lives, and Tom could still find men in the pubs of Stroud to whom Gloucester was little but a name.

As usual he stopped in mid-sentence, as if emotion bound his thoughts; his memory went quiet, he had no more to say. When he got to his feet we followed one by one, unwillingly. Frank and Colin set off up the ladder and the rest of us gathered by the elevator, waiting on our forks for Father to bring in the next load.

The hay, tightly packed from the sweep, burst our muscles as we jabbed and levered down. No breath for talking, no ears for listening, now. It was hard, hot work: but Jenny, unbuttoned and showered with hay, and Grace's tired sweet smile, eased the work for me, and for the men too perhaps, though it was beer they wanted most.

Hours later Father called a halt, not by his watch but by the perch of the sun over the black barns, the cooling air, and by the woods coming up the bank. Around the damp bald field lay little rolls of hay, made by the sweep, and these I gathered for my rabbits and came home as tired as two men.

Haymaking was a quickish business up here; few fields were level enough to cut and even the ones that were had little oases dotted over them, steep little depressions left rough and flowered, like neglected gardens.

On the other hand, harvest went on so long we could never remember doing anything else. It was easier than haymaking but the hours were long and farm workers got extra rations for it. Mother made a special journey to Nailsworth to fetch the harvest rations as they were called, and she had the job of weighing out the portions: extra cheese, butter, sugar and tea for six. She rioted about the amounts as if she herself were responsible for their meagerness. 'Look, it's only a mouthful, hardly worth fetching or bothering with!'

We gathered round the kitchen table for this seasonal ceremony of the ounces, witnesses of lament and anguish. 'I don't know why I have to do this every blessed year; the grocer should do it.' Yet she was pleased to, and when the job was done looked sighing on the little piles, vexed and doubtful. 'Lord, I hope they won't think I've done them down!'

The rations were packed separately and out I went to the shining field to distribute this once-a-year tribute, which with care might last two days.

Father on the binder, Grace on the tractor, the rest of us stooking the dry, thistle-riddled sheaves: that's how it was. The binder twine reddened our fingers, the stubble raked our naked legs, nettles left us in welts, and the icy sap shocked like acid. Harvest bugs settled in the hot places of our arms and legs and drove us to convulsions.

Down and up the tractor passed and the following quiet was very deep and soothing, the rustling corn sounding like many silk dresses, with sharper sounds like splashing water as we made the stooks secure.

Tom and Colin were solo builders; worked alone and carried four sheaves at a go when they were of a mind. Frank and Jenny worked as a pair, silent age and quiet beauty platonically teamed, the best of us all, the most hushed and the most diligent.

Myra and I flaunted our free labour and worked in spasmodic cohesion, took long rests, sought distraction in the woods and stayed there till we heard them calling.

Occasionally we had extra help, men up from the village, but none stayed long. Except one called Fairfax who lodged next to Frank; a tall dark film star of a man who one evening I found kissing Jenny.

Then I knew she was no longer mine, and dearly I loved her still. I had seen her in the sway of men; yet not injured so much as I. When we were alone it seemed that one word might open that feverish secret we shared, that deathless sensation which bound us. But shame made me vacant or garrulous, and sometimes she looked at me curiously, as if she knew or guessed my thoughts.

When the sun was brick red down behind the farm, up came the village women gleaning. They came uninvited, in packs, and kept to the edges of the field, their arms swinging like scythes as they stuffed their pinafores. Backs arched and bulging as if pregnant, they waddled home through the shadowy Park without a word or a glance, and we never dared question their impudence.

Last of all came the men with guns. A pint at The Ram the night before had secured Father's permission. The last small island of standing corn was set upon, besieged, shouted at, struck with sticks, till it disgorged its patient quarry. Old hares zig-zagged through the ranks of stooks, unhurriedly shaming the marksmen. Rabbits did the opposite and went like arrows, or lay still with flat ears till we stepped on them. Foxes there were too, loping away with uneasy backward glances, puzzled, contemptuous and sorrowful.

That is how harvest ended, with the dull thud of shotguns across the hill at dusk, the stars out, and the tractor hot in the shed.

With the corn in and ricked, we waited for the colours in the woods. Now the burning dazzle of the hedgerows came indoors, in the windows, on the stairs: autumn tints of the dying summer. Myra made it a memorable festival. 'Look, Mam! Look what I've got! Look at this! Did you ever see anything like it!' Yellow and red from the dingles dripped from her encircling arms. 'That red's nice. Should like a dress that colour,' said Mother. (Oh, that red dress always wanted and longed for, and never more than now.) But morning brought the reality of nature. 'Oh, Mam, they've all gone over!'

'Nothing lasts,' said Mother, and her abrupt kitchen philosophy signalled a definite change of mood. She stopped singing, sealed all the windows again with newspaper, and began muttering about coal and mud. Once more the white sun drew back behind the woods and stayed there half the day. Came anew the jagged northern blow over the deserted common, and the frost on the five-barred gate turned our thoughts down to nights and Christmas.

First and last was the wind on the hill. Benign or violent it signalled the changing weather and we knew what to expect in the fields next day. We thought of it then as 'our' weather, set in the dry pools of summer and the rough rains of the streams.

Our isolation was in reality modest: one could walk to the village in five minutes, to the main road in ten, be in Stroud in twenty minutes if you were lucky with the bus.

Nevertheless, its comparative solitude was important, and even the village was too close for comfort, too cluttered for our tribal tastes. The hill was like an island with a hostile world beyond, and we returned to it not just thankful at coming home, but relieved and grateful to escape into it again, like ships to a safe deep harbour.

Only the wireless and cinema had influence on our self-imposed tranquillity, made things brave, dramatic, beautiful or absurd, and one way and another their pull was considerable.

The cinema especially let we children fake another life. Our one-andninepenny Saturdays at the Ritz, in the soaring black, with strangers, drew out our biggest, most monstrous desires. Some good, some sinister, they were forced by dark and heat, and of course destined never to survive. In the crush of loners we shared the make-believe, were heroes or villains by choice. The changing lights on the curtains set the spell: the devil dark, the hot plush seats, the timid exit signs the only reality in a trance that would last far beyond the afternoon.

To some extent the pictures and wireless also brought us our war, projected the balance of what we could see and hear for ourselves, for that was never very much. We turned it on or off with a switch, or bought a ticket; take it or leave it.

When the siren wailed down the valley no one ever took cover. We had had our bomb in 1940 and were not expecting another. London could take it, but that was the other end of the world and no one had ever been there except Colin.

Winter nights: they were when the war seemed closest. Mother bought a battery for the wireless, Father had the accumulators charged, and we switched on nearly every night. Our hill lives shrank to the kitchen's width and we played the part we had. Father snored in front of the fire, bootless, the *Stockbreeder* crumpled in his hand. Mother huddled at the cluttered table writing letters to the War Department, composed comic rhymes about her hens and the Bolwells, cut out recipes for whale meat and pictures of the King and Queen, or rubbed her feet and stared restfully into the fire.

Myra was on the sofa by the window, behind her knitting needles, working hard for the soldier, sailor and airman funds.

'Oh, Mam, I've dropped a stitch – made a hole miles back!' The frown would descend more rigid than ever, and she would start her lip-biting and have half-audible conversations with herself as the balaclavas, scarves and snoods piled up around her.

'Have we got any more of this Bouclé wool, Mam? Just a bit to finish off?'

Socks were attempted and as quickly abandoned. A four-needle puzzle which tangled one's fingers was not worth pursuing if it made you deranged and blind, so it was straightforward plain and purl from now on. She promised stuff for all the family and half the old ones in the almshouses, but little of it ever got finished. The wool was used over and over, knitted and unpicked, knitted again, unpicked again, rolled into balls, put aside and finally used for darning.

I of course had my lead soldiers and farmyard, tail-less cows and three-legged pigs propped against the breadboard in the shade of sauce-bottle trees. Match boxes were the pens and the forty-watt bulb was the sun over it all.

What went on outside made all the difference: a storm could add luxury to a winter's night. The howling wind, rain hitting the window like gravel, things crashing about the buildings, tin torn loose and beating like a Zulu drum, buckets leapfrogging the yard – these were all charm and sadness on the ear, like high music. 'God help anyone out in this!' Mother's thought for the lone traveller out in the night was a kind of lifeline prayer. The remark underlined our luck, magnified the wind over the banks; both hazard and sorrow, it bound our kitchen tight and made it everlasting.

These nights could play tricks with us, and through the thriving passage of sounds one would stand out, sensational and perplexing, like the two or three occasions when we heard Godsell barking in the wood.

Then there were days that came to their end thick and cold and as black as pitch. The farm, everything, failed under it, and there was nothing alive or light except our lonely dwelling, and we were the world's last pin of light, one frail and forgotten refuge and nothing elsewhere that was not dead or empty. Where the people of the day had gone was a mystery, for the night – our special hill night – took their shapes and names from our memory and only their imperfect images drifted in our thoughts of the day just gone.

Before I was too tired, 'Monday Night At Eight', 'Bandwagon' and 'I.T.M.A.' joined us in our clock-ticking kitchen. Coming from somewhere far away in the bombing, they beat forever among the ruins of those days, and fill me yet with a hopeless wish to return again to those bleak comforts, richer than any I shall ever know. Alvar Liddel told of raids on Coventry, London, Plymouth; of ships sunk, enemy raiders shot down; of shortages, Cabinet changes, attacks and retreats; of Alamein and Stalingrad. We would watch the wireless like a face: it talked and we listened.

'Are the Jerries comin' Mam?'

'I didn't hear him say so,' said Mother with her timeless sensation-proof humour. War, of which I had heard so much from my beginning, seemed as natural to me as the seasons, a recurring shedding of lives, like leaves in winter. Our history books said as much, and, through our wireless, places flew, ships sailed, soldiers marched. Unexplained and worldwide, it thrilled through all the years of my recollection and in some ways seemed to fit our lives better than the poor peace which followed.

I'd curl up at the table and lay down my head.

'If the Jerries come, Mam, shall us still 'ave t' go to school?' I grunted and mumbled, a sum waltzing over and over my brain. Tired now, beyond mere happiness, my eyes started to close as my general fingers traced paths over the battlefield for my lead army to follow.

We were a silent lot; no one had much to say. Father woke, snored and woke again, smacked his lips and tasted the tea pot; then he'd drop off again in seconds.

'Stop our Dad snoring, Mam. I can't concentrate!'

Myra held up her knitting to show us the wreck, and the sighing and the lip-biting began anew.

'Oh, look! Ohhh! Wake 'im up, Mam, before I go off my 'ead!' But Mother never did; just sometimes she'd gently touch his feet.

'There, there. Shhh!'

Softly, in the breathing, the kettle simmered for our bottles, and sudden gusts, like a choir, drew up the coals.

'Hark at that.'

Repeated over and over, Mother's soft remark was a litany of all known storms, and half the comfort of them.

Sometime in the silent evening I became amorphous; one by one limbs lost sensation and every thought was stilled. The light above my head grew brighter than the sun, and I slid off the chair onto the mat, curling up like a dog.

'Don't go falling asleep now, there's a good boy. It's up the wooden hill for you.'

At last my eyes closed on the day; yet I did not want bed or the cold, moon-struck stairs. Here I wanted to remain, in the shade of the table, by the fire, with a gale marching outside if it would. A calf bellowing at the end of the yard was a faraway reminder of 'out there' that barely reached me, though it was only twenty yards away. Boxer thumping his stall and the sound travelling through the bricks to our fireplace was like someone trapped beneath the house.

At last Myra bundled up her knitting and came round by the grate, rubbing her frozen fingers and staring at the setting coals with a long, despairing passion.

The bottles filled or not, I finally reached my bed. I felt Mother unbutton my shirt and pull off my socks. High and far, Dorniers throbbed through the bitter sky, on their way to the Midlands. She switched out the light and drew back the curtains, a little shape against the window.

'The searchlights are up,' she'd whisper.

That was always the last I heard.

~ MOTHER ~

When thinking of our Mother, remembering how she was, one faces odd extremes. She did nothing by halves. When she laughed she laughed for a week; when she cried she cried for days. Her anger was never a moment's outburst but long coming, slow building. Gladness and grievances were not soon over and done with, but stayed for months – years sometimes. Melancholy and often irrational, she was trapped in a world of unjust laws, agreements and boundaries, and fought all her life to change them. In her time she did battle with the army, police, solicitors and furniture manufacturers. Winning was never in her mind; it was taking part that mattered most, a chance to exercise that obscure ethic which only she ever really understood. We were genuinely surprised that she did not end up in court or in the Tower.

Her abiding wish was for quietness, lonely dells, things apart behind high walls. She had a nun's heart for old stones, forgotten places, sheltered lawns, flowers and the mystery of woods. She found most of these things on the hill and that is why she loved it.

Born at Waterly Bottom in Gloucestershire in 1900, she was the sixth child born of George and Lucetta Butcher.

Her father was a man of many occupations who finally settled as a keeper of inns and hotels. He was as thin as wire and just as flexible, not poor and not really rich. A quiet, fun-loving man, unlike her mother who was a fire-blowing dragon, totally humourless and excessively strict. Mother told us that as children it was very unusual for a day to go by without at least one hiding all round. These bare-knuckle contests were often public, and supplemented by anything she could get hold of: a length of clothes line, skipping rope, switch torn out of a hedge, or even a stick of rhubarb wrenched from someone's garden as they came by. Their own patch of rhubarb, as large as four long tables, was never eaten but used exclusively for flogging. When that was out of season she resorted to a thin cane kept hidden in a huge aspidistra behind the piano. When her temper boiled up (about every half hour), she'd lunge at this plant, slashing at it like an explorer fighting his way through a jungle, cursing husband and children and all the wretched consequences of procreation, till she found it.

For the girls these hidings went on until they left home, or were driven away; but the boys, becoming grown men, used to tie her in her rocking chair till she cooled off.

Mother, thankfully, followed her father's care-free nature, good humour and sense of fun, and from him too she took that arm of solitude which was the strongest part of her nature.

They moved to Blakeney when she was two, and five years later came back over the Severn to the Bell Inn on the Bristol Road. It was here that Mother grew up.

The Bell had a history. Charles Dickens once stayed there; it was also supposed to be haunted. She told us of wild dark nights (wilder and darker because they were so long ago), and of strange noises and shapes encountered on the unlit stairs. In the warm rowdy ale rooms and around the eerie landings that she so loved to recall in after years, she grew into a lively, laughing, grey-eyed girl with black hair down to her bottom, much confused by the ways and winks of the customers. She pulled pints, knew why men drank and what they talked about, rowed daily with her sisters (though never with her brothers), took long walks down empty lanes, slept till noon, filled her days with dreams and her nights with plans beyond her earthly reach, then or ever.

She went to Berkeley school, played up and down the stepped front and trespassed in the castle grounds next door. What could she have been looking for? Was it here in those after-school summertimes that the clear vision of past and future broke down? Did the reality of her plain life tilt then to encompass heroic views and prospects that only she ever perceived, and which she felt all her life to have been denied her? She was always wandering round the castle, looking through the windows and being driven away. 'I strolled right inside once. Opened the blessed door and in I went! I saw the dungeon where Edward the Second was murdered. The gardener bent me over a wall and walloped my backside, but it was worth it.'

In the shadow of the castle, under the elm trees, her brothers settled their differences, clouted each other senseless while she refereed their fights. Laddie *v*. George; George *v*. Chris; Percy *v*. Will. She invariably gave the decision to the loser, out of sympathy, which only led to more determined encounters along the road home.

At fourteen, just after she left school, they moved again, to The Lamb at Dursley, and Mother got her first job in a little newsagent's shop at two and sixpence a week. It seemed curious that she who was to become so muddle-headed over figures in later life should once have been thoroughly grounded in pounds, shillings and pence behind the bar of a pub, and afterwards in a busy shop, rising to senior assistant by the age of eighteen. In those days she must have done her sums conventionally, but in later years she evolved a mind-numbing system of adding the pounds first, then the shillings and lastly the pence, with a mass of calculations that would have stupefied Einstein.

'Lord, those were the days,' she told us. 'Rushed off my feet all day I was, never stopped. Never gave the wrong change either – wouldn't do. And of course we were that polite – all 'sir' this and 'madam' that; not like now.' Sighing and half dazed, she recalled that first job with a voice ringing with the magic of youth and the strength of the unknown.

'Old Mr Crisp cried when I left. Said I was like a daughter.'

'Why did you leave?' we asked.

'Oh, well, it was the war I suppose. Everyone had to go into the factories.'

In the meantime they moved again, for the last time, to Lower Wick, where they lived in a converted mill among five acres of apple trees. It was from here that her brothers went off to the Great War: Will into the army, Percy the navy and Chris into the Royal Flying Corps. Somehow or other they all survived, though in fact they were the only ones for miles around who did. Will became a company sergeant-major and Chris a warrant officer.

By now her sisters and friends were all in the factories making shells for Haig's armies, and Mother thought it was time to do her bit as well. So a couple of months after her eighteenth birthday she said goodbye to her friends at the shop and set off with her sister Eva to walk to Newman and Hender near Nailsworth.

It was a ten-mile walk and it was as keen as could be, but they dawdled through Dursley and Uley. They sang all the way to take their minds off their blisters and keep up their spirits. Along the music-winding miles they hobbled out tune after tune.

'*It's a long way to Tipperary, it's a long way to go . . .*'

Mother loved the soldiers' songs and sang them beautifully. People surrendered at every house they passed and offered glasses of water which they guzzled like bandits expecting their due. They stopped a man on a cart in Uley and he carried them away up the hill. They serenaded him all the way and chose a splendid finale: '*There's a long, long trail a-winding . . .*'

Giggling at their sauce they hopped off the cart, fought off his attempts to kiss them, and finally watched him grind away down the road defeated. Bursting with impudence they took off their bonnets and ran like the wind across the fields.

'Lord knows what made us do it,' she recalled. 'All that blessed way to see about a munitions job.' She sighed in that lovely low way. 'Ah, we were just daft I suppose.'

Half-way down the lane they were suddenly aware of the church bells: a teeming clamour sounded faintly from all directions. Just ahead the convent bell started clanging and two nuns ran out and grabbed them.

'Peace! Peace at last! God be praised, the war's over!'

Taking Mother and Eva round the waist they waltzed them down the lane. Then laughing like schoolgirls, the nuns left them and raced away down the hill, throwing wild kisses and shouting at the top of their lungs, their skirts raised high.

The bells rolled down the valley, Mother and Eva linked arms, danced, laughed, threw their hats in the air, then turned round and went home. Mother rocked with mirth whenever she remembered it. 'We never did go on to that blessed factory, though we were nearly at the gate. Well, there was no point was there, not after that. You should have seen those nuns!'

Of all her family she was closest to Percy, perhaps because they matched in so many ways. It was hard to accept the world as it was and neither of them ever did. They had blinding bursts of energy, then for days never got out of bed. Their good moods would be high for weeks, before the old destructive slide which had no sense or reason to it. Their stubbornness was admirable in many situations, but a fatal hindrance when it came to their own well-being. No one ever heard them say they were unwell, though they were, more often than the others. Because they were weaker physically it became a point of honour to seem stronger. This play-acting taxed their strength and over the years seriously undermined their health.

Percy served on the *Warspite* at Jutland, and after the war went with the British Volunteers to Russia, fighting with the Whites against the Bolsheviks. He came home a changed man. His nerves gone, the jobs he took were poor substitutes for the war. He was a handsome man by all accounts, with straight dark brows, a strong gaze, and lips damaged romantically by fist fights. He had the broad, steady power of all the

Butcher boys and would take on any man alive, drunk or sober. Yet he fell to pieces in the end and his slow decline worried our Mother into a harrowing state of nerves. When he died of neglect, still only in his forties, much of her bloom and vitality went with him.

From Russia he brought back a bear-skin coat and the hair on it was a foot thick. It was the only thing he left her, that and his Jutland medal. She got it out and aired it every spring; spread it out above the hollow and sat there among the pear trees, dreaming. In winter she'd lay it on their bed, pull it round her, watching the moon slide over it through the icy window.

'I'd have died last night without that coat,' she'd say, and she was talking to him when she said it.

At each anniversary of his death she would go to Dursley, put pansies on his grave and a poem in the *Gazette*. These little verses, smudged with tears, kept her up half the night, and Myra would rewrite them for her next day in her neat round hand. Afterwards Mother read them out to us with a mixture of pride and embarrassment. 'I couldn't get it right. My head was like feathers. He'd know what I meant.' She cut them out and stuffed them behind the clock on the mantelpiece, where with time they curled limp and yellow, like chestnut leaves.

Depression gripped her at these times and nothing we said or did made her better: it took hours in the woods to do that. She complained of the heat, the flies, the isolation (which she loved), and plagued herself with imagined wrongs.

Tired though she sometimes was, she was always last in bed. 'I shall be up in a minute,' but we knew that meant one o'clock in the morning. Though in later years she hardly slept at all, in these hill days it was hard to wake her up. Father would shout a dozen times up the stairs before she finally padded down to the back kitchen and splashed her neck under the big brass tap. It was half-way through breakfast before she really woke up.

When we were gone she would sit at the table among the wreckage of our cups and plates, sipping creamy sweet tea, which might be all she would have all day. Half her mind cared for, the other half clouded and muddled; it lay not long without worry or grievance.

When the war came she said we were all going to starve; she remembered 'last time' when they had once eaten potato peelings. And there did indeed begin those strange wobbles of fortune when we ate well and at other times went very hungry. For a while we lived like Bedouins, covetous for the day's bounty, eating for the time when there would be nothing, or next to nothing, except our Sunday dinner of beef and kale tops.

At last she decided something had to be done. It was a sudden decision as always, without a trace of thought or plan, and she flung herself into rearing hens, cockerels, ducks, geese and turkeys. On the face of it we could have fed the entire village, but it never turned out that way. We had eggs in plenty and dozens were given away, but we never tasted the meat. For having struggled to rear her precious birds she refused absolutely to have any of them killed. 'I like seeing them around,' was her final word on the matter. So they became unexpected pets, gobbling buckets of oats every day, staggering round the rick yard till they finally dropped dead of fatty hearts or old age.

They wandered all over the farm, laid where they pleased, in ricks, nettles, behind piled wood and in old machinery. Some nests we knew of, but others only became apparent when a clucking hen brought out a string of chicks to swell the number.

Mother began making frequent mysterious trips to Nailsworth, where by some unexplained alchemy a dozen eggs changed to sugar, butter and cheese. We never did examine this magic too closely; it was Mother's secret and we let it go at that. We'd watch her pack the eggs in newspaper as she tried to keep her back to us.

'Where you goin, Mam?'

'Ah, never you mind.'

'When you comin' 'ome then?'

'When you see me.'

Whatever it was she was doing we knew was illicit, under the counter and furtive, and carried a conviction if found out. She'd be whiter than usual, and strained, like an agent going behind enemy lines. When she came in, the stuff she brought with her disappeared at once to the back of the cupboard and a Shredded Wheat box dragged in front to conceal it; then she'd sit on the arm of a chair drinking a cup of tea and say nothing for an hour.

More or less by accident and in-breeding the number grew to sixty, would indeed have grown larger had they not been regularly culled by foxes. Shutting them up at night was a frustrating and depressing exercise. We were sent out in large sweeps below the cowsheds to poke among the billowing nettles, and came home rubbing our welts with dock leaves. 'There ain't none missin', Mam.' We were guessing of course, but wanted our tea.

'Just have another look round, you might have missed one. Go and have a look by the big house.'

We slashed at brambles, flung stones at branches, yelled ourselves speechless. Myra bit her lip and led off to the big house, like a mountaineer making one last desperate bid for the summit. A half hour round the garden and cellars ('I ain't goin' in there, tis too dark') and we were home again, in the doorway, waiting to be dismissed.

'Just have one more look round the rick yard and I'll make you a dish of custard.'

So off we went again in the wetting dusk, scrambling under steps, in rat-infested sheds, under oily engines, in the granary and stables, and came home with the same story.

The trouble was she never really knew how many she had and they all roosted where they pleased: the ducks in top cowsheds, the turkeys in the old dog's kennel, the geese in the tractor shed and the cockerels anywhere that took their fancy. It was a fox's dream, for nothing was secure and the wonder is that so many survived his nightly prowls. Only the laying hens were really safe, in the barn, and we wedged so much stuff against the doors that it took her ten minutes every morning to shift it.

A great many people came up at Christmas of course. They'd admire the stiff-legged geese, the circular turkeys and pugnacious cockerels, and come to the door flashing wads of money. Mother sent them all packing. Her stock was famous around the village, but no one understood her disdain for profit or her extraordinary maternal instinct for her animals. 'I could have sold the lot ten times over,' said Father, coming in late from The Ram.

'They're not having *my* birds,' snorted Mother, and that would be the end of it.

At first she would not even allow one to be killed for our own Christmas dinner, though we got round that fairly easily. One Christmas Eve Father came in sharpening a knife. 'Let's go and 'ave a look at them birds,' he said. At dusk they were as tame as kittens and we waylaid them in the tractor shed. We never considered anything but a cockerel; retribution, if we were ever found out, would be commensurate with the size of the bird, so a cockerel it always was, and only then when Mother was at Nailsworth.

Father grabbed among them and held up a Rhode Island Red – a striking thing with feathers like painted glass. We felt its chest and legs while it blinked stupidly at our deadly interest. 'This'll do us,' said Father, and tying its legs we dispatched it there and then behind the cowsheds. A bucket of water washed away all traces of the crime, and afterwards I was sent to spill feathers down by the bushes, as if a fox had been at work.

Father hid the body under a pile of straw and brought it in later that evening, coming in from the village.

He held up the cockerel under the light. 'Look at this. I was lucky right enough. Nearly the last old George Fowler 'ad.'

He held it by the yellow legs and a spot of blood dropped onto the table cloth. His eyes under his cap glittered like a criminal's, and he never looked at Mother at all. I dug my murderer's hands deep in my pockets and never looked away from the fire.

'Not bad eh? About eight pounds I reckon,' said Father.

Carefully, expertly, Mother felt the bird all over, examined its feathers and comb. 'Mmm. Not bad,' she said at last. 'Not a patch on mine though!'

These hill years fell softly round Mother, though she did not always want to be content. The quarrels between her and Father, which had their roots in things long ago, momentary and passing though they were, left us wary and troubled. The sudden bitter tears, as if the rows had been made for that purpose, and Father's dark silences as if he were wrestling with some moonlit plan to leave us, were the worst of it. The thaw of course, after a week or two, was always sudden and splendid, like unexpected relief from pain.

Her depressions were crafted for days at a time and nothing she said or did then could ever be explained. She made important decisions effortlessly, yet agonised for weeks over nothing at all. Frivolity reduced the sting of serious matters, whereas trivial things were built like towers. Loud and long was her laughter then, which we joined without knowing why; and her benign tears were abrupt signals of the war, bad news, sentimental songs, or merely for inward things half forgotten.

When she was worn out with us she would go off into Stroud alone, have a cup of tea in a café for that simple pleasure, look at clothes she would never buy, and go to auctions.

Sales in fact were one of her few pleasures, and when old Miss Crimpton died she took me with her to the sale. 'They say she's got some nice things. You never know, we might be lucky.' So upstairs she hopped that day to get her secret egg money, and off we went.

The house at the top of the lane was a crush. 'I didn't think there would be so many here,' she said as we elbowed our way into the hall. 'I wish we'd come earlier; stay close to me.'

The bidding had started, moving from room to room, and we were fighting through a throng of bodies. We ran our fingers round the backs of mahogany chairs and looked under the seats for woodworm. We saw ourselves in the glassy depths of polished tables, lifted rugs and mats, hovered over the silver, blew on the brass. Mother tested the weight of a salt-glazed tureen.

'Staffordshire. That'll fetch a bit.'

She nearly dropped it too, when a fat man came sweating through with a bronze statuette. 'Mind yerself missus,' he wheezed. 'Mind yer backs.'

'Know him,' whispered Mother. 'Seen him at the auctions. He'll never get that home.' She was right as a matter of fact.

We lurched into his space as if propelled by springs and found ourselves by the paintings, watercolours on the left, oils on the right. Mother was half an expert on pictures and there was plenty to look at: a girl in blue sitting on a rock, a waterfall at sunset, wild Spanish horses, jars of flowers losing their petals, an old lady in a window.

'Don't know the artists. They might be worth a bit one day though,' she said. She mumbled something about an old master and nudged me in the ribs. 'See! That might be a Rembrandt. He did one just like that. They didn't always sign their real names you know. Might be one of his.'

I doubt if she really believed it, though she looked at it with a rapturous expression, like a lover she would never see again.

We were shunted past the paintings and joined the queue for the stairs. It was half an hour before we reached the bedrooms.

'Oh, just look at that wardrobe. Walnut. Matching chest of drawers, too. All this stuff she had.'

A yard at a time we edged round the rooms through a sea of villagers. At last someone opened a window; it was stifling. But it was too late for one old lady who turned funny, shouting she could hear the bath overflowing, and when she fainted they laid her out on a bed, very stiff, straight and pale, like a corpse.

If she was dying we ignored her, for the bidding was hotting up. Mother did bid once, for a nice copper warming pan, and shot the price up no end. At the last minute however she dropped out and it was bought by a man from Minchinhampton. 'I knew I'd never get it,' said Mother. 'I wanted to see his face with a bit of a woman bidding against him.'

She lifted the lid of a teapoy and sniffed loudly. 'It's had woodworm at sometime,' she said, and we passed on to a little bedside table, admiring the brass handles. Suddenly she stiffened, straightened up as if stung, and there were little red spots on her cheeks. 'Its her po,' she whispered. 'No one's thought to empty it!'

This was like ice down our backs and our enthusiasm was blasted beyond repair. Somewhere unseen old Miss Crimpton's spirit hovered angrily above, and we felt her shame and indignation. I knew what the tug on my sleeve meant, and we pushed and kicked our way downstairs. 'I've got my head coming on,' said Mother as we barged out into the lane. The quiet and fresh air was like a hymn and Mother sat down on a chair with SOLD written on it. Bits of furniture lay all over the lawn with the owners' names chalked on them.

'There's that nice table I had my eye on,' she said, and ran her hand over it in farewell.

Men trekked away under their loads, smiling and nodding, and we knew them all by sight if not by name. Nearby, the fat man with the statuette lay under the box hedge in the shade, fanned by a little girl with a catalogue. Mother asked how he was; she was sure he had ruptured himself. But the man never spoke and the little girl just giggled. He passed out eventually and they carried him over the fields in a chair to the district nurse. On the way he fell out ten times, once into a brook, but made a complete recovery, though somewhere along the way the statue was lost forever.

This emergency was very low key however compared to Miss Crimpton's po, and Mother brought up the matter again going back up the fields.

'All that going on and no one thought to tidy up! Such a refined old lady she was too. Used to be a governess. What on earth would she have thought!'

So because of Miss Crimpton's po and a dearth of egg money, we bought nothing that day; but there were other days, other sales, and in time Mother filled a tea chest which she covered with a piece of red damask and kept by her bed. On summer afternoons she would unwrap these treasures, polish and love them and lay them out on the bed for us to admire: cracked willow pattern plates; delicate cups lovingly fondled, as thin as paper, and held up to the summer window for us to see how lovely they were; painted bread and butter plates; large dishes with flags or fruit round the edges; a tiny silver tray ('That came out of a big house'); a porcelain chimney sweep with one arm missing ('It's here somewhere – I shall have to stick it on one day'); a brown and white dog; silver forks and spoons; bits of brass and silk and polished wood. She called these things her 'antiques', her nest egg, her box of yesterdays, and they reminded her of that other age she had known and forsaken. She would hold up a little silver cruet, a statement and symbol. 'We had one just like this down home.' But 'down home' was long ago; the hotels, servants, pubs, horses and trap, wooded acres and money, belonged to her maiden life, not so splendid as she remembered perhaps, but comfortable and carefree, and now she was just a labourer's wife making do.

Somewhere over the years she at first ceased adding to this collection and then one item at a time sold or gave away what she had so painstakingly acquired. When we left I found the empty box with just a few bits of tissue paper littering the bottom; but she would never say where all these things had gone.

For such a delicate and muddle-headed creature, our Mother had surprising interests. Antiques, real or fancied, were natural and expected, tokens of a grander life that disappeared forever when she married my Father. Her tiny hands belonged with fine things in them, and beautiful china received its due from Mother. Her preoccupation with crime and criminals was therefore all the more startling.

Murder fascinated her as much as a lovely picture or exquisite ornament. Not the tame, story-book murderers found in novels, but real, historically sound killers who for a week or two shone briefly in the world's light before the final walk with the hangman.

She talked of these famous criminals as if she had known them all personally: Charlie Peace, Palmer, Rouse, Smith; these were some of her favourites, and she had her own ideas about them which invariably clashed with accepted opinion. She thought Seddon grievously wronged, an innocent man hanged on nothing more than suspicion, hanged because he liked money and was more than a match for the Attorney-General. 'Where was the evidence, tell me that?' We shuffled our feet anticipating the coming argument as she began to warm up.

'They charged his wife too you know; then acquitted her. Hanged him and let her go free – what sort of justice is that?'

We shook our heads: there was no sense in it.

'It was a poisoning case – you remember – that old lodger woman they had. They said he doped her with arsenic soaked from fly papers, and he never did anything of the sort, poor man.'

She looked round her court and summed up for Seddon. 'A very funny business if you ask me, to hang him and let her go free like that. All he did was stick up for himself.'

The clock said it was late, the fire made little sounds, Father was in bed and the kitchen was listening.

'Tell us about the 'angman, Mam!'

'Oh, there have been lots, going right back.' Ancient tragedies, terrors, remorse, lives sliding inexorably towards the drop, and the last hand to touch them the hangman's! They might have been neighbours the way she spoke of them: Calcraft, Marwood, Berry, Pierpoint. She'd shake her head sadly over their grizzly business; but I was frankly thrilled.

'It's terrible of course, and I've often wondered what they feel at the end – the murderers I mean . . .'

Between hangings she fell silent as if searching for answers in the range's white fire, coming back to us with a little cough.

'I expect they're glad to get it over though; and of course they deserve it, most of them.'

All the same, she said, there were no last goodbyes, nothing to comfort the poor wretches; and their wives and children left at home, desolate, waiting for the dread hour. For mother's murderers never killed their wives: except Smith whom she excused because he had devilish eyes and women are such fools.

She placed these monstrous people around us; we saw them sitting at our fire, haggard and forlorn.

'Why do 'em murder people, Mam?'

'Oh, passion I suppose, and greed. Lots of reasons.'

It was the Thompson and Byewaters case we heard about most though, and I felt sure we all must be related the way she used to talk about them.

'Byewaters was only a lad – nineteen I think – and she nearly thirty. He got smitten I suppose, and she led him on the way silly women do; wrote all those love letters; and he killed her husband. It was tragic. It got out of hand. She wrote him things – silly things, made them up – and Byewaters believed her, poor lad. It was all untrue, about her husband beating her and that. It was a sort of game with her, to keep his interest. But what an outcome!'

Then she'd sigh as if it were her last breath. 'They hanged them both.'

After a long pause she would blow her nose and ask whether we wanted cocoa or Ovaltine.

I could never get enough of these matter-of-fact calamities. It had happened years ago anyway, and slipped easily into the mind with the Princes in the Tower and the Maid of Orleans. Shelf history but dramatic the way Mother acted it out. We sighed when she sighed, made faces when she made faces, wept when she wept.

I was especially drawn to these murderous pastimes where quite ordinary people had gone crazy, and had mind-flashes of keen knives plunging into yielding flesh, smoking revolvers, powerful hands crushing soft white throats, bottles of deadly green poison slurping into innocent sick-room broth.

I saw dead bodies too, twisted in alleyways, in dustbins, naked on commons, trussed up in trunks, or mouldering in dreary woods. For years I suspected anyone with a thin mouth, heavy moustache, eyebrows that met, or piercing eyes. I was particularly wary of hand carts (these were especially sinister) and of men who raked their gardens after dark.

She not only entertained us with murder: ghosts and hauntings enlivened our winter evenings too, before we went up the dark stairs with our flickering candles. Borley Rectory was a habitual fright. Far away in Suffolk it was, but that only added to its mystery. She said she wanted to poke around there after dark, and threatened to take us just for fun.

One night we sat up very late, she and I, listening to a wireless broadcast. Microphones had been placed in the haunted rectory, and we hoped at last to hear the authentic wailing and manic laughter, the slow fatal tread and heavy bumps; but all we heard was static and wind in the rafters.

'They've messed it up,' said Mother. 'Too much noise and fuss I expect.' Harry Price was in charge of the broadcast and she wrote to him then and there, expressing disappointment and wishing him luck in future attempts. Naturally it did nothing to lessen her enthusiasm for the uncanny and inexplicable. She was never much worried by the dark, with or without ghosts.

One afternoon we came home from school and found Mother scribbling a long letter to Madam Tussauds. She had heard that they were offering a hundred pounds to anyone with enough nerve to spend the night in the Chamber of Horrors, and was about to take up the challenge. Father hinted at a meal (his stomach was touching his backbone) and muttered for hours about empty-headed women; while we coolly leaned on her arm wondering what she would do with all that money. We had no doubt she would go through with it given half a chance.

'I must write it properly or they won't take me seriously,' she said. 'I don't see why blessed men should have all the fun.' However, either she had been misinformed or Tussauds withdrew the offer, for nothing happened. We waited weeks for her to go off to London to win us a fortune, but she never did.

There are loving memory pictures of Mother, parts and habits more startlingly remembered than the whole. She was tiny, no stronger than a flower, but her thin arms had a winter and summer strength and somehow she kept going in spite of wavering health. When finally she started to falter her will alone carried her on, until that too failed, then a little she broke away from us and we from her. It was as if she had reached the end of her purpose; given to us to wear out, take for granted and sometimes love. There was something queerly primitive in her quiet acceptance of this, and she never complained or condemned us.

More than anything the hill kept her going, softened and steadied those tremors which raged at her nerves, making her careless and wild.

In the brimming evenings she'd want to be alone, and in good weather climbed the slope behind the farm. She would sit on a gate in the clover field, singing quietly to the hushed valley. There, late, I would find her, looking down the woods, sad with tangled thoughts that cried out for content in the slumbering fields.

Or she'd just perch on the garden wall above the hollow, her hands screwed in her pinny, dazed with bonfire smoke and blossom, listening to the blackbirds filling the dusk.

Other nights when the ground was like iron and the moon had washed the hill colourless, she would suddenly say she was going for a walk and did anyone want to come. Only I ever took up the offer, and wrapped up like sherpas we jumped out under the burning stars, climbing briskly to the top of the bank.

The bare, blacked-out valley would already be filled over with mist, and down in the smoking garlic dingles, above the village, the badgers prowled their thickets and made for the lane.

Up here though we saw only the fox, the same one, and old by his trot. We knew his run, where he paused on a low wall, and if we did not see him his stain was always there in the empty field.

We never spoke on these walks, never said a word. We just listened to night and made it poetry. We were born for these nights, she and I. Day was far flung, wide with noise and people, but here we passed alone and unseen, known only to the dazzling stars, the trail of the woods, and the bare arms of the wind.

Mother might have walked on till dawn. We surmounted fences and gates yet she seemed merely to glide right through them, her eyes high and bright with cold; and when at last we turned for home it was like a flight of birds, instantaneous and without collision.

The moon was in our faces now, hanging over Roaborough, and we were here, high and open where the air was cold and clean and sweet like water. Bombers droned tonight and searchlights waved from Minchinhampton. Grass crunching under foot was the only other wide-awake sound in our air world.

We came down the drive, the dead farm patched by the moon, the bank rising blackly behind us.

We bound in like puppies, into the empty kitchen, home of the softly singing kettle. The cat climbed onto my lap, and by the last of the fire we sipped our tea in the flickering.

At the end, upstairs, Mother leaned out of the window for a last good breath of air, watching the quiet fields.

'It's lovely out, as bright as day . . .'

These moments were best enjoyed before what Mother called her Expeditions: the shopping every Tuesday and Friday at Nailsworth. These tranquil walks over the hill at night were the tonic that kept her going, the anodyne to stiff banks and three bags of shopping.

She prepared herself slowly for this ordeal, and with a certain form, like a duellist. She put on her hat first, then got out the ration books and tucked them securely in her bag. A long look down the valley for the weather would make the decision: sandals, shoes or Wellingtons. Mostly it was Wellingtons, and she screwed up wads of paper to make them fit. The cold never counted with Mother, so a light raincoat finished the preparations. The laborious counting and re-counting of money, bus fare in her pocket, a last look at the range, and she was off.

From the main road it was a twopenny bus ride and the buses ran every ten minutes. Green National, Red and White, Stratford Blue: draughty double-deckers filling the narrow roads, making slipstreams that ravaged hedges and trees and sent cyclists spinning into walls.

It was a bitter ride in winter, colds and influenza guaranteed with the ticket. A fan lightly warmed the first four passengers; the rest froze with the speed of an arctic night. We jammed our tickets under the metal edge of the seat in front and if the inspector got on he had to sort them out himself.

On the platform, in charge, were conductresses – war novelties painted up like film stars. The belts of their ticket machines and money bags crossed in front and their breasts stuck out like bumpers. Mittens and heavy overcoats beat off frostbite, but sometimes they were so cold and unwell that they never bothered to collect the fares at all.

The buses were full in those days and if one went by we just walked on to the next stop. At times we walked all the way. Mother's routine was to leave home at eleven and be back indoors by two.

'I like to see myself coming back before I leave,' she would say.

But it was not a rigid schedule, and she often collected me from school and off we would go to get the weekly rations. This was in winter when the mud-slick banks made shopping penal servitude. We got the bus at the piano works instead of the station, an extra half-penny on the fare.

Our system was a crisp drill, a careful haste; yet for all that it often took a long time, though of course one hour in the town seemed like six at home.

Fawkes Dairy, on the corner, was the first call. I was never quite sure why; I suppose it was like testing the water. We'd look at the bread and cakes and come away with nothing except the satisfaction that we had clocked on. It was our entrance, our beginning, and sometimes we did buy cream slices, though we had to vow on oath that we were war workers to get them.

Then we went next door to Burton's grocery.

There are not many shops like this now, no relishes of wax polish, bacon, tea and cheese; no places of varnished wood to give a brown underlying stability; no deep shelves, wide counters, clutters of cardboard and straw. Burton's was more than a grocer's where we went for the rations. It was a meeting place where whistling assistants winked at one like cousins and cheerfully piled food into one's bags; providers who seemed like agents of mercy when there was nothing in the house except potatoes.

The war was on, the shelves were half empty, yet we still came out with two large bags overflowing. The girls wore green wrap-round overalls, greasy on the hips, and the men wore long white aprons down to their polished toe-caps. They added up on sugar packets, and marking the ration books was a half-humorous mutilation with scissors and pencil. Eight shillings easily filled a bag.

Edith usually served us, Edith who loved love, Edith of eighteen laughing years, round and blonde and cheerfully engaged to a Rumanian soldier. She would give us the headlines of her week so wrapped in charm that the prosaic sounded sensational; then the hot chunks of news sizzling from her thrusting bosom ceased abruptly when she reached under the counter or slid round the other side for the fatty rashers.

'Well, see, we went to this dance. You'd 'ave laughed, I reckon! I 'ad on this . . .' Away she went and fetched the ladder, scrabbling in the top shelves and coming back with a bump.

'Well, Larry – that's what I calls 'im – can't say 'is proper name for a toffee; well, like I say, I looked like . . .' She expanded with giggles. 'Oh, I daren't tell you!' She blushed and fluttered. 'Well, 'e said 'e could *eat* me!'

She whispered the secret across the counter, then rushed off to see if the dried fruit was in. She came back panting and rubbing her leg where she had knocked it against a box. She rubbed the place vigourously with a wet finger. 'Damn! That's the second time today . . . Sorry, only raisins, Mrs Roberts. Anyway, like I say, it was a do I can tell you. They 'ad a real band an' everything. Played Glen Miller . . .'

She shot off once more to find the black lead. 'We 'aven't got none, sorry. Try Marshall's. Anyway, like I said we missed the bus 'ome, but I didn't care.'

Larry wanted to take her back to Rumania after the war, but she was not very happy about that. 'Me mam's only got me an' it would kill 'er. I don't think I could do it, I really don't. Anyway that won't be for ages. Larry says it's goin' to last years.'

When the van driver was called up they taught her to drive, and her driving was the talk of Nailsworth. She cracked with laughter trying to remember all the things she had hit.

'You should have seen me yesterday – or was it the day before? Anyway, I bashed a lorry full of soldiers. Ooops! I went right up on the pavement an' round in the road. Didn't they 'oot!'

Driving with the steering wheel under her chin, her forehead on the windscreen, she was determined not to miss anything and seldom did. After barely a week the Ford van looked a pile of scrap, but she shrugged it all off as experience.

'They keep getting in front of me,' she said

The bags were loaded and she helped us to the door; opened it just wide enough for us to slide through, because of the blackout.

'S'long, Mrs Roberts, see you next week. Mind the step.'

We staggered along the pavement in the dark, knocking people into the road, till a slit of light showed the butcher, and we skated in on the sawdust.

Different odours here: wet meat, scrubbed wood, spices, sharp steel, boiling offal. Mr Hallet, with his bleeding apron and bandaged fingers, leaned on the counter. Without a word he took up an old worn knife and sharpened it smartly. Ration books scribbled on, the pencil back behind his ear, he looked about for a joint. 'It'll have to be beef again,' he said. 'I haven't set eyes on a pig for weeks. Nor veal.'

He called to his son in the back room. '*You done that order yet, Geoff?*' While talking to Mother he yelled at his ten-year-old son, out of sight down the steps.

'What's it like up your way? A bit on the rough side I expect? *You swept them steps yet?*'

Mother cautiously asked about corned beef. 'Not this week. I'm waiting for it to come in. *You brought that bike in off the pavement?*'

He fought furiously with meat and paper and dropped it in our bag, shaking his head. 'Can't get any help, that's the trouble; only lads. That'll be four and two.'

Next door was Marshall's the ironmonger's and we went there for the candles. We had little need of them but Mother was sure they would become scarce and valuable, and started a hoard. She tucked them away in the bottom of the bag to conceal the useless expense, half ashamed of the petty impulse to buy what we would never use.

Along the street to Hillier's for the pork pies, and then we started back for the bus.

'Won't be long now,' said Mother.

'Won't be long now,' I repeated. It was a joint conviction that the day was already too long and the shopping far too heavy.

Just one more stop, the best, at the newsagent's. The bell clanged over the door as we entered, and we waited for old Miss Allen to shuffle through from the back room where she lived. The little shop was a bright bloom of glossy paper and annuals, a dim, paraffin-warmed grotto which I wanted to stay in to the end of my days. Hard round were mint books, cards of pencils, penknives and paint brushes, which begged you to buy them.

She came through in her slippers, tugging a shawl about her bones, squinting over her spectacles to see who we were. She mumbled something and began a slow careful search for our order among the piles of magazines: *Farmer and Stockbreeder*, *Nursing Mirror*, *War Illustrated*, *Knockout*, and *Chips*. Licking her bony blue fingers she counted each item twice, and tied them in a bundle with green string that had her name on.

'That'll be two and a peeny,' she croaked. It always was, always had been. She passed the roll to me, very deliberately and gravely, as if she were presenting me with a diploma.

This was the last stop; now we were for home, and the closing of Miss Allen's shop door closed Nailsworth for half a week.

The bus was in and we sat half way down on the left. The blue painted bulbs gave just enough light to sort out our fares and there was nothing now but the journey home. The bus filled with shapes and red cigarettes; the cold raced round like a river.

'Won't be long now,' said Mother.

'Won't be long,' I said, and the two halves of the wish were like a rope around us.

The bus lurched sideways as the driver climbed in and the conductress rang the bell. We grabbed our bags and thought of our home in the hills. Slowly, out of the bus station down to the main road, the speed increased to twenty-five miles an hour. Every inch of the fifteen-minute ride known by the gear changes, sharp bends, close walls, branches that flicked the windows and the separate smell of each factory: all more sure than a compass. The brakes whined at every stop and every stop we resented except our own. At night, without lights anywhere, this short ride seemed endless till, always very suddenly, we were on our feet bashing our way out.

No matter how ready we were, there were these prickly delays, the sum of a rising panic, and back on the bus today I hear Mother start a commotion.

'I think it rolled under that seat. I'm *so* sorry. Yes, under there. Dear, it's so dark!'

A man struck a match, the driver revved his engine, the conductress hacked her way through with her torch. She flashed on boots and wet bus tickets and at last a man's heel kicked out a tin of peas. 'There, I *knew* something fell out,' said Mother. Flushed but vindicated, she renewed her charge down the aisle, breaking knee-caps as she went, and joined me in the road. Feeling like lepers, glad not to be stoned, we had one final grope round the bags. 'Hope we've got everything,' said Mother.

Breathing diesel and cold we shouted goodnight at the back of the bus and braced ourselves for the long climb up the hill.

Over the level crossing and the little brook, merry in the dark, we started up the rise and our hearts woke up. We changed over bags every hundred yards, one in each hand with the heaviest in the middle. The lane was about forty-five degrees and would have downed a team of mules, but we climbed on into the star-lit sky. Panting and rubbing our fingers, we rested by the garden walls, invisible to each other in the dark lane.

Leaving the road behind, we were in the fields, and the lank grass, bowed with rain, wet us as we passed. Mother was so small that it brushed her shoulders in the little cuttings and she came in with bits of pollen stuck to her cheeks.

The banks were mud: one step forward, four steps back, and the labours of Sisyphus seemed ordinary after all. Breath was for the fight and there was none for talking, even had we felt inclined. To fill this hour, Mother furnished the mansion one room at a time, elegantly, painstakingly, each room different from the other, and in eleven years had not done them all. A mind trick, like being at the pictures: she wandered the carpeted halls, saw light shooting from glass, wood and marble, heard the ducks splashing along the lake; and always, of course, she was alone. 'I couldn't drag up that hill without my bit of daydreaming,' she said. The champagne of that vision got her to the top of the bank and we cheered the dark shape of the farm cut out of the sky. The wind off the ridge was a blessing if not too wild, and today it was just right. Our leaking blackout guided like a star, cattle scampered away unseen in the dark, and the bags were half a ton lighter.

'Let's hope Myra's got the kettle on.' This was a whistle hoot just before the cowsheds; and when did Myra ever let us down? We crashed into the kitchen like half a platoon and Mother pounced on the teapot. It would be hours before she took off her hat and coat; she kept them on, fluttering like battle flags, sitting on the arm of the chair. Her sighs were always of a very long and heavy calibre after Nailsworth, and she kept looking at her hands and feet with a pity for their trials and wear.

'That hill's a real killer!' She said it half to herself, or probably wholly to herself, though it was like a warning that she hoped we would take up; but it was a long time before we did.

She was increasingly unwell in the years before we left. Her animals dwindled, became less sacred as her interest in them faded. Ducks and geese went missing, and no longer were there hectic search parties mustered at dusk, or frantic saving of ducklings in cloudbursts.

Talk in the kitchen late at night was a matching of symptoms and age. They loved the hill but it beat them in the end, and the decision was made to go.

So, one cold rough day in December we left and went to Wiltshire. Here there were no steep hills to strain her heart, just woods and meadows high with elms; and we were out in the middle of a field again. Mother never liked the place. The village was four miles away and you had to use the road. A bus ran twice a week to Malmesbury but sometimes never ran at all. She grew old very quickly.

In an effort to rekindle something of her old zest, and as usual without a word to anyone, she bought three goats. A lorry backed up to our gate one day and dumped them in the garden. There was no question of keeping them of course and by great good fortune a farmer took them off our hands. Mother made no fuss. From the beginning she had had little interest in them, and had bought them, I suppose, to remember the old days when all was well and settled, if settled they ever were.

We moved again after that, I scarcely remember how many times, and along the years her dreams for us faded and finally fell to pieces.

Bob was married and living at Pagan Hill. He seldom wrote, but biked up once or twice to see us, and sometimes found the house empty because we had moved again. In ten years we saw him only three times, and by then he was so far from us that in some ways he was rather like a stranger. Only Mother kept alive his name, dusted it off, made sure we never quite forgot who he was.

In the last years she bought a great dane, a final defiant surprise to her badgered spirit. He was big and indestructible, that was some of it; a balance to her own precarious hold on life. She took him for long walks over the fields, till the farmers complained and made her keep to the roads. Much of her days were lost, feeding sparrows and remembering things over and over.

'I was just thinking about Godsell,' she would suddenly say. 'I'd give anything to know what happened to him. I'll never believe he went off, just like that, all on his own . . .' She'd play with her hair, now turned silver. 'Proud of my looks I was then. It was down to here and all the men making eyes. I never bobbed it like the others.'

She grieved for her poultry. 'Remember all the ducks I reared? Aylesburies mostly, as white as could be, and that little Khaki Campbell that got mixed up with them? He was my favourite.'

The years came again and she was standing on the rick-yard gate watching them feed . . .

'That old cockerel – the one with the wicked spurs! Remember? He was an old devil and I've still got marks on my legs from him. How I used to curse him!' Her face opened with the thought of it all. 'Ah, he had lovely feathers though. A real beauty.'

Aunt Tina came up from Bromyard to see her, the only connection she now had with her family. But Mother was shutting down, pestered by spasms of mountainous optimism, talking of money and mansions like a baroness, though there were bright happy moments still, when her humour flared like rockets and lit us as it had of old.

Yet all the time, in ways we never really understood, she and Father grew ever more distant, sealed inside themselves, waiting for the other to make a move, waiting for the reconciliation, the gentle hand, the kindliness that never came.

Then suddenly that day she left us. She was alone even then.

At Leckhampton she lies, by the silent fields sloping up to the ridge. The quiet she craved is there too, and the wind from our old hill blows that way every day.

℘ YANKS ℘

When the war began Selsley Hill grew bristles of round concrete blocks, to stop German gliders. Later, when the threat of invasion had receded, they were removed and the flat parts ploughed up for barley. We had room enough for football and cricket though – until the American army arrived in 1944. Round the edges of the crop, in the rough dips and margins, they crowded thirty tanks, forty lorries and a hundred and fifty men, part of an armoured division.

The doughboys were casual soldiers, very relaxed. There was none of the intrinsic smartness and discipline we expected. They chewed gum and were homesick. The N.C.O.s were busiest and keen-eyed; the officers were rarely evident and saluted only on Sundays.

Starting their tanks, shunting their lorries, racing their jeeps up and down the road, had no other purpose than to use petrol. They were idle, impatient, on the whole subdued, and the random thrashing of engines was the only exercise allowed.

We had heard they were generous. 'Shall us go up tonight?' said Sparrow, the moment we heard of their arrival. We tested their vulnerability that same night, and met along the road.

'Ain't it great you! Look what I got already!' Sparrow held up four sticks of gum and gave one to me – a reasonable share of the windfall he thought. Then we strolled about, watching the men brew coffee, gambling or sleeping in their lorries, part of the long queue that would take them all the way to Southampton and Normandy.

Two or three tanks started up and we ran to look. The smoke belched and the woods held the sound, amplified it right to the bottom road. Like a flashing fairground, it was what we expected, and we started begging shamelessly. If we failed with one we succeeded with another, though only 'Dottadun' had a one hundred per cent success rate.

He got his name from a queer hitch of speech. His opening shot to any American, regardless of rank, was always the same: ''Ave you dot a dun? Dot any dum?' His hollow face would droop pitifully and they'd give him all they had and more. He was a fountain of manna, a treasure of contraband, and his bulging pockets always looked as if his hips were broken. We'd crawl round him saying we would be his friend for ever if only he would tell us how he did it, tell us his secret. But none of us ever learned or ever could have learned. We did not have his gifts of nature, his pinched wistful look, his toothless winning smile or springy confidence.

So we just followed him around, deferring to his natural superiority, our leader and provider, a harbinger of good luck and tasty surprises.

They'd even hand over their Colt pistols, remove the clip and let him work the slide and click the trigger, while we stood round in awe and admiration, envious of his rags.

They were easy-going but we did sometimes fall foul of dark-chinned sergeants.

'Get them gawd-damned kids away from there!'

But authority in despair we knew how to cope with, and, feigning retreat, ducked under the lorries to make a stand elsewhere.

In a week we were indivisibly one of them, and until Sonny Blatchford got himself wedged in the bottom of a tank we were getting away with it. The armour could stop bullets but not Sonny's howling, which held one's ear like a screaming bomb. When finally he emerged red and vengeful, saying that we had sat on the hatch till he cooked, we thought we had lost everything. Quaking with malice and cursing like a veteran he raced off to tell the captain. His wretched story got us rounded up in a drag net, and while we waited for the firing squad we mouthed threats and made fists at Sonny and he knew what he was in for.

They lined us up and the captain gave us a lecture: keep off the tanks and guns, keep out of the tents and lorries or he would have us sent to Leavenworth. We accepted the conditions without protest and Dottadun got five shillings out of him for good measure; but we dragged Sonny into the wood and beat him up just the same.

As solace to these new restrictions we started smoking Lucky Strike, under the wall. They were a change from Woodbines, and Dottadun, that great expert in low tastes of every kind and instructor of high sensations, gave his verdict to our assembled clan: 'They ain't bad,' he said, 'but look what I got!' He drew from his ragged trouser pocket a long, shining cigar, rolling it expertly between his fingers and passing it under his nose. He got it from a cheery New Yorker who sometimes made us coffee and sang opera to the cows.

That first time, that first cigar was like the seduction of a woman or a wound in battle: pleasure and pain and exultation. He leaned on the wall, confident and showy, clenching the thing between his teeth.

Expectant and half-mad with envy, we watched him suck and blow, like a chimney: it was the best thing he had ever tried, the very best he said.

We closed round in air as thick and sweet as a Sultan's tent, dizzy and edgy, fighting for a go. When quite soon the lovely thing fell from his trembling fingers, we pounced on it like dogs after a bone, snarling and drawing blood.

With his face turned cabbage and his shirt stained with ash like bird droppings, we watched him collapse and slide down the wall. He howled and reached and we gathered in a knot at his life's end, wondering who on earth would tell his mother. He was apparently dying, he whom we thought immortal, and, mourning the loss of gum, biscuits and chocolate, we started looking round for a replacement.

Yet we all had a go at that fatal cigar, all tried to survive its hammer impact, and one by one turned the colour of old, very worn washing, croaking like toads and fit only to be led home and thrown into bed.

We were saved from this self-inflicted torture by a giant negro who found us rolling about under a bush. He took away the cigar, still only half smoked, and crushed it under his size eleven boots.

'Ah neva did see anybady so hell bent on misery,' he said. 'Dem tings am poisin. Y'hear. POISIN!'

His massive hands descended and he swung us onto our feet, shaking us like kittens. When our heads cleared he gave us gum to take away the taste of tobacco and vomit.

George, whose home was in Detroit, ran every evening to Nympsfield and back for the sake of his wind, and coming home had found us lying in the grass like sick dogs, hunched back and whining.

After that we sought him out, not because he was nearly the first black man we had ever seen, but because we found out that he had once been Joe Louis's sparring partner, and we asked him about it. 'Shua, ah trained wid Joe,' he said, 'trained wid him till he was drafted I guess.'

He told us he trained with Louis for the Braddock fight. He sat on the wall above us, flashing smiles, and took us to the fights.

'He stopped Braddock in de eighth roun' wid a right, like dat [a short hook]. Yea, guess he did all right.'

'What about Tommy Farr?' we asked, for we had heard from the men that Farr had beaten Louis and been robbed of the title.

'Yea, it was a close fight all right,' he said. 'Tommy was a good boxer, clever and quick; a bit small for a heavy though. Guess Joe pinched it that night.'

The world was bigger then than now; the sportsmen in it giants. But could Louis really beat any man in the world?

'Well shua; guess ol' Joe can lick any man in de ring. Guess it means dat or it don't mean nothin'. Course he had trouble now an' then.'

Then he told us of the Conn fight; three years ago it was at the Polo Grounds, New York.

'Yessir, dat Billy Conn wa' some fighter. Only a light heavy too; but he nearly beat Joe; had him licked for twelve roun's.'

We sat in the grass, his shoulders filled the sky, his voice melted with the wind. 'Lord, but dat man w' slippery – fastest man I ever did see – some sort o' Jack in the Box I guess.'

He got off the wall and showed how, bobbing and weaving and ducking and swaying, Conn had nearly beaten the Brown Bomber.

'Yea, he'd feint an' move and jig about, kinda like a shadow; and he had a good jab, fast and hard. Good counter-puncher too. Joe couldn't catch him. Roun' after roun' dat ol' Conn jabbed an' moved an' weaved an' jabbed; guess he shua enough figured it out. Chappie Blackburn, Joe's trainer, say to Joe: "Hit him in de middle; git to his body." But every time Joe gets set, dat Conn would slip away like smoke.'

Linked in combat, ears stinging with punches, throats dry as dust, we battled with Louis and Conn. We pressed up, rubbed against each other, leant on shoulders as the arc lights polished our vacant faces . . .

'Yessir, dat title wa' slippin' away an' ol' Joe knew it. Conn w' cocky an' gittin' faster. In de twelfth, Conn staggers Joe; staggers him so bad he don't know where he's at, an' his arms dropped like he was tired.'

We sucked hard through our teeth, there were no distractions now and we clenched our fists waiting for the bell . . .

'At de end of de roun', Blackburn say to Joe: "You lost it Joe, if you don't knock him out." Course Joe know dat; we all know dat. Anyway, dey come out fo' de thirteenth, an' dat Billy he comes out fightin' mad. Yessir, he comes out like he was ridin' a rocket, swingin' an' growlin' an ol' Joe couldn't believe his luck. Joe got in a good left to the jaw – a good solid shot, an' Billy w' hurt. His eyes kinda glazed an' his legs wobbled. He tried to hold, but he had no chance now. Quick as this (an arm swept over) Joe threw another left an' right an' Conn was out. Man, dat w' some fight!'

George taught us to box, under the spreading trees. The G.I.s made a circle and watched us sparring, bawling advice and encouragement and daubing our bruises with Vaseline.

'Yo gotta be balanced,' said George, so we practised stance, footwork and counter-punching. We flung our jackets in a pile, wrapped towels round our fists, and set to. Swinging wildly, we hammered air and ribs ferociously, till we laughed or hiccoughed, called peace when we were winded, fell over, or just walked off. We snorted like bulls, danced like antelope, collided like rams as the grass turned black under our boots and the woods rang with noise.

We learned the value of a good straight left, how to bob and weave like Billy Conn, how to punch with our chins tucked in. Groaning with pain, holding our stitches, we tried every trick we could think of to get our opponent's sympathy. We never rested between rounds, but licked our bloody lips, blowed hard, eyed the opposition for signs of damage or death.

We were held in the breaks like fighting cocks, encouraged yet restrained, given advice which we never heard, and came out swinging till we dropped or simply got fed up.

George showed us how to skip, hitherto thought cissy. He did this in the middle of the road. At sixteen stone he was as light as air and as fast as a cat, and never seemed to move his feet at all. The blurred rope whistled round him and beat a rhythm that never faltered; now on one foot now the other, a smooth and well-worked effortless jig. These demonstrations always ended with a long flourish, a tremendous burst of heart, legs and arms, and then he'd stand there smiling down, black and massive with the sweat rolling off him like oil.

'Yea, yo gotta skip if yo wanna be fighters,' he said.

He would get on his knees and box us two at a time, let us clout his arms and with the gentlest of shoves send us cartwheeling in the grass. Sweet biscuits and gum was our prize money, and, after he had repaired us, he told more stories of fights and fighters over there in the States.

There were fields above the village which we called Albert Hall and Madison Square Garden; little flat places under trees or between brambles. 'I be Joe Louis an' you be Tommy Farr,' we'd say. There was no referee; such refinements looked weak, a contradiction almost, since we expected to win by a knockout. There were no rules; the punches landed anywhere between knee and scalp.

'I won!'

'Ya, you didn't! I slipped!'

The loser would look round for support but of course never found any, for already we had learned to spurn the defeated.

'You buggers! I ain't comin' up no more I ain't!' It was a threat we treated with indifference. We cared little what we did or where we went or who with, and such reactions were normal after a good punch had dropped us.

The training was going well, but war's sudden priority took George away with his lorry. Without our trainer, without his spur, the drive to bash each other senseless without good reason deserted us, and we threw away our skipping ropes and started scrounging again.

In the end we even tired of that and Dottadun renewed his assault with fresh recruits. It was a drag up to the common anyway, and when a brigade of American infantry took over the mansion grounds it saved me the trouble.

Rows of tents went up by the lakes, tons of supplies blocked the tracks through the woods, a hundred lorries pulverised the ground to dust, the lakes washed with boats, and the gargoyles were shot to pieces for target practice. There were so many that they finally spread out into the fields, half a mile from the farm.

One day three of them came over to see what they could buy. Mother brought out a straw-lined bucket half-full of brown eggs and they bought the lot. Helmets served as baskets; they spread a handful of change on the kitchen table and sat on the steps outside drinking warm milk and eating the eggs raw, like oysters. They told us that they had been in England only a week and had been continually on the move till now, always under canvas, and were tired of rough and ready. They especially craved fresh bread, and an heroic impulse made me contract to supply them with loaves, twice a week, carried up from the village in a sack.

I got to know a few of them quite well. Paul from Kentucky was one, a pony rancher. 'Prairie ponies I guess you'd call them; not like your cart horses. What wouldn't I give for those two!'

Frankie came from Iowa, Doug from Chicago; conflicting personalities both, though backbone buddies through thick and thin. Frankie was a dumb, homesick lad with a huge Adam's apple, who seldom spoke a word except to say: 'Guess it'll be noon back home,' or 'Guess the ol' hooter would be soundin' right about now . . .'

Doug was loquacious, a cab driver of extraordinary memory. Sprawling in the grass, buttering bread and sharing a tin of peaches, he would tell us of the famous people he had had as fares.

'Got 'em all in a book – all their names I mean. Got 'em all there and one day I'm going to write about it all so my kids'll know the kinda people I had in my cab. All class.' Millionaires, senators, film stars – so he said.

'Picked up Al Capone once. All alone he was – no bodyguard, nothin'! Flags me down sweet 'n' easy. Tells me this joint and I'm away. Course I saw straight off who he was. I mean – the scar and hat – it couldn't be anyone else. I says to him, "Hey, ain't you Big Al?" and he plays like he don't hear so good. So I says again, "Hey, ain't you Big Al?" and he leans forward kinda confidential: "Yea, I am," he says, "and I don't want no blab see." He had a dame somewhere – somebody's wife, a real bit of class – and he wants it kept secret. Anyways, I drops him off and he says I'm to keep buttoned about where I took him. It sure would surprise some folk. He gave me fifty bucks for the tip.'

He bragged and invented and passed the glamour round. Truth and fiction mixed with a bright imagination can be wantonly seductive. We never believed all his stories, though there was nothing that made them unbelievable. It is just that we mistrusted anything too extraordinary from a private, first class, laying on his back, undone, and cramming his mouth with bread.

The bread orders increased and brought me in touch with Al Cossetti from Boston and Sam Mathews from Philadelphia who were both big story tellers: truth highlighted, I suppose one might call it. They fired my mind with stories of moist blue plains stretching from sea to sea, sun-blasted deserts, crumbling red mountains, wheatfields that took days to cross, buildings sitting in the clouds, yellow cabs, trains a mile long that never stopped. Chicago, New York, Washington: well there was nothing to compare with them except London, which they grudgingly allowed was largest of all. There was plenty of work over there for lads like us they said; we'd be millionaires in no time. 'Were they millionaires then?', somebody asked. They hedged: well, just maybe they would be one day, after the war.

We sat in the grass, or in branches, or on groundsheets listening to these flamboyant stories. In any case picture books and the cinema half confirmed what they said and we were not cheeky enough to argue. Yet their very presence there in our fields was astonishing in itself, and although we knew America was mixed up in the war, it scarcely explained why they were so far from the action (we thought they were in England permanently). These infantry, and also the tank men on the common, never left camp, never got much of a chance at the women.

Their reputation indeed seemed somewhat inflated. They were generous certainly, but no more so than the British tommies had been; they were lustful, yet no worse than any group of men, and certainly not as bad as the Italian prisoners confined to a large house and grounds in the village, who carved us wooden rings and guns and handed them through the iron gates with dubious invitations.

However, the Yanks weaved strange patterns while they were there and the remnants of their influence stayed a long time, especially when it came to sorting out the girls later on. We boys suddenly began talking with our noses blocked, as if we had colds that stubbornly resisted snuff and smelling salts; a long nasal drawl that got us lines at school and contempt from our betters. Myra laughed when I said I was off to America.

'You wait our Myra! You just wait till I'm rich 'n' got bloody dollars! You wait 'n' see!'

She is still waiting.

Of them all I liked Texas Johnny the best. He was a thin, slow-nerved fellow, an ideal soldier but born a hundred years too late: for his was a free spirit which belonged to the wilderness. Rifle and pony were his natural companions and rough living a blessing and glory. He'd talk for hours about himself and in time we dragged a whole string of stories out of him. I hope he is still alive and well, though I doubt he will ever read this, for after the war he said desert or forest would have him, there to end his days.

He told us many strange tales, and the one which we often asked him to repeat was about an Indian, the desert and a gold mine. The significance of the Indian's prophecy could not have been apparent to him; certainly of course it was not apparent to us. It was only years later, remembering what he had told us, that the name Omaha sprang to mind; for it had been the secret code name of one of the American landing areas in Normandy. It perhaps was coincidence; all the same I've often wondered.

Here, as well as I can remember it, is what he told us.

He had led an interesting vagabond life, roaming all over North America. He was actually born in Canada of an English father and Scottish mother. When he was fifteen his parents died in a fire. He escaped the blaze by climbing onto the roof, and as it collapsed beneath him, he leaped in the dark to a tree, and was saved.

After that he went to stay with a farmer out in the sticks where he scraped a living. 'I never went to school much after that,' he told us. 'Guess I never thought it was worth it.'

He cut wood from dawn to dusk and slept in the attic. 'They weren't real friends; just someone my father knew. I worked for my food I guess, and that was about it.'

One night when the farmer was in town getting drunk, the wife went up to his room . . .

'I left before it was light; walked to the highway and got a lift south.' He went down into the States and stopped off at Detroit. For a time he worked at the Ford plant and hung about for a couple of years saving money, before moving on. He had wholesome dreams of wealth and thought that here might be the place to find it. But he was not trained, had not even finished school, and it would be wealth by sweat, instinct or accident. Indiana, Illinois, Missouri: he took jobs where he could get them, and it was not easy during the Depression.

'Got a job down from Jefferson; it was good money and I sure needed it. I dug ditches, set drains and slept in a trailer. After a while I had enough to buy my first jalopy.'

There was a diner along the highway and one night he went there for a beer.

'These guys came in. You could see they meant to start sump'n. They were kinda edgy and hardly touched their coffee. Suddenly one pulls a forty-five an' I guess that's when it all got interestin'.'

It was a quiet night, only two customers in the place, but they were ordered against the wall anyway. He laughed: 'These guys were amateurs, nervous as kittens, waving their guns crazy. There wasn't much in the till; like I said it was a quiet night, so they came over and robbed us. I had only four dollars which was lucky. The other little guy must have stuffed his somewheres or spent it, or maybe he didn't have no money anyway, and they starts beaten' him up. "Don't do nothin', don't do nothin'," he kept sayin'. He was real scared at first. "Look here," he said. "Look at this. That'll fetch around three hundred bucks. Take it! Take it!" It was two or three small nuggets in a handkerchief. Real gold. Well these guys are dumbfounded and starts arguing, 'cos it don't look much; not like gold see. "Come on," says the little guy, "I ain't waitin' all night." An' they argue some more and finally one of 'em says "OK we'll take it, take the nuggets." So this little guy just throws 'em the handkerchief; just throws it, casual like. But this screwball panics an' starts shootin', and the little guy is hit and drops down right next to me. Then they all panic and runs off into the night. They had an old truck in back an' made off like all the devils in hell were after 'em. They operated on the little guy but he don't walk no more. I used to go in and kinda cheer him up. That's when he told me about the mine.'

He was never certain whether the old man was just making it up, and paid little attention to him. It had been a dream once, digging a fortune, but he had grown up along the way and knew that things like that did not happen any more; but he let the old man ramble on.

'I thought it was all just hokum. But he had them nuggets right enough, no denying that.'

After the old man died he moved on, down through Oklahoma, getting work where he could. 'I was kissin' the girls and burning gas, always on the move, but goin' nowhere I guess. I wanted to get rich but didn't know how.'

He had saved money and bought a lorry; started hauling loads right through to New Mexico. Staying awake was a problem on long trips. If he picked up a hitch-hiker who could drive, that was fine. If not he went without sleep.

One night he was nodding off when an old Indian stopped him. The old fellow knew nothing about lorries or how to drive them, but kept him awake chanting to the moon hanging over the desert.

In the end, overcome by sleep, he lost his way and stopped. He fell asleep immediately.

'It was nearly dawn when I woke up, just starting to get light, and I guess the cold roused me,' he told us. He was in the desert but miles off the road and of his companion there was no sign.

'I got out and looked round. Hell there was nothin' but sand and rattlers; no road, nothin'. Just rocks.'

He shouted for the Indian, but there was no answer. He still had his money and his pistol, and the load was intact. He fired a shot, putting up some prairie chicken, but no one came; there was no one to hear. As the sun burst over the empty sand he climbed a knoll, but there was no sign of the Indian.

He went back to the lorry and started the engine. The tank was half full, he had a canteen of water, and there were tracks to follow. But the tyre marks finally gave out, and he was uncertain of the way. So he followed a track, rising on a low hill, and quite suddenly came to the remains of an old mining town, sheltering under low cliffs.

But what instantly attracted his attention was the freakish sandstone pillars overhanging the place like cow horns. Even now his face brightened when he recalled the find.

'The old guy – the one with the nuggets – told of just such a place. The red outcrop, the old sheds and the canyon leading into it were all exactly as he described it. I sure wish I had paid more heed. It was weird finding it like that, sort of fateful, and I sat there a long time taking it in.'

There were several sheds, some without roofs, filling with sand; and he saw signs of horses. He looked about and found fresh boot marks. As he started back to his lorry a shot rang out, and he heard the bullet whine away among the rocks. The sniper's aim had been deliberately wild, and, thus encouraged, he turned and roared back down the trail, hoping the springs would hold.

'That was real scary,' he said. 'They were probably doin' a bit of illegal mining. Mexicans most likely. I never did see that Indian again though. He just kinda vanished. Indians are like that.'

Twenty miles on he found the road, but the delivery was late and he lost the contract. 'Kinda got discouraged I guess. I sold the truck and went down to Texas, ranching.'

But he never forgot the old man or the mine or the strange events that seemed to link them.

'I used to spend a lot of time in the libraries,' he told us. 'That way I picked up a lot of stuff about prospectin'. Guess I was still thinkin' on it when Pearl Harbour happened and I enlisted. Yea, I'm goin' back to that mine some day though. There could still be rich pickins – a vein maybe missed by the old prospectors. Might go back to Canada. They say there's a heap of that yellow stuff up there in the McKenzies if you don't mind the solitude.'

The Indian though had told him that his days would end in Nebraska, at a place where gold ran like water.

'Guess he must mean Omaha, where they purify the gold. I ain't likely to get up that way though, not now.'

They went as they came, silently all in a night.

The common was empty and all they left behind were a few rags, oil patches and Camel packets.

The barley ripened, the wind thrummed again through the dips, and their passing slipped back a century.

They left a mound of debris by the mansion. I picked up a hundred cartridge cases which I flung into my box with bits of grenades and aeroplanes. Also I found things of utility: tins of jam and meat, which my Mother kept in the top of the cupboard for emergencies that never came, and when they went rusty she threw them away – but that was years later.

Gallons of paint, boots, shirts, rope, webbing and petrol tins lay round the flattened undergrowth amongst mountains of rusting cans.

We boys wandered in the bones of their camp, wondering why they had left so abruptly and where they had gone.

A week later, on the sixth of June, we knew.

⇜❦⇝ OUTINGS ⇜❦⇝

Father, that captain of labour and routine, that dove of the placid backwaters who could scarcely even be tempted into Stroud, came in one night from work with the shattering announcement that he was taking us all to London the very next day.

We stared astonished, as if he had suggested mass suicide, wondering if he was ill, babbling such rubbish.

Broadening this thunder clap he went on to say that he had never been to London, that he had always meant to go, that things were slack and now was a good time. Laughter might well have followed this unexpected news, but one look at Mother's face told us it was no joke. She was downright alarmed, and brandishing the bread knife which she happened to be using, beat out her argument like the leader of a band.

What about old Hitler? What of the flying bombs? She said there was not a brick left standing anywhere in London – she had heard it on the wireless – and we would spend all day in the shelters or in hospital; this was her opinion and she flatly refused to go.

But Father was curiously deaf to all this and said his mind was made up; and by now so was mine. Absurd though it was, it was an infectious madness – the thought of being bombed and blown up – and in a moment I was all for it. Myra first agreed, then wavered, and finally next day said she was definitely not coming. She had dreamt we were going to vanish without trace, and could she please have my cigarette card collection as I would no longer need them. Meanwhile, Mother was searching a trunk for the insurance policies and muttering about funerals.

So it came about that Father and I set off alone next morning, and to keep our boots clean we went the long way through the Park.

It was yet dark, though daylight was coming and soon the sun would burst like a flower over Rodborough. This was morning night, not shuttered and growing heavier by the hour like that other night, but expectant and full of birds, with the air like cold silk.

Our early legs were sluggish; mine were anyway, and my head, abed and weak with the distant calls of women, had no power at all, and I kept stumbling into bushes, like a drunken thing. Father, a veteran of the early hours, plodded along, head well down, mind far away. He was a man to whom enjoyment of any sort seemed nearly a waste of time and effort – at least if it took him away from home – which made this day all the more remarkable. I glanced his way now and then, every moment expecting him to change his mind, but when we got to the bus stop I realized we were committed, though by now certain also that neither of us knew what we were doing.

Waiting for the bus in the growing light, blobs gathered round us in ones and twos, and men cycling to work with their heads bent on the dawn grunted as they passed by.

The bus came rattling round the corner and swept straight past, full to the platform. The conductress leaned out, jerking a thumb, which meant there was another behind, but it was ten minutes before it came.

We had to stand, and at every stop workers piled on, going to the factories and mills up the valley; black thoughtful faces twisted with last night's war news, chain smoking and staring at their knees.

This morning the ride took a good twenty-five minutes, and when we got to Stroud station the London train was clanking up the track. Its hot vapour sat on the platform long after it was out of sight, and London would remain unexplored for years.

I thought it finished and done with, the next London train was not before noon. But Father studied the timetables and came up with another plan.

'How about Bristol? There's an express in fifteen minutes.' The name 'Bristol' had not the same robe as London, yet for all that it was more familiar. Father had signed on there in 1916 and Bob was stationed there in 1940. It was, of course, no more than forty or fifty miles away, unlike London where imagination put it half way to America. I do not remember even giving a reply, but suddenly found myself packed in the corridor among service men and women. We had to stand all the way.

That first-ever train ride was intensely nerve-wracking. There was no pleasurable release, no reckless abandonment of the old self in new sights and sensations. Only miserable suffocation in tobacco fumes that burned like pepper, and soon I was blind with ophthalmia. I saw the crowd in a flood, people taller or shorter with legs and arms detached through the mist of swollen and sticky eyes. The front of my shirt was wet with tear drops.

At last someone got the window open and a dagger of beautiful clean air lanced through the smoke. Things were better till we got to Wickwar tunnel. There they found that the window, which had been so difficult to open, was now impossible to close, and we choked with engine smoke and started dying on our feet. An A.T.S. girl sank unconscious and another very pretty one clung to the window, eyes closed and pale. When we leapt out the other end she stuck her head out into the tearing slipstream. Her curls went wild and afterwards hung over her face fetchingly. It was she who pulled me forwards over the kit bags and rifles and lifted me into the fifty mile an hour wind, which froze my scalp and sawed lines of colour back into my cheeks.

Resting pleasantly against her pulsating lumps, I immediately stopped wheezing and fell into a beaten idleness. Forgotten by my Father, soothed by the clicking wheels, the swelling fields broke against us like the rushing of a sea.

At Mangotsfield we slowed among a skein of tracks, and at last, very sorrowfully, I slid hotly off the A.T.S. girl back to my distant Father.

The morning was gone as we crawled gently into the belly of Bristol. The train threw us in heaps with its violent braking, and we fell out at Temple Meads and were swept away into the city.

This was my first ever meeting with large-scale streets and its punch was solid. I had grown up in green places, village and market town, and from their streets one could see commons and woods only an arm's length away. Not this black grief of murdered peace hanging like curtains down every street, right across the city, end to end. It lay in heaps, maimed, patched and boarded – yet resolutely alive.

We started for the centre down the cold street, and the ruins left and right were already under weeds. Soot clung in our throats and I had a sudden craving for our open hill and its rough sweet gusts; for my chest was noisy again, like leather needing oil.

Father was in front, I trailed behind, and he'd stop now and then to let me catch up, looking round tile-black jagged walls in the heavy sky. No one noticed us, never asked what we were doing or why we had come among their flattened streets, and we would have been tested trying to explain.

We had lunch in a British Restaurant in Broad Street, queuing for sausages and mash and rice pudding, and ate as if we had no right to be there at all. We had no idea where we were or what we wanted to do; the impulse to come at all had been bizarre and the springs of it dried long ago on the train. However, when we came out Father said we must have a look at the bridge over the gorge; so we struck out for the Downs.

Buses blasted by but we never considered getting on one – not for the four or five miles we thought we had in front of us. We lost our way a dozen times; the day was getting on. After some miles we stopped. Father took off his cap and scratching his head looked as if he had woken from a nightmare only to find it real. Puzzled, he hunched his shoulders the way he did when making a decision.

'Look, why not go to the zoo? There's the sign. It can't be far. What's say, young un?'

The zoo or the bridge – what did it matter? Anything that raised the focus above our blisters would be joy.

The pride of Bristol Zoo at that time, indeed the only thing worth looking at, was Alfred, the largest gorilla in captivity. He sat at the back of his cage with a sack drawn about his mighty arms, nibbling a crust like a lady. Over six feet when standing, he had a chest like a tree-trunk and a head like an outcrop of granite. The keeper came in with his tea – a loaf, half a cabbage and some carrots. Kings deserve better, and Father remarked of the difficulty in feeding him, what with the war and everything. The bowed, yellow-faced keeper considered the matter as if on oath, and nodded gravely.

'Ah, tis an' no mustake.' And he explained how it is with gorillas.

'Tis all this damned bread we damned well gives 'n. Bread, bread, bread day after day. It don't do 'im no good it don't. It bungs 'n proper.' He shook his sallow head and swayed as if very tired. 'Nothin' for it then but rough cider – gallons on't. What a job that is, cleaning up all that damned mess; an' I ain't as young as I used t' be. Don't get na extra for it . . .'

Wet boards and foul air bespoke the unnatural life, the pity of his caged world. Alfred ate the cabbage reluctantly, yawned spectacularly, and went back to sleep in the corner. No one could do more than guess at what lay behind his very watchful smoky brown eyes.

We left him curled in his sack and came out into the weak October sunshine. We followed the path to the lions, two very thin males padding nervously behind high bars, their yellow gaze staring past at the nothing that was Bristol.

The monkeys laughed in their temple, the baboons were spiteful and erotic, the giraffe chewed the cud in a self-possessed heaven, the bison was in tatters, the little elephant conducted music in her head: all listening for the wilderness, the plains they would never know.

Sipping hot tea on the cold, deserted lawn, sharing our biscuits with the sparrows, neither of us knew what to do next. We were as out of place as the animals we had come to see.

'We shan't 'ave to leave it late.'

When Father said that I knew he wanted to be gone. The feeling of strangeness had at last been acclaimed and we rose together as he spoke, taking our cups back to the counter. Sooty red walls, houses sealed and empty, gutted churches, rubble and thrusting weeds made our avenues into town. Other places, untouched and undamaged, were wearing away with neglect: wild lawns where ladies in circular dresses had once played croquet; empty mansions of long-dead merchants; everything large, spreading, unending, street upon street, mile upon mile, ordered, divided, lined, shaking like a nest; nothing recognisable or known. I vaguely wondered whether we were still in England.

On the way back to Temple Meads we passed things worse than anything we had seen: streets of black bricks roped off with bombs still in them. There had not been a raid for months, but bombs there were – and still going off so we were told. Father had seen nothing like it since Ypres.

Except for dinner time we had been on our feet since six o'clock that morning. At home I could have curled up in a bush or climbed a tree or found a barn . . .

'Come on little un, look sharp!'

I was cursing Bristol, the zoo, the luckless day; walking, it seemed, on stumps of legs.

'Come on little un, 'urry up!'

I dredged up some energy and hobbled past him and was first onto the platform. The train was there, the porter slammed the doors. This time we found seats and a carriage to ourselves. The engine whistled and the station slid backwards.

That strange day ended thus, and coming home was best of all. I shivered as if I had a fever and watched the roofs of Bristol flick away in the rain. Before the light faded, fields and hedges came round us; the halls of our country world. Air as sharp as lemon found our hearts, and Father was already thinking of the pint he would have at The Ram on the way up the lane.

We rushed through the green, left the mangled city behind: a place challenging with dark undercurrents, thin alleyways and black trees; a place oddly patterned, shaped and stepped; a watchful place that absorbed people like a sponge.

All day Father and I had hardly exchanged a dozen words in our long walk through the city, and it took our rain-swept fields to put Bristol in perspective. Then from this distance it looked a pretty good day all things considered.

These outings were rare, bright-tailed comets flashing through the years, nervy affairs keyed up with excitement and fear, especially when Mother had anything to do with them. Would we get on the buses? What would happen if we could not? Suppose we got on the wrong one? Would there be an air raid? How would we find our way about? What would we do among strangers and how close should we let them come?
 The day Mother decided to take us to Gloucester the suggestion again came out of the blue, though there had been signs enough that something was about to break for a week or two. We thought it just meant that she was going to buy another dozen turkeys to fatten into old age. She had been looking at *The Standard*, staring hard over the hollow, watching a stain on the ceiling, and letting the milk boil over: all indications that something was brewing. Then one night she tossed us the surprise, not as shocking as the London one, but almost.
 'How d'you fancy a look at Gloucester. It's a nice long ride.'
 Myra needed a new outfit for work, something grown up for the office, her first job. The clothing coupons were saved; it was cheaper in a place like Gloucester, more variety, more to look at; and the very next morning we went.
 I remember how odd it was not getting off the bus at Stroud; the long wait outside Woolworths facing the wrong way and leaving by a strange road. Once more moved those tremblers beating on tension, surprise and curiosity, like little electric shocks. The town turned inside out and at the Cross the policeman directing traffic stepped right back to let us swing down the hill.
 'Wave to Inspector Hobart,' said Mother as we passed the police station at the bottom. The engine thundered like a cataract going up Horse Pools as we crawled round new woods, fields and churches; familiar in some ways but unknown, like things on postcards.
 The sun baked through the window and we fell silent and forgot. I scratched my legs, Myra yawned and Mother said it was too hot to bother with anything. The bus stopped at last without us noticing, and we jostled out quietly, like a crowd leaving church, and made off up the street.
 It was midday, we were neither tired nor hungry nor anything, but

Mother said we had to have a meal. 'Hang on to me and don't let go,' she said. She started her fiddles of worry and they were going well by the time we got to the restaurant. We sipped brown Windsor and hacked at the stringy beef, our guards well up. Custom kept our eyes well rivetted to our plates, yet we noticed the worn carpet, bright wood, waitresses in their smart caps, a woman knitting at the cash desk. In the churchyard-quiet and cellar-black we glimpsed heads and arms, unmoving, poised like statues; till something crashed in the kitchen and we darted glances at each other as if waiting for someone to be expelled for it. Mother gave her nervous laugh, half turning in her chair.

'What on earth . . . ?'

Calls for mops and buckets produced a titter from the girl at the next table, but the officer she was with looked at her so severely that she blushed, disengaged from the peach melba and touched not another thing.

The uproar over, we got on with our dinner, and after every course Mother looked up at the waitress smiling, saying how nice everything was and telling us a little too loudly to eat slowly and watch our sleeves.

With the aproned girls looking on like wardens we finished our wretched meal: no sniffing, no elbows, backs like boards and no sliding off when we were finished.

'I wonder if I've got enough ready change,' said Mother, nose in purse. She tried to work it out five different ways, with five different answers, then gave up and asked for the bill. Sixpence slid under the plate and we scrambled out, flushed as if coming down with colds. The dust blowing in our faces seemed briefly soothing and luxurious after that hour's imprisonment, but even the state of the carpets had not dimmed Mother's enjoyment of it.

'Did you see that officer? He was a captain. That place always did have a good name.'

At the bottom of the street we turned right; or rather I did. When I looked up I found that the woman at my side was nothing like my mother at all. All the wild nights and haunted mansions had not half the terror of that moment. I was lost and alone among hostiles, where everyone except me knew where they were going, knew their way home to their beds. Fear had me a dozen hours ahead, in moon-stricken streets, buried in a black doorway waiting to be clubbed or garotted . . .

It was a moment only, a brain storm of seconds, but it put me off crowds for ever. A hand gathered my jacket and drew me onto a step.

Looking up I saw my mother again, distracting my agitation with talk of ice cream in the British Home Stores.

It was in Eastgate that we bought Myra's starting-work costume of utility red check. It was the wrong size, but then, the lady said, nothing fitted these days, what with the war and everything. They could alter it upstairs if we cared to call back in an hour or two.

Out we wandered through the Gloucester afternoon, looking at the shops till Mother said she felt stifled and started looking for somewhere to sit down.

A service in the cathedral and the pale sound of a choir drew us naturally within the close. We sat on a seat under a tree in a pool of quiet, while the city murmured over the roof tops. A seagull called sharply, circling the tower, wings wide on the breath of the building, then beat gracefully away westward.

'That might be a spirit going home,' said Mother dreamily.

Waves of heat, music and voices touched our receding consciousnesses, and only people sauntering through, sweating in suits or cool in summer cotton, stopped us from falling asleep. Our bond of content mingled with the rustling shade and clattering dust, like masses of fluttering birds.

Mother dipped into her handbag and drew out the postcards she had bought, her thin white fingers shuffling them slowly; then she put them away and dabbed her throat with a handkerchief.

'Didn't think it would stoke up like this. What a scorcher.' (Back on the hill the haymaking would be slow, the brook turned cloudy by thirsty calves, the woods still and empty in the heat . . .)

'Blessed weather! What time is it Myra? I can hardly keep my eyes open.' Mother had a look which said: 'Give me a blizzard and a good north wind.' Not this relentless burning that offered no escape day or night. She flapped her hands, fanned herself with the cards and finally got to her feet.

'Let's go and see if they've got it ready,' she said.

At half past four we were back at the shop listening to the woman.

'It's the war, madam. We can't get the staff, not the sort we used to have, not the best type d'you see.' She poured over the counter, her arms like mutton pieces, looking down an acre of bosom.

'She had your purchase ready. Well I *thought* it was ready d'you see. But anyway it's nearly finished now – just a few tucks – won't be half an hour. It's the war.'

We stalked out thinking murder, saying we would be back at five o'clock – fifteen minutes before our bus. Mother was pale and tight and we knew she was coiling to strike. We found a café and ordered cakes, all of us threatened by Myra's costume, all ready to attack or retreat.

'Stupid woman,' said Mother. 'Why didn't she say there'd be all this bother. We could have gone to Dowlings.'

We polished off the cakes and emptied the tea pot while Mother promoted Dowlings' emporium.

'All the posh people go there. Lady Gower and Henry Workman's wife get their things there. You can't beat them for quality.' She never said how she knew all this and we were too tired to ask, for no one earning less than fifty pounds a week ever went near the place.

Back in the street, we got our heads down and forced a passage up the pavement to the shop. A big notice on the door said 'CLOSED'. We grasped the big brass handles and rattled for all we were worth.

'Oh they'll open up all right,' said Mother confidently. I got down on my knees and shouted through the letter box. Myra banged the glass till her fists hurt. Mother shook the door relentlessly.

'What the devil are they playing at,' said Mother. 'This is the limit, the absolute limit!'

Myra bit her lip and every glance was an apology for her costume, which now I doubted she would ever wear or even set eyes on. We stopped hammering the door to form a battle plan, when a policeman suddenly filled the pavement behind us, thumbs hooked in his pockets ready for action. We blurted out our story in quick packets of panic while the constable stroked his large dark chin. He considered our statements, judged the situation, weighed up the problem with the greatest care and consideration.

'Well, I expect they're closed then,' he said. He rattled the door twice, peered inside, brought out his watch.

'Yes, well past five.'

'But they said they would stay open for us,' said Mother with her nerves rising. The policeman laughed at that as if he had already heard the same story a hundred times this week. 'I expect they've gone 'ome me dear.' He showed us his watch. 'Closin' time see. Gone five. Oh they're closed all right.'

He lumbered into the road and stopped the traffic for us when we said where were going. 'You'd best come back tomorrow,' he said as we passed safely to the other side.

We waited in Brunswick Road for the bus and Myra tried to cheer us up, the way she did when disaster struck. 'Don't worry, mam. I'll come up tomorrow. It'll be all right. Our Gerald can come with me.'

'I ain't,' I said.

'Damn 'em,' said Mother. 'We should have gone to Dowlings like I said and caught the earlier bus. The hens'll be wondering where I've got to.'

The bus came in and we crashed into our seats. The driver and conductress sat on the wall smoking, numb with miles, numb with love, looking at each other as if they wanted to get into bed. The passionate semaphoring of their eyes temporarily distracted us and we had not noticed the young woman hurrying along the pavement behind a large brown paper parcel. She staggered onto the bus.

'Anyone here name of Roberts?'

She dumped the parcel in Mother's lap, blurting that the last stitch had only just been finished, and no they had not heard us knocking, and she was sorry for the delay and inconvenience and hoped we would call again sometime.

'Of course we shall,' said Mother sweetly. 'But not till after the war I'm thinking!' The girl blushed, looked very sorry and ran, and we never discovered how she found us.

As the bus moved off Mother said: 'Did you see the way that policeman stopped the traffic for us.' That little gesture had made her day.

Bristol and Gloucester were rare peaks then, far away and half foreign, blowsy and boiling with pale-faced people. Anyway, the air there was too grey and noisy and we never went back.

Dursley was more like it though, partly of course because of its connection with Mother's past, but also because it had Aunt Maud and Cousin Mabel. Our outings to see them were reserved for our summer holiday, were indeed our holiday, our one sure day away each year, part prize for feeding hens, fox watching, gathering wood, picking pears. For all these things we were excessively paid by this one inexpressibly happy treat. But no surprise this, and we had a week in which to tighten our expectations, till the great morning came and we were loosed off like arrows.

Always the sun shone for us on these Dursley days, as if heaven itself conjoined in our pleasure. We'd wander down the drive singing, to the edge of the common where we waited for the single decker to take us away. Here was the sparkling anti-chamber of our day, the high early air heavy with the crush of summer, and we drank deeply of it. A patch of daisies, like clouds on water, was where we always waited, looking back at the fields as if we were leaving the farm forever. The tell-tale mowing rippled like a lake, the air quivered over barns on the hill, and the breeze in the wood was like the sound of restless water.

As usual we were half an hour early, but eventually the bus rose over the common and gathered speed towards us. Mother was on her toes. 'Quick! Put out your hand. He won't stop!'

But stop he did, with a great squeal of brakes, and we climbed up into dust and hot engine. Off then through verdant tunnels of hazel and ash to Nympsfield, where we reversed and stopped. We waited outside the Rose and Crown very much as Edward Thomas, the poet, must have waited at Adlestrop: no one left and no one came. The bus was nearly empty; just today, on the back seat, a soldier lay sleeping amongst his kit.

'Poor devil,' said Mother. 'I expect he's been on guard all night. I wonder if he knows our Bob.'

She sent me tiptoeing to the back of the bus, but I saw from his badges that he was from another regiment.

'He's in the Worcesters,' I said, and then we were silent.

The sun poured on the little street and nothing stirred in the village; just the ways of birds touched the air from out the yellow meadows. This was slow time in high summer when all the days were slow and long and heat-heavy, and the ride over the hill and down through Uley was half the enjoyment of the day. The road twisted by house and wall, by wood and barn, through guards of elms and fields where horse-powered mowers clattered like machine guns.

We got off at Bull Pitch and sauntered down through the town to Aunt Maud's. Usually they were out – and were today – for our visits were never confined to tidy dates and times, or even to any particular month, but were a frolic of Mother's whim.

The door was unlocked, and we went in. It was like entering a cave. It had the same violent coolness, the same blind treachery, especially coming in from the blazing street. Shivering in the narrow depths of the hall, our eyes were seared by the hard-edged light, like steel, forcing past the heavy curtains and hitting the glassy pattern of the floor cloth, bursting upwards. It pained one to look, till out of the brown wash there fitted around a dingy elegance.

We put the kettle on and went into the conservatory to tease the African parrot in his fetid, paraffin-warmed jungle of ferns, where the walls streamed after every thunderstorm. He squawked a welcome that sizzled the ear drums and came slowly, very slowly, along the perch to savage us, if we cared. He raised and lowered his head feathers, fussing the bars to tempt our fingers; but we had learned by now. He was very intelligent, with a sailor's vocabulary (Uncle Percy had trained it) and after considering us a moment or two shouted for his mistress as loud as he could – and that was very loud indeed.

'Maaauud! Maaauud! Keee! Keeeee! Scraggle! Scraggle! Keeeeeee!'

The house ripped with uproar and we were driven back into the kitchen where presently we heard the front door open and a gush of noise enter from the street.

Aunt Maud came wearily in, back from the woods where she spent half the day, and the branch she had dragged for three miles lay outside blocking the pavement.

'Well I never,' she said as soon as she saw us. 'I was saying to Mabel only the other day . . .' She had a habit of leaving sentences unfinished, which the listener completed at leisure.

Cousin Mabel followed her in, hurrying to the sound of our voices.

'Well I'm blessed. I was saying to mam only the other day . . .'

Thirty-four and married, Mabel had lived at home all her life, was indeed her mother's companion and would be always. Maud and Mabel, two halves of a crumpy whole; tiny in stature, pale, and never in anything but black, they were ready for any funeral at a minute's notice. Together they pottered about Dursley like sheriffs, always on the lookout for wrongdoers and ready to gun them down. They were the bane of every fishmonger and greengrocer for miles.

You had to watch them, Aunt Maud said; you had to keep your eye on them or they would do you down. Fish left over from the Last Supper and wasp-holed plums – you had to take up arms against things like that. She would pounce on any herring that looked a bit dull round the gills and send it spinning along the sawdust floor.

'The churchyards are full of people poisoned by bad fish,' she would shout; then shaking her gloved fist under the man's nose she'd invite him to sue her. They never did. Once, Mabel upended boxes of yellow plums all down the street and defied the proprietor to fetch the police. 'Wet and rotten that's what they are, Mr S. Wet and rotten and not worth a rag.' The police never came.

The shopkeepers cursed them both but it went no further than that, for most suspected them of possessing ancient powers and did not wish a plague of boils.

Aunt Maud and cousin Mabel laughed loud and long over mischief like that, and their flashing humour was like a light thrown about the gloomy house.

We never knew Aunt Maud's husband. He came from Lancashire and owned mills there, but had left her years ago in a temper and went back up north. He gave them the house and sent regular sums of money through a solicitor; that was all. They were never divorced – few were in those times – but they never met again either and now no one ever spoke of him.

Ern, Mabel's husband, was the man about the house. He worked next door at the engine factory and was as silent as an empty room, nearly the most invisible man I ever knew. Mabel called him 'sweetheart', which in that setting seemed startlingly carnal, like 'sex' shouted loud in a convent. I went crimson the first time I heard it used between them, as if I had caught them in an indecent act. The more so because none of them drank or smoked or swore, or ever went out of Dursley that I know of. Here the three lived in seclusion, never visited anyone and, apart from us, were never visited. They had had the same neighbours twenty-eight years and had never spoken to them; did not even know their names till one of them died and they read it in the *Gazette*.

On this day we sat down to liver and onions in near darkness, poking around our plates for bits of potato and finding liver, or looking for liver and finding onion. Uncle Ern sat opposite me, an outline in shirt sleeves. He smelled of swarf, chewed his food in the same precise way that he spoke, and never once looked up from his plate now that he'd found it. He sometimes grunted at us, but never as I recall did he ever speak directly to us children, and seemed to us like a locked room where no one ever went.

Today, after dinner, he paced nervously around the kitchen, switched the wireless on for the news, then went out in the garden so that the women could be at ease. When he went back to work he kissed Mabel on the neck.

'S'long sweetheart. Cheerio Nance.'

'He's doing overtime,' said Aunt Maud sadly.

'Ah, and that job's too hard for him. He's not that strong, you know,' said Mabel.

Neither for that matter was bony Mabel, and out in the garden the sun seemed to pass right through her. She had solids of sorts, but without her dark clothes I am sure she would just have vanished in the pillars of light slanting over the high walls, or have blown away like a leaf. All day we waited for something to happen to her, for it nearly always did. Once, in the garden, she fell over right in front of us, a sort of hop and cartwheel it was and a sideways roll which took her expertly into the shrubbery without a murmur. She lay on her side looking up through the bushes.

'There!' she said, and with such emphasis that we knew she must have done something special.

It was her lifelong recreation, having accidents, and she practised it to perfection. Curiously enough it all began after she left school, with minor tumbles in the street coupled with a good deal of bashing against walls and railings. From these humble beginnings there quickly developed an astonishing talent for self-mutilation, and falling off chairs and out of windows became everyday events. They bought her a step-ladder to see what she could do with that, and one day in the garden, with nothing better to do, she flung herself off the top step into the kidney beans where she remained impaled upside down for an hour. A couple of days later, still heavily bandaged, and to prove that it had been no fluke, she threw herself down the stairs and rolled till the front door stopped her.

Mabel made bone breaking deft and majestic, but her ability to cut and bleed was Olympian. She could savage herself with any improbable implement: a spoon, comb, shopping list, umbrella, chest of drawers, a penny, the piano or just opening a letter. Haemophilia is unknown in women, but cousin Mabel set the doctors wondering, for she could gush blood quite happily for hours, sopping up handkerchiefs by the dozens and turning the sewers red. Aunt Maud used to time her in case she needed topping up. Once, having badly gashed her finger on a book, she bled for six hours without pause for breath. Her record though was nearer twenty-four hours, and this time they hauled her off to hospital to be replenished. The doctors thought she had tried to take her own life and wanted to call the police (suicide was illegal then if unsuccessful), but stayed their hand when testimonials poured in confirming her extraordinary and unique talent. Apart from giving her an updated manual on first aid, they had little advice to offer.

In time they converted the spare room into a chemist's shop cum surgery stacked with cotton wool, bandages, splints and Dettol; even then they were always running short.

Today in some extraordinary fashion she stabbed herself with a coat hanger and we gathered round to watch her life blood ooze down the sink, vaguely wondering whether she would leave us anything in her will. Aunt Maud went straight into action with stop-watch and rags, rubbing her back, pinching her ears and watching her colour. Through the hiccoughs and screams and threats of being sick, the flow of blood finally stopped. I remember the sense of disappointment that she had not broken her record; nor did she even faint.

With the crisis over and the mess cleaned up we sat down to tea, and Aunt Maud got round to her favourite subject: the war. She was rather keen on Field-Marshall Runstedt who reminded her of an old flame, and she was always a bit vague as to who was fighting whom. She was terrified of a gas attack and quite convinced it was inevitable.

'Mark my words, Nance. Just you mark my words,' she said. 'He'll drop it on us one of these fine days, you see if I'm not right.'

The civilian gas masks were useless, she said. 'I use mine for doing the onions and they're no good even for that.'

By hook or by crook, by bribery or blackmail, she somehow obtained three military respirators which they would use when the gas rattle sounded down Long Street. Thick rolls of matting were ready by the doors and windows, and Ern had even made a contraption for the parrot.

Once, when the Scottish Borderers were stationed there, she got a sentry to hand over all his gas warning paper, a strip of which she had noticed stuck on his bayonet. She took these bits home and hung them round the house like tiny flags. The paper was supposed to change colour at the first whiff of gas, and Mabel went round them twice a day until 1950 muttering, 'No sign yet, mother; no sign yet . . .'

Into the garden we went with our cups and plates – it was that sort of tea-time, that sort of day. Wilds of colour burned in the brash greenery, all piled between the high walls and spilling over the path. As a concession to the war effort, Aunt Maud had planted potatoes, odd little patches here and there grovelling to survive among the flowers.

'I planted thirty King Edwards and fourteen Lincoln. But veges don't do here,' she explained.

Bobbing round her roses, looking at each bloom like a face, each flower seemed to know its name like a pet. Later, Mabel pricked her finger on a thorn and dashed indoors howling and spouting blood again while the two sisters fell into a reverie, recalling people and places long ago when they were girls.

'Nance, d'you remember old Mr Packer up at Woodford? The one with all those goats. I saw his daughter the other day. She says he's bed-ridden . . .'

They wept once more over Uncle Percy and laughed over Uncle Will, who acted as if he were still in the army and drilled his six children morning and night up and down the road.

'Our Laddie's moved again,' said Maud.

'Where to this time?' said Mother.

'He's living in a train carriage. It says 'No Smoking' on the windows and 'First Class' on the doors.'

'Funny,' said Mother. 'I expect he's finding it difficult.'

'He's working at Parnalls making gun turrets. You know, at Yate, where they had all those bombs. Dozens and dozens killed . . .'

They sat down on a low wall among the nasturtiums, like gnomes in the towering greenery, abandoned in the last strength of reckless memories. Now and then Mother looked up, her eyes, drifting without seeing, passed over us and through the garden like feelers, and now and then shapes of past events spilled to our ears.

'Can't imagine what he ever saw in her . . .'

'. . . he was a vicar once, too . . .'

'. . . hung himself . . .'

'. . . everything's so dear . . .'

'. . . I'm cooked . . .'

Maud said she would put the kettle on again and Mother followed her inside. Low voices, the rattle of tea cups, and claps of laughter came from the open windows.

We lay by the goldfish pond, Myra and I, stuffed with Aunt Maud's currant cake, trailing our hands in the starry weeds. Out here was laid down a colour-strewn hollow of sights and sounds; honey memories which made up that brief put-aside holiday, the only one we ever wanted. It dropped easily in and out of summers, regular and dependable like the hours in the day, and when it was time to leave one grew joyful in the achievement of having trod where others dare not go. So we hung back a bit, adjusting the separate pieces of the day, fitting them carefully away in memory to dip in all through the white winter.

Down in the afternoon the five clocks all told different times. The grandfather in the hall struck his long, thin notes as reminders of the passing day, a piling up of hours to lodge with one's reference of buses and shops. When it struck eight it meant four. All the clocks were like that: merely unmarked signposts through a journey of hours and nothing more. Only Ern could work out their collective meaning properly and get anywhere near the right time, so as usual we had to rely on the wireless and Sandy MacPherson.

Our departures therefore, in contrast to our carefree arrival, were desperately fought, and made worse by Maud and Mabel who insisted on coming with us to the bus.

Holding open the door, ready to warn passers-by, we waited breathlessly on the pavement. A quiet was come to the town, all the shops closed, the streets nearly empty; Dursley was ready for the blackout hours away. From inside came salvoes of screams followed by the buzz of near normal conversation, as if time was of no consequence at all. Then out of the hard silences (like the calm before a storm) there came a howling and screeching while the grandfather clock beat out the minutes like a threat.

'Where's my hat?'

'Damn that chair!' Mabel had dented her knee-cap which immediately swelled and went stiff.

'Have you seen my hat, Maud?'

'Where's the blessed iodine then?'

'Half a mo . . .'

'Have I got time to spend a penny?'

'Oh, where's my bag got to? It was here just now.'

'Don't forget your things, Nance!'

'Look at your stocking, Mabel!'

'Oh, we'll never do it!'

The parrot caught the mood and crawled all over his cage. 'Maauuud! Maaaauuuuud! Sodit! Keeeeeee!'

At last they charged out and knocked us over.

'Come on you young uns. Don't hang about!'

Shouting farewell at the parrot, we let go the door and chased after them up the hill. We stampeded through the streets and the few people we met fled at the sight of Aunt Maud.

'What's the good – we shan't catch it,' gasped Mother, and Aunt Maud waved her arms like a charging dragoon.

'Run for it you young uns! Make him wait!' She clung to her hat and dragged Mabel by the coat, and no traction company would survive if the bus left without us.

We got to the top of the pitch; the bus was there, the driver in his seat, the engine running.

'I said we had plenty of time,' wheezed Mabel, pushing us aboard. Aunt Maud just sagged against the wall and gave one of her royal salutes, a sort of half wave with the hand turned inward.

'S'long, Nance,' she called. 'Cheerio you young uns. Come and see us next year . . .'

We pressed on the window like monkeys, watching Mabel draw up her skirt and inspect her knee which had turned black. Then they were waving again, saying something and pulling faces and laughing – we had no idea what about.

Bull Pitch, Dursley, Aunt Maud and Cousin Mabel drifted away and we waved till the houses stepped out and we could see them no more.

Now we were limp, all expectations gone, the day sucked dry and ready for our hill. The sun drilling through the passing elms burned in blue shafts between the seats; our cheeks filled out like petals and our homeward eyes turned amber.

'We shan't be long now,' said Mother. 'He'll rattle along when we get up the hill.'

At Nympsfield the day was losing; the sky wide, soft and white. Hot grass and tar, warm bricks and black woods teased us like prisoners. Never too soon we came out under the last ash trees and stopped at the end of the drive. We climbed down into the grass, the backs of our legs red and hot, and the bus pulled away to Stroud.

We took our Mother's bags and hurried on in front. Myra went back to her speechless seclusion, to premium thoughts of cold milk and Sunny Stories with which she ended every day. I was glad too, for there was red in the windows of Amberley, the air was hot and cold in patches, and the beetles winged towards the night.

We always guzzled our homecomings, whereas Mother sipped hers like vintage wine, and came leisurely into the kitchen half an hour later, clutching a bunch of wild flowers picked along the drive.

But the relief was the same for all of us, and our outings never ended without this calm and longing.

~~ DOWN IN THE VILLAGE ~~

The almshouses were at the conjunction of field and village, at the top of the lane, and, when we were there, four out of the five were still in use.

It was an outlandish place even by the standards of our far-flung village, and the old people seldom went further than their own little gardens. Too weak now to tackle the hill, one found them in the Park on summer afternoons. They'd loiter in the chest-high grass, mute as the stones that housed them, staggered by gusts, frightened by aeroplanes, condemned to the world of the aged where even the language had changed.

No one passed them save us, or courting couples, or lone travellers limping to the common. The low grey dwellings – the roofs of which touched the stinging nettles on the rising bank behind, the inmates fixed at their doors all summer long – were at the highest point of the village: only the farm and heaven lay beyond. There, plagued by memories of a different century, they stared all day long on the valley.

Against the lane, in the first cottage, lived the Duchess. At least that is what Mother always called her, and for years we children believed that she really was of noble birth. She perpetually wore the same old hat well anchored in her wispy hair, a faded pink thing with roses round it. Thirty years of sunlight had turned the flowers drab, like hard-headed rivets. The women said that the Duchess wore this hat because the pins holding it on were twisted and rusty, impossible to shift; since she slept in a chair day and night it hardly mattered anyway.

At any rate, whatever her aristocratic connections she was certainly the dirtiest person we had ever set eyes on. Down in the village they would tell you that her skin had not seen water since her christening, a remark more humorous than cruel; but the truth was that her shoulders had turned stiff and at ninety-two she saw no sense in doing anything about it. She just gave up washing. She still had grace and style though, and now and then one noticed in her poise of head and careful speech something of the woman she had once been. She had dignity even now and the ravages of age had not entirely obliterated the beautiful slender woman she must once have been. We children believed she had been sent here by the king, years ago, to keep an eye on the village, and we looked out for her on warm days, in her high-backed chair by the door, where she curled her blue fingers together and slept till sundown.

She came from Wotton-Under-Edge, the sly product of a servant girl and a squire, the cousin of a lord, who chased her out and paid her off. Whatever the truth of it, men thought that she had connections and money and many proposed. Finally, though, she settled for a no good farmer who seduced her and carried her off to his ramshackle house at Miserden. When he discovered that he had not married a heiress after all, he beat her and took to the bottle.

Six years later, her husband and two children all dead of the Cough, she sold up and was once more fancy free. She had two hundred pounds and spent the lot on her friends travelling round the country. Penniless, she came back to Stroud a year or two later and began her long inexplicable slide into hopelessness. Her good breeding, genteel appearance and agile mind at first secured her good situations as governess and lady's companion. After that, when she started to let go, she went into service and then the mills: steeper and steeper steps down, her bright mind gone, her will for better things withering against the sixteen-hour day. This and ill health lost her job after job, and at last, in desperation, she set off in the snow to walk back to Wotton. Somehow she found her way to our village in the middle of the night, demented with fever and rattling with cold. A farmer abroad late caught her in the light of his lantern, curled up in a doorway half covered in drift, and lifting her gently onto the cart took her home to his wife, cheating her of the death she would have welcomed.

It was a fresh beginning of sorts. The farmer gave her a job as milkmaid and put her in a tiny thatched cottage on the bank. The narrow river of her days flowed on at this level until she was old, though she liked to think – and often told them – that it was only temporary, that one day she would get her settlement and be gone. By one means or another she kept alive this promise to herself to climb back, though neither she nor anyone else ever understood how she had ever come to fall so low, or what gods had unravelled her life so.

In time they put her in the almshouses to be looked after by the parish, and there we passed her every fine warm day, fussing about her little garden, talking to the flowers and watering her tiny patch of herbs among the thriving groundsel. Stiff and respectfully, I took off my cap whenever I met her, and Myra always curtsied.

Not knowing how to address a Duchess, we put her in the same league as our teacher.

'Afternoon, Miss,' we cheeped, straining our ears for the soft reply. 'Good - afternoon - children - have - you - had - a - jolly - day?' We always said we had in case the King found out; then we'd back away, bowing.

We'd watch her stoop again on her sticks, pressing back the grass from some treasured plant, cooing sweetly as if talking to a baby.

These were our first encounters with great age, for our grandfathers and grandmothers were youthful in comparison. They were out there nearly every time we came by, and where they had been that morning they would remain, not having moved more than a yard all day. The midget houses whose eaves even we children could reach on tip-toe, the wild little gardens with, here and there, brown patches scratched in the weeds, the inhabitants fixed and unspeaking, had seemingly all shrunk together to these doll-like proportions, like toys run down and thrown into a corner.

We saw these ancients as curiosities and without any particular reference to ourselves, and I am sure we never thought that they had ever been as we; knew not that we would one day be like them and were already drifting down the same long road.

Feeble and thickly clad even on boiling days, they shuffled out their doors in faltering inches. Toothless, sunk, dim of sight and hearing, and hair so white and thin that you could see the pink scalp beneath; all of them one breath, one hour, one day from their Maker: is it any wonder that they spent so much of their day staring up at the sky, looking for the way home . . .

Of their number, though, one was not an ancient. Cissy Harris was but sixty years of age, and she worked at the sawmill bundling sticks, and had never worked anywhere else. A week after she started there, at fourteen, they put her on a machine which she was neither strong nor quick enough to operate. The guard had been removed to cope with big pieces, and one winter's morning when it was only half light, her sleeve snagged and drew her hand onto the knife. In blind panic to free herself her other hand hit the blade also, and she collapsed from shock and loss of blood, still trapped. Time went by before they could find the switch behind the blocks, then they took her off in a horse and cart to the infirmary, and sewed up her stumps.

She recovered well because she was young, but lost fingers on both hands. Compensation was, of course, out of the question, but the factory inspector made them give her a job for life, if she wanted it. Thereafter, she wore mittens summer and winter, though they did not conceal the amputations but only made them more cruelly obvious. The cold turned the stumps blue, and they pained horribly.

'How are you today, Cissy?' Mother would ask.

'Not good, missus. Not good,' she would reply. 'It's me thingers; they'd ache so.'

This accident so long ago stifled her natural progress to womanhood, and she was terribly aware of it. The little head between narrow shoulders gave her a tortoise-like appearance, and the baggy brown coat and black beret smoothed her to the shadows of the village, unnoticed and uncared for except by a few. Slowly, soundlessly up and down the lane, she'd timidly whisper Hullo, nervously picking at her mittens. She had never married. 'I always wanted a man of me own, missus, but who'd look at me like this.' Sometimes, short of money, she waited for Mother at the top of the lane. 'I got summat for you, missus. Summat you might be interested in.' These soft petitions were surprisingly compelling and we trailed along the cinder path behind her. Her little cottage – it was only one room, as they all were – was a dimly cluttered museum of pretty vases, royal mugs, flowery plates, glittering brass, pewter and stuffed birds that had last stretched their wings when Victoria was a girl. The iron bed wedged under the window covered books, pots, basins, faded tapestries and yellow newspapers. The walls leaped with stags at bay, bouncing spaniels, charging lancers and rearing stallions, top to bottom, end to end.

'Look at this!' And out of the corner today she drew a small picture of an angel child, pink hands clasped in prayer. She held it round to catch the light. 'It's yourn for a bob. I be a bit short this week,' she said. Sometimes it was a cup and saucer or a vase or an ivory-handled knife: all sixpence or a shilling.

'The frame's good and it's spotless as you can see.'

'Oh, are you sure, Cissy?' said Mother. 'It's so lovely. Are you sure you want to part with it?'

'You take it an' 'ave it, missus.' Then she came closer, whispering over Mother's shoulder. 'Only don't let me down, missus. Don't let 'er along the end know will you. I'd die if ever 'er found out.' Where all this stuff came from she never would say. 'I've 'ad me friends missus – ah, an' I still got most of 'em too!'

Among themselves the ancients were a quarrelsome lot, bickering endlessly and watching each other all the time from behind their curtains. When one came out into the light of day another would go back inside; and Cissy had a running feud going with the Duchess.

''Er's no better'n me, no that 'er ain't, missus. Thinks 'erself summat 'er do cos 'er 'ad a good start. Ah, an' look at 'er now!'

The oldest of them all was 'Er Wi' Gout, who lived in the very end cottage against the wall, where the trees lapped over and gave a bit of shade. Very shy and almost never seen, they said that she was well over a hundred and had had a telegram from the King – even Cissy and the Duchess agreed on that. Only once did I ever see her, looking over the wall one hot afternoon where the calves were curled up in the buzzing shade. Usually all that one ever saw were her swollen feet and the bottom of her long black dress as she sat in the doorway waiting for the sun to warm her through. Mother often asked Cissy about her.

'Oh, I ain't seen 'er, missus. I heard 'er though, so 'er must be all right. 'Er'll be out agin come next summer.'

The other ancients were The Couple, man and wife for sixty-eight years. Theirs was really one single existence, a caring whole, drawing the same breath, using the same heart. Out of doors they clung to each other like small children, holding hands and shuffling the few yards into their garden where they planted carrots and onions. If the spring was late they huddled at the window like a couple of owls, watching the wind in the trees, wondering when they would be able to go out, or if they ever would again. Often they did not plant their little patch till August, through forgetfulness, and nothing came up; not that it mattered. The seasons whirled and dissolved, splintered into warm days and cold, which was now all they understood. They had five children, of whom only two boys survived. One was in New Zealand, the other in Rhodesia, and the postman reversed his van all the way up the lane to deliver brief postcards from half-way round the world: great waterfalls and hot springs that were like nothing they had ever seen, from grandchildren and great-grandchildren who were only names. Their card collection grew to a greasy bundle, the writing smudged to blobs, but they'd sit on the doorstep reading them over and over all through the summer, and kept them safe in a margarine box on top of the cupboard.

Then in the course of time the ancients died one by one, though no one seemed to know when, not even Cissy. Nor do I ever remember there being a funeral for them, though there must have been.

The windows clouded over and dandelions sprang out of the

doorsteps; these were the notices of their passing, and they all seemed to vanish with the drift of that one cold winter.

After that, Cissy stayed on there alone for many years, until finally she retired from the mill; she was then well over seventy. Frail now, and more withdrawn than ever, they came at last and took her away to a home, saying it was for the best. They took her to Gloucester, to a place she hardly knew, and there pined away and died within the week.

So the nettles took over the gardens and the almshouses were never used again. Doors peeled and swung open, windows broke and fell in. Without a purpose the old houses aged quicker than any of their occupants had ever done, and hurried on to follow them. Finally, the roofs collapsed after a thunderstorm and filled the little homes with rubble. But the walls stayed up among the thriving brambles and fell down leisurely, stone by stone, over many years.

Shake our village fifty years ago and anything might drop out. We had a clique of sly poachers, men with downcast eyes who slept with guns by their beds, when they slept at all; men with strange addictions to night and dawn, nets and wires. Some were real businessmen with war-time quotas to fill with Stroud butchers, and on moon-wide nights they'd labour up into our fields and not return till daybreak. Their guns bumped day and night round the hill, and every morning on the way to school I would find empty cartridge cases still sharp with powder. They were a nuisance, putting wires down where there was cattle, and twice we had animals trapped by the tongue.

Their undoubted leader was Smoky Curran. He poached anything anywhere without prejudice, and kept all the hotels in Stroud supplied throughout the war. (Some who dined there were quite unaware that they were eating their own pheasants and trout.)

There was no art in it though, not with Smoky. While it was true that he could claim a certain mystical compulsion from his grandfather, a poacher of renown married to gun, ferret and fishing rod, Smoky was driven solely by pecuniary motives. Bej sold rabbits for pennies and thought himself lucky, but Smoky got three or four bob for them, pleading the cost of ammunition. He joined the Home Guard, not patriotically, but just to give himself an excuse to be where he ought not to be. If he was caught he could say he was on exercise, and the uniform served as a pass – a threadbare warrant where trespassers were prosecuted. When at last he ran out of shot he started on his Home

Guard supply, issued for use against German parachutists. The usual small pellets were replaced by steel balls the size of a marble, and the mangled results of this expedient could be found on the butchers' slabs all over Stroud. At the end of the war, though worn out from lack of sleep, he was the first in our village to buy a motor car.

Our poachers developed an ad hoc Freemasonry, like tramps, known to each other by secret signs scratched on the road, dead hedgehogs, little piles of stones and branches oddly broken. They parcelled out the village fields, occasionally rotating so as not to get stale. 'Poacher' added to a man's name (behind his back of course) was never thought slanderous; rather it was a title bestowed, if not with dignity, at least with respect, for it conjured a quiet glamour of nights and guns and daring, like highwaymen, which a century or so ago they probably would have been. It is no wonder that we boys who raided and stole and wrecked, found in them something of our own wildness, and we'd go out of our way to befriend them.

Then there were the terrible black-faced tramps, though we had no friendship for them. Several roamed the village. Vulnerable as we boys were, we quickly learned that even to look at one meant misfortune. Hump Clack told us that he had once seen one, when he was five, and had straightway become misshapen; not an inch had he grown since. When one of us was late for school someone was sure to say: 'Perhaps 'e's met a tramp you!' Then the terror of his end ran among us like electricity and we would spin round three times and spit twice for luck: a ritual guaranteeing safety. Occasionally we did meet them, always when we were alone, always in the loneliest places. If we could escape we did, legging it back the other way. But if the encounter were too sudden and inevitable, we charged right through like a rugby player, head down and eyes averted.

Fortunately these meetings were rare, and the lucky survivors of them, playtime heroes, were besieged with invitations to tea. For some strange inverted reason the girls never minded them quite as much. Dinah Marsh in fact had a curious liking for them. She'd stop and look them over, even speak to them, drawn close by their mesmeric power, close enough for them to touch her, close enough to smell the straw and earth of their bones. One day they will have her, we said, and I believe in the end one of them did. She said they were sweet and just unfortunate; and whenever she spoke like this we kept well away from her, unsure of how people became mad. Some said you could catch it just by holding hands, so she lost out in games as well and had to stand by the wall sucking her thumb.

These tramps were the yeti of our village, much spoken of but seldom seen. Fascinating and feared, they tormented our young lives like nothing else, salted all our early days with an appetising danger. If not actually encountered, we would get in a group and watch them climbing the high fields, making for their secret camp. A creeping, hanging menace, they came into our minds suddenly with a shadow, a cloud, a gust of wind, and always when we were full of delight with ourselves. But bad as they were they were nothing when compared with the Mad Woman.

Our young lives then seemed half-filled with terrors of one kind or another, which were polished and handed on to those coming after us. The Mad Woman was different though and needed nothing but her own wretched and formidable reputation to put us to flight, adults and children alike.

She lived in the south part of the village, half way down the street and set in a dip, and we ran past the opening, turned away our heads in case she was out there by the door. Just one look we believed would turn us instantly to stone or red-eyed bats. She was volcanic; dormant for months then suddenly erupting in flame and steam. Then she would start her prowling and no one knew where one might find her.

Her appearance fitted the mortal turmoil beneath, was the exact outward manifestation of the twisted fright within: white hair like a briar gone wild, clothes hung on back to front, legs and feet bare, shutters half closed over her reason. Terrible were her eyes: deep and black like damsons set in a skull; fiery and bottomless, they both fascinated and repelled. She talked to walls, gate posts, trees and flowers; barked at dogs and hissed at cats; wandered the village holding her head and planning massacre. Or sometimes she would just stand in the middle of the street gently rocking and crying in some deep and terrible grief.

These moments were the worst, the most difficult to gauge and cope with. The village women would approach her gently: 'There, there, let's get you down home,' and there and then they would be instantly pounced upon, punched and scratched and pulled to the ground. At other times she let them lead her home like the lost child she was, clinging to their arms and trembling with the fear of their voices.

Her piercing screams jarred the village end to end, flashes of awful pain that made horses leap fences and cows go dry, and when daylight came they would find all her doors and windows wide open and the old woman asleep in the street. Yet she was not that old, perhaps no more than fifty, but her life tugged in all directions at once and to the world at large she looked haggard and archaic.

I once had an encounter with her at the top of the lane, coming home from school. She was sitting astride the gate arguing with the hedge, and when I looked up and saw who it was I thought my end had come. She glowered at me and extending a thin, richly veined arm beckoned me to come up.

'Here, I want you,' she said.

Her voice, so soft and reasonable, quivered with fire and had power, like the cocking of a gun. I had no intention of going anywhere near her, and as I backed away she rose screaming.

'Here you! Pick up all this paper! Pick it up this instant!' There was, of course, not a bit of paper to be seen anywhere, and like a fool I told her so. She fixed me with those deathly eyes, fiery drills that made the blood go cold, and sliding off the gate like a python coming off a branch she charged me, raving.

I turned and fled, convinced I was done for. I hurled myself at a couple of doors near the bottom of the lane, for no one would have refused me sanctuary. But she was gaining and I did not wait to be admitted. The distance between us was down to ten yards and there was nothing to do but run. Gathering her skirt up to her waist, her bony legs seemed to dangle helplessly beneath; yet she chased me very hard for a mile, shouting bloody murder, while everyone rushed in and locked their doors. I ran nearly back to school, and came home round about, over the common.

I staggered home like a furnace from my four mile race, babbling that I had nearly been set upon and done to death by ''er' and that she had chased me over all the fields and tracks and would have murdered me.

'Oh that poor woman,' said Mother calmly. 'I expect the heat's gone to her head again.'

That September, after she had been up and down the street smashing windows, they finally put her away, took her to the asylum, and the village was relieved that it no longer need dance to her madness. In fact, we quickly forgot all about her, and no more did Bri Hayes, Mary Finn or Swaddy Hughes, who lived closest to her, rush indoors the colour of lettuce gasping: ''Er's a comin' you!' and straight away dive under the stairs.

There were brief alarms, heart-stopping rumours that she had escaped and was making for the village to take revenge on all of us. For a day or two we went about in packs, looking into trees, behind hedges and under walls, but it soon passed as other gossip filled the waiting vacuum.

Not that there were any gaping, raw scandals in our village in my day, though I have often wondered why that was when all the elements were there. Perhaps it had to do with the war; for although there was more temptation there was also more excuse, and its very presence in our lives seemed like a temporary amnesty of morals, compensating the loss of other luxuries. One need not join in of course, but those who did soon had the tongues wagging, unless they were very careful or lucky. But these bed and body liaisons, because they sprang up in wartime, deferred spite, and nothing seemed at all odd or outrageous or tragic or adulterous for very long. A tenth of our number were outsiders anyway, transient orphans of the blitz. Mouths from strange towns, other counties and countries, speckled our village then, and it was on these that gossip mostly centred. If one or two local girls left the village suddenly to visit aunts in Scotland or Wales, for nine months, we accepted their mothers' downcast eyes as both confession and repentance, a downpayment on curiosity and blabber that would last years.

The townees were different of course, and for them we had sharp hooks, before they disappeared in name and memory. Their affairs were likened to a good book or film, something extraneous to our lives, a pleasurable drama. Mostly though they were laughed at, and few were condemned outright.

Our fields at dusk were a haven, a verdant stage where couples could act in a separate world, and casual love could be enjoyed and remembered, or regretted and conveniently forgotten, a war thing beyond measurable standards. There was Mrs L whose husband was a prisoner of war. She reacted strangely to this news by accommodating thereafter every man in uniform she ever met, and even postmen and railway porters were said to have passed through her hands when there was nothing stronger available.

Another lady, who we called United Nations, kept her sly trysts in our copse at twilight. Pleasure swelled through the startled night in lavish foreign tongues: Norwegian, Polish and Czech. Their low love-talk echoed like sermons among the dense trees, especially in the still before a thunderstorm; and she was cursed by every poacher for miles, for they caught nothing when she had used their night. Afterwards, her perfume lingered on about the quiet dells, pleasurable and sensuous, till the wet chill of morning wiped its stain away.

Coming home late from Scouts I had several encounters of that sort. Twice I passed the captain's lovely young wife in the dusk at the top of the lane, and afterwards watched her wade out into the moving corn with an American Negro, and with him sink limply into its rustling depths. Coming on up the bank I heard her love cries in the stillness, desperate and mortal, like a wounded vixen, and perhaps for the first time I began to realize how hopeless the world was.

There were things never directly talked about, too dreadful likenesses to fatal illness, and we knew of them only by innuendo, instinct and observed suspicion. Like the family where incest quietly heaved, and no one seemed to care, as if it were the most natural thing in the world for a man to sleep with his daughters and give them babies. The Yanks were blamed by some (a lucky convenience), but most knew the truth. The irregular offspring grew up as pale as milk, limp, beautiful hybrids of that complicated family, stared at and talked about, the whole thing a lurid puzzle. The father hurried at terrific speed about the village, head down, unspeaking, shaved to skin and bone, burning with a compulsion that few could comprehend. His massive wife gave him five children, his daughters produced four more, all popping and simmering in the erotic heat of their one overcrowded cottage, withal liked if not treasured – our one undercover curiosity.

There was a common village wish to keep such things to ourselves, an unspoken desire born centuries before, and the old strain was even now still active, largely undisturbed by laws and regulations. Good and evil were sick adversaries, too smart by half out here in the country where nature ruled. When we passed the policeman on his bicycle we knew that all he was doing was putting up Foot and Mouth notices or superintending the dipping of sheep. The war extended his duties to the blackout code and catching men without rear lights on their bicycles, for which they would be fined two-and-sixpence at Nailsworth Magistrate's Court: that was the extent of our acknowledged crime. The rest of it was just the village. The brawls, infidelities, thefts and rapes were occasional events which never seemed to gain or need a wider public. Disputes were settled indoors, out of sight, within the parish; revenge exacted by fists, arson, character sabotage or a solicitor's letter. Most of us had the wireless, yet some did not, and the final end of isolation came as always from without, through the ether and along the main road, where cart-horses had to pull aside for cars. In fact when cars came, banks had to be cut away, hedges grubbed up and walls taken down to make room for them. Then it was that we yearned again for the Mad Woman, for tramps, for dangers we understood; not these road accidents which began taking lives all round us. The first one I remember was the army lorry coming down the hill from Amberley. Its brakes failed near the bottom and it crashed through a fence and turned over in a field. The driver was killed and the load burst down the bank: Carnation milk and corned beef – hundreds of tins that vanished into cupboards and we all knew which ones. We went along from school, searching for loot, but the wreck had been picked clean long before then.

Not long afterwards another army lorry, this time an American one, took a bend too fast, burst through the parapet of the road bridge and plunged ten feet into the brook. A girl waiting there for the bus was killed outright and the black driver, seeing people running, thought he was going to be lynched, and fled to the woods where the MPs caught him three days later, half starved and about to cut his throat.

We did in fact have several spectacular suicides during the war and each one was sensational. The news, got going by unknown mouths, would be amplified in stages round the village. Most of our news came from The Ram, brought home by Father. In fact when he came in we were disappointed if all he had to deliver was a couple of packets of crisps. What we wanted was bad news and plenty of it. Blood fights, heart seizures, desertions, adultery and visits by the police were all more or less welcome. But suicides were top of the list, in another category altogether, chiefly because they were so sudden and unexpected and the participants generally so youthful and well liked.

One lad, in agony with toothache for weeks, went upstairs, dressed himself in his Home Guard uniform and shot himself through the mouth with his rifle. The bullet passed through the ceiling, joists, rafters and slates and smashed the insulators on a power line across the road, putting out the lights for hours. He left a note saying he feared death much less than the dentist and hoped to meet them all in hell.

Full moons took their usual toll and so did fire watching. A man in the mad, still hours of early morning, watching the starless sky, tried to brain himself with his boots, and afterwards completed the job by flinging himself under a lorry along the Nailsworth road. He had married the prettiest girl in the village, an unblemished treasure worshipped by all, and no one ever understood why he did it.

A girl killed on her bicycle outside the walking-stick mill put an end to this line of tragedies, all those sudden, remembered deaths (apart from those self-inflicted) that came by machines, in the air or on the road. For men killed by horses and bulls, or crushed under carts, evoked the commonplace, were no more extraordinary than a bee-keeper being stung to death. And because the girl on the bicycle was the last of those accidents, we recalled it avidly, remembered it longest, and it was the one we always spoke of. There was some talk of stringing up the driver of the car, if we could only get our hands on him, though he was blameless and the inquest said so. But justice had no power over emotions and the thing rumbled on for months, always certain to be mentioned in the pub or street.

'That devil 'e got away wi' murder 'e did!'

'Ah, 'angin's too good for 'n, that's what I says!'

She was not even from our village, but she was young and beautiful and now she was dead, and birth and death we understood best of all. The dead pilots, the soldier, the girl on the bridge – even poor Pansy killed on his paper round – had not half the impact of this one life so carelessly ended, and some of the old ones still talk of it today.

Through all this drama of course the village got on with its business, and all round were its ties, like Sid and Arthur the piano tuners. Blind from birth, both had felt their way through the streets and lanes and knew their parts unerringly. There was never any need for we boys to speak. We were recognised instantly by our footsteps, our sniffs and coughs, by our Brylcreemed heads and Vicks-plastered chests.

'Hey, Arfur! You be goin' the wrong way! The piano works is t'other way!'

He'd cast his head in our direction and fence towards us with his stick: 'Off to school you young buggers, or get your trousers down!'

We'd watch him shuffle on along the road, high stepping, touching the walls and the edges of the pavement, more sure than an engine on rails.

'S'long, Arfur.'

'So long boys. Don't forget to wash behind your ears!'

Once, Tatty Hollis snatched Sid's stick and ran off down the road with it. When we caught him, Dipper floored him with one punch; then we gave him Chinese burns, twisted his arms off and threw him in the brook where the sides were steepest and slippery – a gang justice meeted out to idiots such as he.

They were bachelors both, in lodgings, and told us that they knew the size and shape of most things, but regrettably knew nothing of women. 'I never 'ad the chance to feel one, so I don't know 'ow they're put together,' said Arthur. 'But I'd tune one up, given the chance.'

They held their chins high and leaned a little towards you when they spoke, smiling always. They thought life not too bad.

One day Cissy told Mother that she had passed Sid going to the Jug and Bottle, and that in spite of the very dark night he had known who she was.

'They be marvels, missus,' she said. 'But it beats me 'ow they do it in the blackout!'

Another such, over there in the north end, was Brandy Black, the deaf and dumb cobbler. Round his little sunlit porch we'd watch him working: knife, file and hammer sliding through his nimble hands like a conjurer. Getting him to understand what we wanted was a problem and could take longer than the repair. He was better when drunk, and the pub was where we waited for him. It was all done with mime, with hands semaphoring through the smoke of the lounge, and Brandy tapping his head saying that he understood, holding up fingers for the number of days that must pass before we could collect our boots. By these signals he would also find out what you did for a living so that he could fashion the repair accordingly. An office worker would find himself with paper-thin soles, enough for scuffing about among tables and nothing more. Boys' boots were built up fore and aft with great wedges of leather, for football and tree climbing. If you were a postman, God help you; the soles of your boots would be so thick that falling off them became a daily hazard.

The district nurse wobbled round the village as if on stilts. When riding her bicycle the weight of her shoes acted like cams, forcing the pedals round, and a set of brake blocks burned out in a week.

Once, I remember, I took him a pair of Father's boots for repair. Brandy turned them over and over in his hands, felt the quality of the leather, pressed the welts, frowned at the wear. Tapping his head and chest like a tic-tac man, he asked who my Father was and what he did for a living, and I drew pictures on his pad while his little light eyes twinkled with amusement; yes, he understood. To make sure, I mimed loading carts, tractor driving, walking, climbing ladders, and he squealed and grunted and laughed, tapping his head again to say he knew what I meant. Three fingers meant call Friday, and on Friday I went along and he handed me a large, shiny brown parcel lashed with string, holding out a large calloused hand for the half-crown. The package was heavy and cumbersome, more than seemed right, and when I got home and Father cut the string the boots crashed to the ground like lead. They lay on the kitchen floor, one upright, one on its side, and we gasped. There was something of the circus or music hall about them; they were props designed for mirth or sensation, a giant's cast-offs still hot and sticky from their journey in space. The soles were two inches thick, clustered with dazzling groups of studs, with tips front and back for self defence. Father picked them up, handling them gently like explosives, and removed himself to the yard. We followed dumbly, hands over our ears. He sat on the steps and the boots swallowed each foot with a burp; then he tied the laces loosely and stood up. He lumbered over to the concrete, sending up whorls of dust, and set off up the path. He banged and smoked and the sparks were like fireworks.

'Watch the straw!' we shouted, collapsing with laughter. He sounded like a platoon drilling, a grating rumble designed to terrorize and overcome. Once he got used to the weight Father quite liked them, but we always stood well back when he took them off and sent them skidding away under the chair.

Those boots never wore out. The tops eventually cracked like metal, curling and turning as hard as steel, but the bottoms remained as lethal as ever and we used them afterwards to jam open the big barn doors.

We who remember will be sorry for the village now, without its Brandy Black, Duchess, and Sids and Arthurs; without the tramps, the lame, the mad, the lovely and unloved. A wider world killed their roots, disturbed forever the wild ground in which they thrived. But then in the thirties and forties we were just the villagers, shouting with one chest, protecting our lusts, nursing our grief, binding our blood, cooling our savagery, laughing at ourselves, weeping. I do not suppose we ever wished to be different; and if progress was inevitable it also came too fast for some. In the long term it had compensations of course; kinder perhaps in some ways, but hard to love as we had loved the old. For these were the last days before we strayed beyond the village, and its distinctive life ended forever with characters such as these.

❧ END DAYS ❧

The war ended, all the workers left the farm, and in six weeks we were on our own. We thought one or two might go, but not the whole team, and the emptiness foreshadowed a peculiar regret.

The fun ended with the war, and a joyless self-interest took over from common effort. Whatever it was we had in those years ended on VE Day. It was not just the Germans who surrendered; we all did one way or another and no one was even half as friendly as they had been.

There was another sound now, one not heard before, like faint vibrations before an earthquake, and people panicked. They changed wives or husbands, home and work, and some left the village to emigrate.

As the last rifle kicked and the final bomb burst, Frank came to Father and said he had had enough, it was time to go; and a week later, without ache or pleasure, wandered home through the fields for the last time, closing sixty years of work. He closed the door of his little cottage by the Yew Tree and never stirred outside again, except to dig his allotment down by the brook. He died six months later, propped on his pillows looking across the banks. The track he had made through them for over half a century became his slab, his memorial, and for all I know may still be there. Rabbits and foxes and cattle used it, and we did, too, on our raids to Mrs Gerrar's daffodils. Boxer knew his old pal had gone for good, and for the first time in his life came eagerly to the gate to be brought in. Ears pricked, he would listen for the boots hobbling up the yard, but would never hear them again.

That started it. Grace got a job in a market garden at Kings Stanley; Tom went back to his old boss at Didmarton; Colin to the fairground.

Jenny had already left us to go into munitions. Her young man, Geoffrey, had gone missing in his Lancaster over the North Sea and the loss of him struck her hard. She stood that day in our kitchen, eyes downcast, pale and distant, holding in the tears. 'I've got to get away and try something different now,' she said; and Father sent on her money and cards.

Rumours about her came back to us now and then, all of them believable: that she'd married a millionaire; had gone off and joined the WAAFs; had had a baby by a stranger; and, best of all, that Geoffrey had come home safe and well and they had married and settled down.

But the baby story persisted, the infant supposedly conceived one reckless moon-mad night on the bare of Selsley Common.

'I don't know where they get such stories,' said Mother laughing. They all laughed at that, except me.

For two months Father worked the 500 acres by himself, and then they sent us three German prisoners to help out.

Karl and Erich were both young and spoke fair English, but Walther was a grandfather and stubbornly refused to learn anything new, except a few necessary words. Mother of course gave them all names. She called Karl, Don Ameche, because of his dark good looks. Erich became Master Daddy (he had six children in Dusseldorf) and Walther, at forty-nine, the Kaiser. They bunked in our old cottage and were punctually in the yard at seven o'clock every morning for inspection and orders, lining up at attention when Father appeared. However, they had not reckoned with his Gloucestershire accent, which at times could drop below the level of comprehension into a made-up vocabulary, a bumble of words, a fit of speech. Disc harrows became 'discarrers'; motorbike, 'mudderbike'; will you?, 'oot?'; cut, 'razzer'; throw it , 'chuck'n'. Give me that one will you, might sound like: 'Gi I 'e oot'. When preoccupied or warm-tempered he slipped naturally into these word puzzles and the Germans floundered in them like a bog. For all the good it did he might have been speaking Urdu, and the German/English dictionary they always carried went sailing through the air that first morning. So they had to resort to sign language, drawings in the dust, prayers on the wind. And if all that failed, Mother would be called out to explain everything in her good clear English.

They were a serious lot, by custom humourless, and rarely talked of anything except the war. Karl, the youngest, was crippled with a natural arrogance that had constantly to be pricked if he was to be of any use at all, and, of the three, he found it hardest to come to terms with defeat. He was vain too, and his carefully groomed hair, parted straight down the middle, was like spite or an unspoken challenge. He combed it carefully and smoothed it while he talked. He talked rather too much in fact, and about the wrong things, and, once, he and Erich came to blows in the rick yard. After that Father put him working by himself and threatened to send him packing if there was any more of it.

The Kaiser held the balance, bellowing and threatening like the sergeant he was, keeping them in order like a father. His only desire

now was for peace and quiet and to get back home to his Frau; he was
not having any nonsense from these two. At nearly fifty a depression had
set in that had nothing to do with the war.

'Germany ist kaputt. Walther ist kaputt. All ist kaputt,' he said. 'Kaputt'
was the key of his every conversation, the dirge of all misfortune. If it
rained too much or too little: 'Es wird eine schlechte Ernte geben.
Kaputt!' When he felt unwell he would go to my Father clutching his
stomach, half destroyed by a mortar bomb. 'Ich habe Bauchweh. Kaputt!
Oh, ich will meine Frau haben! Dieser verdammte Krieg!' For all that,
he was strong and hard and the long hours he had to work meant
nothing to him.

Only the blonde, bustling Erich looked to me as a German should.
He had played hard, played well, but in the end the game had been lost.
He regretted his thin leg and the limp a British bullet had left him with,
but had no desire at all to go back to a country laid waste. If he had had
his way he would have stayed with us for ever. He'd rove the fields and
hedgerows looking for things to eat, for he believed nothing should be
overlooked or let go waste. He made tea out of nettles, poultices from
leaves, and laxatives from grass. On hot days he paddled in the pools of
the hollow, saying that it eased his frost-bitten toes. He would roll up his
trousers, mash mud and water into a thick paste, smearing it round his
feet, and lay in the grass till it baked hard. Afterwards he chipped it off
saying how much better he felt.

They had been with us two months when a directive came from the
War Ag. saying that prisoners might be allowed out under supervision,
though they were not permitted to use public transport, visit cinemas,
shops or pubs. Father looked at it and said: 'What about public toilets?'

Anyway, he passed the message on and one Saturday they asked if they
could go into Stroud, and would I take them? They had a bath and put
on their best battledress with the yellow patches. We had to walk of
course, and going through the village people edged up to the walls to
see these men, their first Germans, the terrible Hun they'd been fighting
for years.

In spite of his limp, Erich swung along in front, reassured by the sight
of men digging their gardens, women gossiping, the little two-coach
tank train smoking along the valley, and cattle coming up the street for
milking.

Karl and Walther observed none of these things, felt nothing but
hostility and spleen. They were chain-smoking, lagging behind, arguing,

signals from their nerves hoisted like bunting, and I called Erich back to find out what it was all about.

'Zey don't vant to go on,' he said. Then he explained. 'Ja. Zey zink people mide . . . vell, zey mide nod like it zo zoon after ze var.'

'Dies ist falsch,' said Walther.

We stood in the middle of the street conscious of staring windows and listening walls. The splashing water trough nearby thundered above the dissension. We drank from it, trailed our hands in its brimming pool, and pulled ourselves together.

'Ja. Ve go on,' said Erich.

But we had not guessed how conspicuous we would be. Eyes followed us like searchlights and our boots crashed arrogantly, like storm-troopers. We fell silent long before we got to Stroud, cowed by the glaring looks and remarks as sharp as arrows thudding into our backs.

'Who be they then?'

'Where be they vrom?'

'Jerries ain't they, or Ities?'

'Jerries? Don't know – I never zid one.'

Two men the worse for drink turned round and followed us up George Street. Our skins seemed to heat and peel. The lynch mobs were gathering, word was being passed round: 'String 'em up outside the Subscription Rooms!'

So I led them up into the garden, a stone's throw from the church. If need be, a retreat and stronghold. No one followed, and we held a brief council under the yew tree. The decision was unanimous.

'Iz best ve go, Ja?' said Karl.

'Ja,' I said, and so after barely half an hour we crept out of Stroud, expecting every second to be surrounded; but when we looked back, coming along the Cairnscross Road, there was no one behind except a grandmother with the weekend shopping.

Yet that uneasy feeling never left us till we got to the common, and then we started singing. First Erich, then Walther and Karl, then me; a tuneless bawling of Lillie Marlene flung at the wind and Selsley. Still singing, we came home along the drive, and never again did they ask leave to go anywhere, not even to the village. When we left not long afterwards, they remained there alone, looking after the farm for nearly another year before they were repatriated.

The farm, the hill itself perhaps, would never be the same. The cottages were hardly ever used again, and the workers, the few that would now be needed, would in future come from the town in their motor cars. Tied cottages, tied employment, had had its day up here; here especially, where the buses were too far away and in winter you could not get to them at all.

In these years, when we knew nothing else, we lived in the relics of a fading community, and were the last undemanding tenants of those bleak cottages and windswept banks. Yet the hill never gave as much again. For those coming after it was just a place of work; whereas we breathed it, lay on it, pulled it over us at night. Our separateness over the village was a privilege, but we were villagers all the same and moved in the ebb and flow of its tides. When we left, a tradition ended and the Park and Long Ground ceased being highways for food-hauling and coal-carrying, or the springboard for distant towns. Farms had not become factories then, and the production of food was almost incidental, a job habit; horses still pulled carts, tractors were not machines but skilled tools, animals foraged under the moon, yards were mud or dust, the fields sheaved or ricked, and walls and hedges had been where they were for hundreds of years.

Over the farm the skies were quiet at last, the hollows still and stifled, and, in the pause, like an interval in a play, we noticed that things around were no longer as they had been; they were greater or lesser with our growing, but not the same. The marks on the barn door where I was measured every birthday were still not high, but their numbers told, and the hill that had brought us up, Myra and I, was ready to turn us loose.

She was seventeen now, working at the incubator factory by the station, learning to type. Every evening she pushed a space on the kitchen table and got out her Pitmans: slow, laboured hieroglyphics which hung on the paper like noodles. It meant something, she said, all that scrabble. Sighing her end-of-the-world sigh, biting her lip, rubbing out, she drew the jagged symbols over and over. Her mind was quick but her hand was slow, and she never did quite master shorthand. She came in from work telling us of Mr Ruckman, her boss, and Mary that other girl, and the boy William who whistled at her through the window. All weekend she stayed on the farm, never went out. She cranked the gramophone for Diana Durbin, steamed her eyelashes like the film stars, dreamed in her solitary walks over the common, as Daisy had done a hundred years ago. She built up her fancy of course, but there were no young men very near and always they would be just out of her grasp. It was a bald interest at best, and love and marriage quickly succumbed to a virulent independence; she let it go without regret and became a sort of second mother.

The Old Man was back from the army, people coming and going, cars parked all day outside the big house. Father would come in to his dinner looking hunted.

''E's on about them damned walls again. I told 'im t' get more men, but 'e just won't listen; never 'ould.'

They sparred every day over one thing and another, and sometimes over the treatment of the German prisoners.

'Drive 'em harder, Roberts! Drive 'em harder!' he used to say to my Father. 'Be damned to regulations!' Nothing was meant. It was all part of the sudden dilemma.

Father gave as good as he got but it was wearing him down and he knew there could only be one outcome. 'I shall 'ave t' watch meself,' he would say. He saw the changes coming and hoped to head them off while there was still time – and did, but only just.

About now Mother lapsed into one of her periodic fanciful romances, and thought we ought to ask the Old Man to provide a car for us so that we could get on and off the hill in comfort.

'A little Austin Seven would be nice. I'll ask him when I see him.'

'You won't! He'll think you're mad!'

'No – he'll understand.'

'You'll get me the sack, that you will!'

'You don't get anything if you don't ask.'

By now though she had made up her mind that she did not want to leave the hill, that after all there was no need if we were going to get a car. She had it all worked out. Father could carry on until he retired and then we could retreat back along the fields to our old cottage under the wood where we began. It would all be as it used to be; nothing need ever change. The Old Man barely came into her reckoning. Not only that but she had abandoned my name again and for some reason started calling me Ernie.

'Ernie, let's go down and have a look over the mansion,' she said one day.

'What for?'

'Oh, I just want to look round.'

We wandered along in the heavy summer day, the thundery air pressing on our faces like warm fur.

'I want to pick some lily of the valley,' she said. She knew just where they were and I followed her in among the birch trees to white drifts between the bracken. She bent for the flowers in raincoat and pinny, the yellow sun splashing through the trees across her back and arms, like a Renoir painting. She straightened slowly, holding her hip, her nose buried in the posy. Her face was like that of a sixteen-year-old girl.

'There was a wood just like this down home,' she said. 'We weren't supposed to go there of course – it was the squire's – but we did, and came home with bunches and bunches.'

We strolled back to the path and headed for the mansion while she recalled the old days, her brothers and sisters, schoolfriends, that first job in the paper shop.

'Did I ever tell you about Uncle Paul? He used to sell wild flowers round Dursley. He used to pinch them from the woods and orchards – never did a stroke of work in his life. He was a proper rascal.'

The wood had gone quiet and there was a bump of thunder away over Nailsworth as we came out in front of the house. She stared up at it and gasped.

'There, just look!'

She stood there unspeaking for several minutes, swishing at the flies with a bit of fern. The silence was grace, symbol of a dear wish, unobtainable, so all the more cherished.

'It's falling to bits,' I said, to draw her away.

'No, no. It just needs a bit of attention. It was never finished. They ran out of money. Shame what the Yanks did.'

We turned down to the lake. Mother was a keen fisherwoman, an improviser of rods and hooks who once had decimated the squire's perch. She shielded her eyes against the sun's glare, looking up and down the water. Something plopped a dozen yards out.

'There'll be trout in here I expect. I used to catch any amount with a nut stick and a bit of string. I used a cork as a float and boiled rice as bait. Our Percy and me – all the stuff we caught!'

The lakes, the woods, the old house, the watching silence: forgotten, lost and unknown – it was here that she belonged.

But come home we must, and on the way back she was preoccupied with moulded clouds, sun dazzle, insects in her hair, purple shades, the blazing trees, and had half forgotten I was still there. She entered the kitchen as if returning from a great pilgrimage and was unsettled for the rest of the day, talking of footpaths, fishing rights, money and

Father's retirement. Between times more immediate matters cropped up, like the loss of the village shops: Gorton's and Browning's had closed; Turner the butcher and both bakers all gone. If we ran short now it was Nailsworth or nothing.

But the village had changed more than that, for the faces one saw there, familiar from countless playtimes, were grown bony and spotty and shaven, with voices rasping like horns. Heap was happily driving a grocer's van, and even happier committing adultery, till he was found out and shot in the street by an avenging husband.

Swaddy, who always meant to be Prime Minister if he could not be King, had to make do with a bit less and went to work at the tannery. Samson was a telegram boy and Dave Walby took his brawn to the timber yard. One way and another we all had to make do and settle for the little strength and brains that we had.

Dipper took up cabinet-making like his father, and football like his uncle, and was good at both. He was a good cricketer too, with his left hand outswing, and was unplayable on our village pitches. He married young, became captain of the cricket team, built his own house and became a church warden.

Sparrow with the brains, Sparrow of the tree-climbing records, arse-out-of-his-trousers Sparrow, survivor of scarlet fever and twenty broken bones, took his head off to grammar school and confounded all by marrying a rich widow, older by twenty years, who taught him chess and communism. Unfortunately, the widow had two daughters who, although their minds did not amount to much, were certainly quite lovely. He ran off with one, grew tired of her and took her back, then ran off with the other, all the time keeping up a stimulating correspondence with his red wife.

Some like the Dalby boys stayed single and permanently out of work; others like Alfy drifted away. Pansy was in his grave, and Phil was fighting his father for a tractor, though only got his way when his old nag dropped dead in the shafts pulling a massive load up piano works hill.

The girls were women, fat as ricks or as slender and feathery as willow. Trissy grew into a beauty, and no longer took off her clothes on request but became prudish and untouchable – she whom we had touched so often at her bidding, the pleasure seed of our first trembling flesh. She married a vicar and went to Africa to convert the heathen; she forgave her husband's moral lapses, got him off the drink and made a man of him.

Sheila Forrest, Margaret Thule and Doreen Carter all married farm labourers. Maureen Cole, the Pet, stayed single and moved in with a shaven-headed woman.

Dina March used to wait for me in the lane. All the tramps were gone, but I was fit and black enough coming home from the garage, and she flung herself round my neck.

'Let's go up the dingle,' she whispered.

I followed like a slave, full of shame and curiosity, melting in her musky odour. In a shallow dip under the fir trees she squatted down, unbuttoning her blouse.

'Come here. Oh, aren't you *dirty*,' she purred.

She drew me down for the kiss, a thin partial surrender of her senses to my oil and grime. Then: 'Oh no! It's too much!' and, thrusting me away, jumped up, buttoning her blouse in a temper while I blinked in astonishment.

'Bringing me up here! I know you Gerald Roberts! I'm going!'

She acted out this idiot thing three times before I understood the game, and was not surprised when finally she took up with a coalman and raped him on the sacks in the back of his cart.

As yet work was still a pastime idling among my dreams. It dragged on my wilder fancies, but never I think completely extinguished them. I would be a poet, a soldier, a boxer, a great artist – all things told me by the wind and the woods. I carried a sketch pad everywhere I went, painstakingly drawing sections of the hill, for I knew that all breath and light must change forever when we left.

With the ending of the war and starting work, my anchor broke free and I was left adrift. Days and weeks were no longer separate, life no longer an event of incidents but dramatic with tumid emotions in which I seemed to be drowning. My core was still and watchful, everything else disturbed as in an illness, as I floundered in the suspense-filled days and cried aloud in nights of crimson labour. Then I awoke at last at sunrise, bedevilled by images that I strained all day to remember.

I was troubled by energy and, foolishly aggressive, I picked a fight with Buck Mawle who lived at Selsley, and threw down the gauntlet.

'Let's settle it with the gloves,' I said.

I started training earnestly in one of the cowsheds. I pulled myself up and down on a beam till my strength was gone – not long – and afterwards, exhausted, sat in a water trough to cool off. A sack filled with old clothes served as a punch bag. I skipped on the concrete path, shadow boxed, ran down to the main road every morning and back up again at night.

We met in a wood, just the two of us in a clearing. We slipped the gloves on, tucking the laces inside. It was agreed that the rounds would end when one of us was knocked down, as in bare knuckle days. Then we began.

Straight away I saw how imprudent had been my challenge. He was four inches taller with a correspondingly larger reach, and outweighed me by two stone. Also I was as weak as a kitten from all that training. In less than a minute I found myself on my back among the roots. This triggered my temper and for a moment I was invulnerable to his blows. Smirking, he came in for the kill. I copied Dempsey and tried a double left hook. The first rattled his ribs, the second made his nose bleed, and we called it a draw.

After that we sat on the gate talking about girls: those who would, those who would not, and those who might.

'You bin with Violet Dodds yet? 'Er's all right they say. Do anythin' 'er will.' She lived in Selsley, so I had not heard. In any case I was thinking of his sister Barbara, a red-headed, freckled-faced temptress who in some ways reminded me of Anne. It was she who was the current focus of my lust and the reason for picking the fight: I hoped to meet her afterwards and a few bruises seemed cheap for such a privilege. Still, there would be no harm in a bit of practice first.

He said that Violet took the dog for a walk over the common every evening, and that was where we would waylay her.

'Right then. I'll meet you up there next Thursday night,' he said.

'Yea. Let's keep our fingers crossed.'

There was nearly a week to waste, and as the grand expectation of the first days dwindled, there came in its place a morbid dread, like a sentence to be carried out at a definite place and time. I went, though, stern like an executioner, hoping there would be no nonsense.

Buck waved as soon as he saw me; we were two dots converging from either end of the common, and in a few minutes he was up to me breathing hard from the run.

'Hiya. Seen 'er?' said Buck.

'No I ain't. 'Er mightn't come.'

''Er will. 'Er always do.'

We strolled a bit and sat down on a tump watching. Presently we saw the dog bounding along, and a moment later she bobbed into view out of a dip, sauntering our way. ''Er's comin',' said Buck, rubbing his hands. 'I be ready for 'er too!' He swallowed hard and my legs shook with nerves.

'Shall us 'ide or what?' I said. He looked at me sharply.

'What, an' jump out on 'er you mean?'

We considered it: manhaul her, arms and legs into a dip; but the dog, an alsatian, was an unknown quantity, so we abandoned that plan.

'What we goin' to *say*?' I wanted to be prepared, well rehearsed, not tongue-tied like this.

'Just ask 'er. 'Er knows what's what,' said Buck.

So we stayed where we were and waited, and in ten minutes she was nearly up to us. Violet was twelve, not particularly pretty, but she had a kind mouth and a nice bottom and had been serving the Selsley lads for years.

'Hiya, Vi. What you doin' then?' She knew Buck but had never seen me before and gave me a quick bashful glance.

'Hiya,' she said quietly.

She kept walking and we fell in beside her. The dog lead jangled in her hand. Her seasoned power was tremendous, unconsciously exerted and all the more potent, and when we spoke our voices were half strangled.

'It's comin' on t' rain,' I croaked.

Buck looked at the sky and started whistling 'South of the Border'.

'Let's go up the barn. Comin, Vi?' he said.

She made no reply, but her head sunk a bit and her eyes were suddenly dark.

We helped her over the fence into the harvest field where the stooks stood in ranks. The rain came harder, hissing across the stubble.

''Ere, let's get under one of these fer a minute,' said Buck. We pulled apart and rebuilt a stook and Violet crawled willingly into the narrow tent of sheaves. Tony wriggled in after her, half across her, while I held the thing to stop it collapsing. Then I dived under another, steaming and indignant. I heard them muttering, heard the straw rasp when they moved. Buck's legs were sticking out, wet to the knees, and I watched his legs jerk about, as in a fit, saw his elbow searching under her dress.

The drumming rain increased the delirium, and the ground quaked under my stomach. I felt it shake and throw itself up, pressing each separate nerve of my loins, sweetly.

Then suddenly the stook broke in two and I saw heads and arms, bare legs, backsides and hands struggling under the lashing sky.

'Blast and bugger!' cried Buck, throwing off the sheaves. Violet was somewhere beside him, pushing herself clear with her feet tangled in his braces. I pulled at a sheaf and there was her face, eyes closed and smeared with rain – and on an impulse I stooped and kissed her.

''Ere, what you doin!' cried Buck. 'Bugger, give I a chance!'

'Stop it! Stop it!,' shouted Violet, scrabbling to her feet, pulling her dress down.

Buck looked surprised and hurt, and the rain dripping from his face was like tears of frustration. Violet ran her hands over her sodden, untouched body and started crying. I grabbed Buck's jacket and put it round her shoulders.

'We'll take you 'ome. It'll be alright.'

I tried to sound normal, but the tiger was loose and even as I said it I wanted to drag her down.

Buck jumped to his feet, slipping his braces up over his shoulders, twitching like a drunk, his eyes blood red.

'Let's go on up the barn like I said!'

But the magic moment had passed and Violet had had enough of us.

'I be goin' 'ome,' she said. 'An' don't you dare follow or I'll tell our dad!'

The dog came out from cover when she whistled, she flung Buck's jacket away, and as she ran hard down the field the dog lead tinkled like a fairy bell.

'Well I'm buggered!' said Buck. 'Another minute an' I'd 'ave . . .' He did not finish the sentence and looked about him, bewildered and half savage.

We slunk away up the field, looking back now and then at our disappointment, a black dot racing away over the rain-swept common.

We sheltered in the shepherd's hut, lit the stove and spread our clothes out to dry.

'It don't matter anyway,' said Buck. 'We'll get 'er next week. You game?'

I said I was, but in fact I was learning, and knew that she would never look at either of us again after such bungling.

I got round Barbara though and took her to see 'For Whom The Bell Tolls'. Later, in the woods, I kissed her like Gary Cooper, and in my mind started building a palace of such life-long intensity that it frightened her off. Also her father, a passionate, quick-tempered drayman, got to hear about it and threatened to whip me if ever I went near her again. It little mattered, for I hardly heard or saw anything now that was not extravagant, and the threat of a beating, or any physical violence, seemed less fearsome than a knock at the door from a policeman, and we lumbering youths looked favourably on such threats that denied the law.

Dina Marsh, Barbara Mawle, Margaret Thule all offered, all fumbled over, all reluctantly escaped my careless net and passed on to older, surer hands.

I saw the village lads less and less, and in the end they were almost like strangers. The girls too, with whom we had once been so free, grew serious and hardly spoke.

So the village once more receded and I passed through it unseeing on my way to the town. Once again the hill was more important than all, the place that best gave me the fever I sought, burdened and uplifted as I now was by cycles of rising strength.

More and more I lingered in the hollow, sitting in a tree with a book. Bars of sunlight and the green enslavement of woods and water held me captive hour upon hour.

They begged me stay forever, called me all day long in the rattling town, and coming back at the end of the day I'd loiter with them and come in late, half dazed, to my supper.

I began a little to be what I am; and something, perhaps the uncertainty of all those tomorrows, made me seek what shadows remained, and then it was that I began wandering the hills at dusk.